T0339732

Work Simply

Work Simply

Embracing the Power of Your Personal Productivity Style

Carson Tate

PORTFOLIO / PENGUIN

PORTFOLIO / PENGUIN

Published by the Penguin Group
Penguin Group (USA) LLC
375 Hudson Street
New York, New York 10014

USA | Canada | UK | Ireland | Australia | New Zealand | India | South Africa | China
penguin.com
A Penguin Random House Company

First published by Portfolio / Penguin, a member of Penguin Group (USA) LLC, 2015

LIBRARY OF CONGRESS CATALOGING-IN-PUBLICATION DATA
Tate, Carson.
Work simply : embracing the power of your personal productivity style / Carson Tate.
pages cm
Includes bibliographical references and index.
ISBN 978-1-59184-730-4 (hardback)
1. Time management. 2. Ability. I. Title.
HD69.T54T374 2015
650.1'1—dc23   2014038624

Paperback ISBN: 9798217045150

Set in Univers LT Std
Designed by Daniel Lagin

To Andrew and EC

Contents

Work Simply

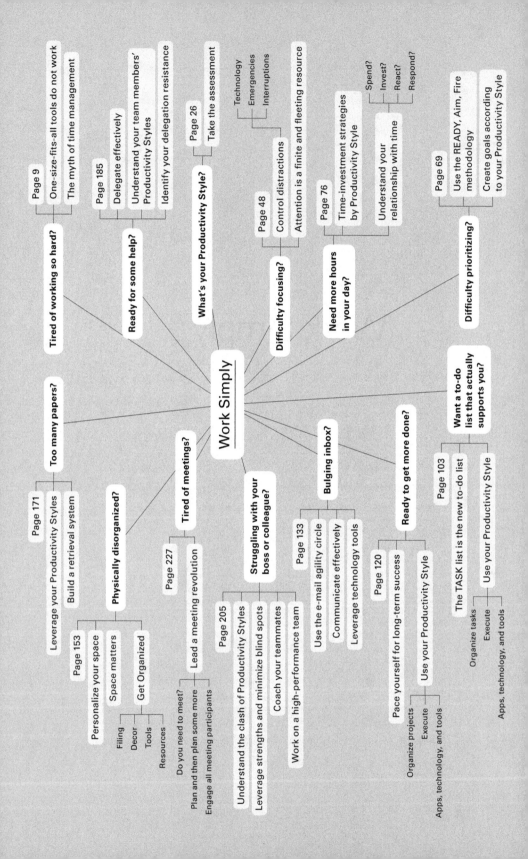

Work Simply

Tired of working so hard?
- Page 9
  - One-size-fits-all tools do not work
  - The myth of time management

Ready for some help?
- Page 185
  - Delegate effectively
  - Understand your team members' Productivity Styles
  - Identify your delegation resistance

What's your Productivity Style?
- Page 26
  - Take the assessment

Difficulty focusing?
- Page 48
  - Control distractions
  - Attention is a finite and fleeting resource
    - Technology
    - Emergencies
    - Interruptions

Need more hours in your day?
- Page 76
  - Time-investment strategies by Productivity Style
  - Understand your relationship with time
    - Spend?
    - Invest?
    - React?
    - Respond?

Difficulty prioritizing?
- Page 69
  - Use the READY, Aim, Fire methodology
  - Create goals according to your Productivity Style

Too many papers?
- Page 171
  - Leverage your Productivity Styles
  - Build a retrieval system

Physically disorganized?
- Page 153
  - Personalize your space
  - Space matters
  - Get Organized
    - Filing
    - Decor
    - Tools
    - Resources

Tired of meetings?
- Page 227
  - Lead a meeting revolution
    - Do you need to meet?
    - Plan and then plan some more
    - Engage all meeting participants

Struggling with your boss or colleague?
- Page 205
  - Understand the clash of Productivity Styles
  - Leverage strengths and minimize blind spots
  - Coach your teammates
  - Work on a high-performance team

Bulging inbox?
- Page 133
  - Use the e-mail agility circle
  - Communicate effectively
  - Leverage technology tools

Ready to get more done?
- Page 120
  - Pace yourself for long-term success
  - Use your Productivity Style
    - Organize projects
    - Execute
    - Apps, technology, and tools

Want a to-do list that actually supports you?
- Page 103
  - The TASK list is the new to-do list
  - Use your Productivity Style
    - Organize tasks
    - Execute
    - Apps, technology, and tools

Introduction

A Road Map to the Book

MY HOPE IS THAT THIS BOOK CAN BE A TOOL THAT SUPPORTS you as you reclaim your life by using personalized tools that can make you more productive, creative—and happy.

To assist you as you read this book, I have included a road map of each chapter to give you an overview of the chapter contents and help you quickly determine the reading order that suits you best. By following the links from one balloon to the next, you can see how the ideas in each chapter are connected to one another.

You may find that the ideas in certain chapters quickly grab your attention because they relate so closely to challenges you're facing in your daily life and work. Feel free to jump from chapter to chapter as your needs and interests dictate. But I recommend you start by reading chapter 1, "Work Smarter, Not Harder," chapter 2, "Get Ready to Work Smarter," and chapter 3, "What's Your Productivity Style?" to assess the root causes of your stress and to identify your Productivity Style. That style will be referred to throughout the book as you develop your personalized path to productivity.

Prologue

The Day After Christmas

IT WAS DECEMBER 26, 2011—THE DAY AFTER CHRISTMAS. IT was also ten days after the first birthday of my beautiful daughter EC. And I was tired. Very tired. I am sure that's normal for the mother of a little toddler, especially in the midst of the busiest time of the year and a very special birthday celebration to boot. But I couldn't help wondering, "How did I end up sitting on the floor, my bones aching, wondering whether I would be able to stand up again?"

Andrew and I had waited a long time after marriage before deciding to start our family—eleven years, in fact. So when I got pregnant, it came as just another challenge for the two of us in the midst of two very rich, very busy lives. Our careers were well established, our friendships were deep, and we were heavily engaged in our community. I was running one successful business while making plans to sell it, launching a separate consulting practice, and working on a master's degree in organization development, all at the same time. Yes, it felt hectic at times—working on airplanes, juggling homework and client conferences, saying good night to my husband by telephone from halfway across the country. Andrew and I loved our lives just the way they were, and we had every intention of keeping them intact, baby or no.

When the news of my pregnancy was confirmed, I promptly decided that nothing was going to change in my life. In the months that followed, I was true to my word. I did not slow down at all during my pregnancy. I did not cut back on work, school, family, social, and community activities. I even kept up my usual exercise routine, including outdoor runs, right through my thirtieth week.

EC was born on December 16, and the three of us enjoyed a wonderful holiday season as a family in our home in Charlotte, North Carolina. By the end of January, I'd resumed work on my master's degree and was back on an airplane headed to Phoenix to work with a client for a few days. My total time off after EC's birth: less than six weeks. I told myself, "After all, if I don't keep pushing to build my business and make it successful, who will?"

I maintained this pace for the entire first year of EC's life. I finished writing my master's thesis, continued to work with clients across the country, and stayed relentlessly focused on building my consulting business. And of course there was the adjustment to motherhood and the joy of being with EC as often as my crazy schedule would allow. I am lucky to have a wonderfully supportive husband who filled in for me as much as humanly possible—but, yes, it was tiring. There were a few too many nights when my hours of sleep numbered four or five instead of seven or eight; a few too many jet-lagged evenings when I smiled at friends or colleagues over dinner table conversation without really hearing a word they'd said.

By the time December rolled around again, I was running on fumes. I'm sure that family and friends, and especially Andrew, were wondering when I planned on slowing down. But in my own mind, the plan was clear. "I can't stop now!" I thought. "I have to plan EC's first birthday party, the holidays are coming up, I have a thesis to defend, and clients and employees to entertain."

But occasionally even I had to admit there were cracks showing in the façade. I recall Andrew staring at me in concern one day that December as I was rushing to set the table for a dinner party we were hosting. "You know," he finally said in a gentle tone of voice, "you've missed a few things this holiday season. Are you okay?"

I was deeply shocked. I remember thinking, "He says I've missed a few things! Is that possible? I don't miss things! That's not who I am!" When the denial finally wore off, I admitted to myself that of course he was right. I'd forgotten to send a present to his grandmother in Kentucky. I'd forgotten to call our favorite caterer to plan the holiday party for Andrew's work event until forty-eight hours before the event—during their busiest time of year. I had even missed a conference call with a key client. With all these thoughts whirling in my head, I smiled reassuringly at Andrew, finished laying out the last place setting, and dashed off to tackle the rest of that afternoon's to-do list.

Somewhere inside me I was wondering, "How many balls have I been dropping? And if Andrew has noticed, who else has noticed? Am I really out of control?" But there was no time to focus on questions like those. I kept going at full speed—or maybe a little bit faster.

I made it all the way through Christmas—and then, on December 26, I crashed headfirst into the wall of my so-called life. And that's when I found myself sitting on the living room floor, staring up at the twinkling lights on the tree, oblivious to the sounds of EC and Andrew from some other room in our house, aching with an inner weariness unlike anything I'd ever experienced before.

This was more than just physical fatigue or sleep deprivation. This was soul fatigue. I'd achieved what I'd wanted—to keep my rich and busy life intact while being a new mom too. I'd proven I could do it, and there was satisfaction in that. The image of a successful woman that I'd always carried with me was that of a woman who was smart, driven, professionally accomplished, a Mary Poppins mom, a loving wife, a leader in the community—and someone who made it all look effortless with her calm, impeccable style. That superwoman was the gold standard I'd spent years trying to live up to. And in the past year, in some sense, I'd achieved it.

But now, on December 26, I'd woken up and realized I wasn't living. Not really.

It wasn't just that I was tired—tired of trying to do it all, tired of trying to live up to some bogus notion of success. It was my memory of EC's first birthday, ten days before. As I sat there on the floor, I remembered watching EC blow out the candle on her first birthday cake, which was the size of a small castle—one of those telltale symptoms of working-mom guilt. "Isn't it amazing?" I'd thought. "I have a one-year-old daughter!" And suddenly I'd realized I couldn't remember a single significant detail or moment from her first year. EC was the single most important thing in my world—and I was living a life that left me fundamentally out of touch with her.

Another memory popped into my head—a conversation I'd recently had with one of my closest friends, whose son had recently turned ten. "I only have eight years left with him at home," she'd said with a sigh— "only eight more years." And now I'd just missed the first year of my precious daughter's life. Was I going to blink and find myself suddenly celebrating EC's tenth birthday, wondering where all the time had gone?

That was the moment when everything changed for me. The moment when I knew it was time for me to reevaluate my life. Time to get real about who I was and who I wanted to be.

I'd spent the past year frantically racing around the country to build my business. And what was the name of that business? Thinking about it, I didn't know whether to laugh or cry. My company is called Working Simply. I teach people how to work more simply, more purposefully—to use smart planning to achieve much more with less effort.

Ironic? Yes, painfully so. But appropriate too. A wise woman once told me, "We teach what we need to learn the most." Suddenly I grasped the full truth of that saying. Suddenly I realized how much I had to learn along with my clients.

I am very grateful that I woke up the day after Christmas, looked at my beautiful daughter and amazing husband, and decided that my busyness was no longer serving me. That the drive to achieve my idealized notion of success no longer served me. It came with a cost so high that I no longer chose to pay it.

And I realized that "working simply"—the promise I make to my clients—is about more than simply being efficient, well organized, and productive. It's about moving beyond being busy to reclaim purpose and meaning in life.

In the weeks that followed, I made a number of important changes in my life and work style. As I'll explain later in this book, those changes and others I've made have profoundly enriched my life and my relationships with colleagues, clients, family, and friends. So now my work is more important to me than ever—because I'm on a mission. A mission to change the way we work and to support individuals, teams, and organizations in working smarter, not harder. A mission that I share with my clients.

If you've ever found yourself in the same desperate place I was in that December 26, I hope you'll join me. To get started, please turn the page . . .

1
—
Work Smarter, Not Harder

I SPENT NINE HOURS IN MEETINGS TODAY. MY E-MAIL INBOX has twenty-five thousand messages. I did not have time to use the restroom until 3 p.m. When I got home, my daughter threw my iPhone across the room and told me she was tired of me always being on it. It takes me hours to fall asleep at night because I cannot turn off my brain. I do not remember the last time I did something fun. I feel overwhelmed, stressed out, and frazzled. *My life is out of control.*

Does this sound familiar? Life in the twenty-first century is busy! We have access to unprecedented amounts of information. We are connected to one another twenty-four hours a day, seven days a week. Technology has blurred the lines between professional life and personal life. We *can* do more, so we do.

Statistics confirm this reality. About a third of Americans who work full-time say they work more than fifty hours per week. According to the National Sleep Foundation, moms who work full-time and have school-aged children say they spend less than six hours in bed on weeknights. John de Graaf's handbook *Take Back Your Time* reported that dual-income couples say they can find only twelve minutes a day on average to talk to each other.[1]

This epidemic of busyness comes with a pervasive belief in time management. We tell ourselves that if only we could make better use of downtime (read e-mail in the elevator? At a stoplight? In the line for coffee?) or multitask more cleverly (I can do this conference call *and* walk the dog *and* pick up the laundry), we'd get ahead of the busyness and reclaim our free time. But the stark reality is that we are not going to become any less busy. The demands on us at work, at home, from our friends, and from our community are not going to diminish—if anything, they are only going to increase. As we work harder and harder, we invest more hours and energy trying to fight a losing battle. Something's got to give.

If you're reading this book, your efforts to solve your busyness problem have probably not paid off. As a result, you're probably feeling frustrated. Or worse—you feel like a failure. Why can't you stop procrastinating? Why can't you get more done? Why isn't your inbox under control?

The truth is that the problem is not you. It is *how* you are trying to overcome your busyness that is the problem.

THE MYTH OF TIME MANAGEMENT

Within weeks of starting my first job out of college, I was sent to the in-house time management training program. Everyone in the entire organization attended the program, which was designed by a world-famous company that specialized in time management strategies. On the first day, the instructor handed out a planner and instructed us to use it to plan our tasks. We were told to prioritize our tasks, using numbers and letters, and record them on the left-hand side of the page in the planner on the date when they were to be completed. If a task was not completed on the designated day, we were instructed to move it to the next day by rewriting it on the left-hand side of the next day's page in the planner.

I dutifully attended the class and used the planner as instructed. But as the weeks went by, I noticed that my productivity hadn't seemed to improve. The time I spent filling out the pages in the planner felt like a needless waste. And I wasn't the only one. As I looked around at my colleagues, I noticed that many of them were really struggling with the system. Busyness, stress, and the feeling of being overwhelmed quickly crept back into our lives.

What happened? Now that we were armed with the secrets of a popular time management program and its specially designed planner, why weren't we all productive, efficient employees living balanced, purpose-filled lives?

The reason is simple: Time management programs do not work. Such programs teach a process focused almost entirely on how to plan and exercise control over the amount of time spent on a specific task or activity—for example, "Set aside adequate time to prepare the quarterly sales report before your meeting with your manager." This stems from the erroneous belief that poor allocation of time impairs performance. But such a one-dimensional approach does not account for the reality of work today, which is multifaceted, fast-paced, and constantly changing.

For example, at many companies, corporate goals are often only broadly specified. When I worked for a hospital foundation, one of the corporate goals was to be the preferred provider for cardiac care in the region. I worked in development and was not directly or indirectly responsible for providing patient care. So how did I organize my time to support the company's goal? I focused on employee giving and exceeding the target for our annual fund, which supported the operational budget of the hospital. As an employee, you must ascertain how to align your individual goals to the larger organizational goals. The numerous demands placed on you require that you not only increase your efforts but, more important, deploy those efforts wisely—otherwise the increased effort is not translated into performance gains.

Time management training is not going to teach you how to work more productively. And that explains why time management training in fact has not been proven to have a direct impact on performance.[2]

If you want some firsthand evidence, look around you. How many people in your office, in your neighborhood, and at your gym talk about how they are working to manage their time better and then frantically pull out their smartphone and rush to the next project or meeting because they are just so busy?

In my work as a productivity trainer and consultant, I have plenty of opportunities to see for myself how ineffective time management training is.

Andi waited to have her son, Jonah, until later in life, when she was already the managing partner at the largest of the regional offices in the Northeast at one of the top four consulting firms in the country.* After his birth, her world started spinning out of control. In the past, she would work long nights and weekends to catch up on work. With a child to care for, this was no longer possible. Suddenly the crushing weight of her workload seemed heavier than ever, and as an overachiever and perfectionist, Andi now felt as if she was failing to meet her professional and personal responsibilities. She could not remember the last time she'd gone for a run, her inbox was about to explode, she was behind on almost all of her reviews, and she felt completely out of balance. She was composing e-mails with her son in her lap and falling into bed exhausted.

Of course, Andi didn't simply allow these problems to overwhelm her. She did everything she could to fight back. By the time she called me for coaching, she had purchased four books on time management and enrolled in an online seminar. She had written an extensive to-do list, prioritized it using numbers and symbols, and blocked her calendar in fifteen-minute increments to complete her work. When her calendar was triple-booked and she was spending more time creating her to-do list than completing actual work, she realized that time management was not the real problem. She was going to have to radically change the way she thought about her work, how she structured her workdays, and how

---

*Throughout this book, I'll be telling the stories of clients and acquaintances who illustrate the ideas and principles we'll be studying. In the interest of privacy, their names and identifying details have been changed.

she took care of herself and her family. Everything had to change—
and fast.

As Andi experienced, the problem with time management is that it is
inherently limited in its effectiveness. Though she blocked her calendar in
fifteen-minute increments, very little of her work could actually be completed in this amount of time and it left her no time to respond to her
team's requests for her input, an essential component of her job. Andi's
time management seminar did not support her in considering the broader
context of her work and the need for a comprehensive overall productivity
strategy. She needed a productivity strategy that addressed how she
prioritized her work responsibilities, how she planned ways to meet her
work objectives, and how she allocated time and effort to enhance her
work performance. By contrast, Andi's time management course was
myopically focused on increasing her perception of control over time and
increasing the time available to pursue her activities. Time management
applies a one-size-fits-all solution to a very complex problem whose di-
mensions are different for every individual.

As Andi realized, time management is not what impacts productivity;
rather, it is our *work strategies* that impact our productivity. Andi stopped
making assumptions about how long it took to complete each component
of the review cycle. Instead, she timed herself so she could accurately
plan her work and manage her effort. She got very clear on how she
uniquely contributed to the bottom line of the company, and she strategically began saying yes and no to requests for her time and expertise. Andi
also realized the importance of self-care; she began running again both for
stress relief and to provide time to reflect and think.

PERSONALIZE YOUR PRODUCTIVITY

Andi realized that she worked best when she had a large volume of deliv-
erables that had to be completed within a short time period. The intensity
and satisfaction of quickly and accurately completing the work fueled her
and heightened her focus. Her analytical, logical thinking preferred working

with specific facts and data, and she realized that she got sidetracked when her direct reports came to her with vague or open-ended questions. Not only was this a source of frustration for her, but it also required a significant amount of time and energy to respond to their needs. Andi knew she was analytical, logical, and fact-based, but it was only upon reflection that she realized that her preferred working style was unique to her way of thinking.

Your work strategy is your approach to planning and allocating effort across goals, activities, and time periods.[3] This approach is usually unconscious and unsystematic rather than deliberate and rational. Nonetheless, patterns can be detected, which generally grow out of your individual *cognitive style*—your habitual pattern or preferred way of perceiving, processing, and managing information to guide behavior.[4] Since everyone has a distinctive cognitive style, you also need a unique set of work strategies. It is the *personalization* of these strategies to suit our individual strengths, preferences, needs, and talents that enables us to be efficient and effective.

You cannot outwork your busyness using one-size-fits-all time management solutions. The latest app, prioritization tip, or e-mail management strategy will not work if it is not personalized for you, aligned with the way you think and process information. Instead, it will only create even more frustration, inefficiency, and ineffectiveness.

Brigham is the owner and chief creative officer for a large national event management company. He purchased the company from its founder a few years ago and has been steadily growing the firm. Brigham called me a few months ago to say that he was struggling to adjust to the growing demands of being CEO and leading his team. He was constantly in meetings, had little or no time to think, and could not remember the last time he had a creative idea.

When he called me, Brigham had begun using a new task app in the hope that it would fix his feeling of being overwhelmed. I asked him, "What prompted you to switch your task management system?"

"Well, the CEO of my largest corporate client recommended it. So I figured it must work well."

"Well," I asked, "has it worked for you?"

"No," he replied. "I am now more overwhelmed and frustrated than ever."

As I probed deeper, it became apparent to me that the app was a linear, analytical tool that was not in alignment with Brigham's big-picture, holistic, synthesizing style of thinking. Of course it was not going to work! Brigham had squeezed himself into a T-shirt that was three sizes too small. He needed a tailored, personalized solution.

Brigham installed two additional large whiteboards in the company's meeting room and deleted the to-do list app from his iPhone. At the beginning of each week he now goes into the meeting room and mind-maps his weekly to-dos on his two whiteboards. He captures ideas on the boards, and throughout the week he goes back to them frequently to see what he needs to shift to respond to the day-to-day demands and challenges of the business. When he is feeling stuck or overwhelmed he goes into the meeting room, gets a marker, and just lets the ideas flow.

WHY THIS BOOK?

The busyness epidemic symptoms are familiar to most people, but we often fail to fully recognize the price we pay, as individuals and as a society, for accepting a way of life in which we are deprived of our most precious resources—time, freedom, and meaning. The loss of these three resources was a price I was no longer willing to pay. Are you?

If you are tired, frustrated, and desperately searching for a solution to the stress and chaos in your life, you have picked up the right book. *Work Simply* will show you, step-by-step, how to personalize your systems using what is unique about you and the way you think. You will be shown proven strategies and tools tailored to your thinking style. You will learn how to work well with others to actually get work done. You will at long last have a productivity system that truly and fundamentally fits you.

This is what my clients have sought and achieved. They are engaged in meaningful, purposeful work, producing high-quality results. They have exceeded sales goals, led wide-scale corporate change, created new, innovative businesses and products, and doubled the size of their companies in a year. At the same time, they are living life to the fullest: taking ballroom dancing lessons, coaching Little League baseball, drinking wine with friends, and reading best sellers. They are present and fully engaged with their colleagues, significant others, children, and friends.

How is this possible? They have personalized their productivity, embraced their individual Productivity Style (as we'll discuss in chapter 3), followed the simple yet powerful strategies outlined in this book, and leveraged their strengths. And as a result, they are working simply and living fully.

It is time to let go of the traditional approach to overcoming busyness—time management—and instead embrace the power of your unique cognitive style to guide and inform the choices you make about planning and executing your daily work. It is time to get personal about your own productivity.

But before we jump directly into personalizing your productivity, you need to prepare yourself for success. In the next chapter, we'll examine some of the key issues that are standing in your way.

2

Get Ready to
Work Smarter

IT WAS LATE AUGUST, ONE WEEK BEFORE THE OFFICIAL START of my freshman year at Washington and Lee University. My parents had just dropped me off at the loading dock outside the gym where I was about to begin the preseason training camp for the university's cross-country running team.

As I climbed into the waiting van and met my veteran cross-country teammates—many of them All-Americans—for the first time, I was suddenly overcome by fear. What had I done? There was no way I could keep up with these women! How could I even hope to compete at a collegiate level? I was convinced I'd made a huge mistake.

But later that morning, as I tied my running shoes and prepared for our first run of the day, I noticed something about my veteran teammates. Each of them had her own prerun routine. Some stretched, others sat on the floor listening to music, and still others did calisthenics—jumps, squats, and butt kicks. Still later, at my first college race, I would see how these routines intensified and shifted when they were preparing for a race.

My teammates had learned the power of preparation. Their prerace routines prepared them for the hard work that was to come and helped them get into a mind-set that enabled them to focus completely on the present moment. During my freshman year, I learned these lessons from my wise teammates, and I continue to apply them today. That's why I believe it is important for you to get ready before we start personalizing your productivity.

ROADBLOCKS TO SUCCESS

To get ready for your journey, it's important to identify the two major roadblocks that may be standing in your way. This analysis will help you to develop strategies to confront these obstacles head-on when they threaten to derail you or undermine your success.

ROADBLOCK #1: LOCUS OF CONTROL

If you are going to get personal about productivity, it means that the solution to the disorganization and chaos threatening your daily productivity starts and ends with you.

Locus of control is a concept developed by psychologist Julian Rotter. It refers to the extent that individuals believe they can control the events that affect them. A person with an *internal locus of control* believes that success or failure is due to their own efforts, while a person with an *external locus of control* believes that success or failure is controlled by other people, environmental factors, chance, or fate.

Where is your locus of control? It's a question most people have never asked themselves—but one that can change your life, as my client Samantha recently discovered.

Samantha is a smart, articulate, seasoned corporate executive who has spent her entire career working with and in Fortune 500 firms as an information technology consultant. She has worked for her current company for three years, managing its information technology support center and training team. Samantha has a great sense of humor, is an avid New

England Patriots fan, and is a working mom to a cool twelve-year-old son, Christopher, who stars on the local Little League baseball team.

Samantha had always been successful and delivered exceptional work. Lately, however, things had started to change. She had begun to receive feedback that she was not meeting expectations, she was missing deadlines, and her planning and follow-up on the training programs she ran was becoming inconsistent. Little by little, her clients were beginning to question her ability to effectively support them.

Lack of effort was certainly not the problem. Samantha was working nonstop, texting and e-mailing with her boss on weekends and late into the evening, even while she sat in the stands at Patriots games. She was busy, but not producing the results that she and her organization wanted. As a result, she had been recently passed over for a promotion—something that had never happened to her before.

When we met for our first coaching session, Samantha spent the first part of our day together telling me how everyone else was the problem. The VP of service delivery never responded to her e-mails; her manager just did not understand her big-picture thinking and her strategic ideas; her team was not supportive.

For Samantha, her locus of control was external. Everyone else was impacting her ability to be successful. At the end of day one, I told her, "If you want to achieve results and reclaim your life, you are going to have to choose to do something differently. And that begins with owning that *you* are in control."

It was like watching glass break. The tough strategic consultant exterior shattered and the fragile, sad woman beneath the surface emerged. Samantha burst into tears. "You're right—I know you're right! I was devastated when I didn't get that promotion. I felt like all my long hours and personal sacrifices were for nothing. What a waste—what a waste!" And for several minutes she simply cried.

It was obvious that the two of us had a lot of work to do together. But it was equally obvious that Samantha's commitment to her career was genuine, and that deep down she knew that she was ultimately in control.

You and only you can change your life. You have the knowledge, skills, and ability to create the life you want. But first you must accept this reality and stop expending time and energy blaming the culture, technology, your boss, your organization, your significant other, your children, or your pets for your busyness.

This doesn't mean that you can expect to change the world to suit your personal preferences. As I have learned only too well on my parenting journey, we really and truly have absolutely no control over others. You might know what I am talking about if you have ever tried to get a three-year-old to eat vegetables. Those vegetables are not going to be eaten if that three-year-old does not want to eat them—end of story!

I can't control the behavior of a forty-pound toddler. But I can control myself and the way I choose to respond. When EC chooses not to eat her vegetables, I simply tell her that is her choice—and as a result of her choice, there will be no dessert.

Deep down, Samantha knew that she was responsible for her own success—she just had to be reminded. In the same way, you probably realize that you are responsible for creating the life that you want. Taking conscious ownership of that reality—internalizing your locus of control—is the first step toward personalizing your approach to productivity and thereby conquering the busyness epidemic.

ROADBLOCK #2: GUILT AND THE SHOULDS

I felt guilty. EC woke up soaking wet because, the day before, I had accidentally bought pull-up diapers for boys instead of girls. I'd been rushing through Target, completely distracted and consumed by a pressing deadline at work, and just pulled a box of pull-ups off the shelf, quickly checked out, and rushed home. During the night, poor EC paid the price for my haste and distraction. No wonder I felt guilty the next morning.

Of course, this is just the minor leagues when it comes to my guilt—I can lay it on myself so thick that it is almost paralyzing. Am I working too much and not spending enough time with my family and friends? Am I undermining my health and my family's health because a majority of the food consumed in the household this week came from a takeout box? Am I letting down my community because I said no to that request to serve on a local board? All I need to do is to spend a few minutes pondering questions like these and soon I am deep in the black hole of guilt—insecure, confused, and miserable.

Emily, one of my clients, was also stymied by guilt. She is one of three female managing directors in the investment bank at her financial services firm. She graduated at the top of her class from Darden School of Business at the University of Virginia and rapidly rose through the ranks in the investment bank, consistently exceeding her revenue goals. She was a success!—until her most recent performance review, when she received a performance score of two on a scale of one to five (her first score lower than five).

When Emily called me, she described her work and the personal challenges she was facing working eighty- to ninety-hour weeks and never seeing her husband and family. She told me she felt incredibly guilty and was failing at everything. Then she said to me, "I realized I couldn't go on this way last Sunday afternoon." She continued, "I was at home, for once, and I was with Tom and the kids in the backyard. It was a beautiful spring day, and our baby Molly was practicing her walking on the warm grass, tottering around the way they do. Then she fell down and started to cry, and I jumped up to help her. But she wasn't crying, 'Mommy!' She was crying, 'Daddy!' and holding out her arms in Tom's direction.

"I felt like I had been punched in the gut," Emily said. "My baby didn't even know me—or want me—anymore. I feel like a failure, personally and professionally." Emily was deep in the black hole of guilt and about to break.

There is a very close cousin to guilt that often is just below the surface. I call it the *shoulds*. The shoulds are those voices in your head—you know the ones—saying, "You *should* be doing this," "You *should* like that," "You *should* spend time on this," "You *should* stop doing that," and so on and so forth, endlessly. There were numerous unspoken shoulds contributing to Emily's guilt as well as my own.

The problem with the shoulds is that they can easily become a runaway train, completely undermining your ability to get clear and focused on what you need.

For example, one of my clients—Colin, an estate attorney with both a JD and MBA and enough real-world experience to make him a formidable adversary if you are in the unfortunate position of being opposing counsel—was succumbing to a long list of shoulds. His firm was experiencing rapid growth, which prompted his call to me.

When we met, Colin was working ninety-plus hours a week and had been for months because that is what entrepreneurs *should* do—their business is their life.

At one of our meetings, Colin confessed that he had just eaten an entire sleeve of Thin Mint Girl Scout cookies for lunch because he was working out of three offices, one of them his car, which had a portable printer in the backseat for use in clients' offices. Why? Because he *should* always be accessible and uber-responsive to his clients.

Colin had every electronic gadget known to man, each of them ringing, pinging, and buzzing throughout the day, because of course, he *should* be in touch via the latest and greatest technology.

Unfortunately, with Colin spinning out of control because of his shoulds, the firm he was building was bending under the weight of the increasing caseload, forcing him to turn new clients away.

The shoulds had completely masked the real issues Colin was experiencing, which were normal business growing pains. He could no longer separate his priorities and goals from the culturally imposed shoulds playing like a heavy metal rock band in his head.

To combat the shoulds and liberate yourself from their tenacious clutches, the first step is to use the three-step evaluation process to test some of the assumptions that are behind guilt. Think about the fears and anxieties that are driving you (guilt is the manifestation of both) and then ask yourself, "What is the worst thing that could happen? Is it real? Is it true?"

For example, while building his business, a client of mine had gone five years without taking an unplugged vacation (that is, a vacation in which he disconnected electronically from the office) because he felt enormous guilt if he was not always connected to his office. Now his family had planned a ten-day trip to Europe during his children's spring break, and his wife and two teenage sons had begged him not to work during the vacation. So he called me in a complete guilt-ridden panic two weeks before departure. During our call, I asked him, "What's the absolute worst thing that could happen if you were not connected 24/7?"

He answered, "The firm could lose all of its major accounts, and the business would fold without me at the helm."

I then asked him, "How real is this concern? Has this happened to anyone you know?"

"Well," he sheepishly replied, "I don't know of any other business in my industry that has lost all of its major accounts in one week. And I have to admit that I have an exceptional chief operating officer with deep industry experience."

"So, it is not true?"

"No, it is not true," he admitted.

We then discussed the processes and procedures he needed to have in place to ensure that his clients and team were fully supported while he was on vacation. He thoroughly enjoyed his family vacation, guilt-free—in fact, while he was gone, his team landed a brand-new major account.

If guilt has ensnared you, use these same self-talk strategies to escape its clutches.

If you find yourself hooked by guilt's close cousin, the shoulds, the best way to break free is to strengthen your own boundaries. Start saying *no* to the voices inside your head, and maybe externally as well, and doing it in a new way—a way that I like to call the "P.O.W.E.R. No." It's based on the anagram P.O.W.E.R.—Priorities, Opportunities, Who, Expectations, and Real. Here's how it works:

- *Priorities.* When that voice in your head says that you should complete this task, lead another project, attend another meeting, or make cupcakes from scratch, evaluate the priority of that message. How does this should align to your priorities, the organization's strategic priorities, and/or your family's priorities?
- *Opportunities.* Explore the opportunities. What opportunities does this should create for you? Is there something that does actually need additional attention in your life? This should could be shining a light on something that you need to address.
- *Who.* Who or what triggered this should? Was it an old script from childhood? Was it an ad in a magazine? Was it your colleague?
- *Expectations.* Whose expectations are these really? Your manager's? Your mother's? Your spouse's? Your child's? Society's?
- *Real.* Get real. What is this should *really* about? Are there real priorities that are driving this should? Or are you taking on societal expectations that are not in alignment with your priorities?

Only after you have worked through all five sets of questions in the P.O.W.E.R. No are you in a position to make a really informed decision about whether or not to listen to and follow the should.

Shoulds lead us to overcommit—and when you overcommit, the quality and impact of your work suffers. When Steve Jobs returned to the helm of Apple in 1997, he quickly recognized that the company's employees were spreading their creative talents far too thin. He reduced their product portfolio from three hundred devices to ten, in the process saving Apple from bankruptcy. Follow Jobs's example—say no to the many things that threaten to distract you and derail you so you can focus your energies on the handful of things that will really lead you to success.

The P.O.W.E.R. No enables you to think carefully and critically about all of the shoulds so that you can consciously and thoughtfully respond.

It puts you back in the driver's seat, enabling you to *respond* rather than merely *react*. Stop shoulding all over yourself and take back control.

READY TO RUN

The two major roadblocks are behind you. You have learned that you and only you can change your life. You are at a choice. You choose to respond versus react. You know that you do not have to listen to the shoulds in your head and can say no to the many things that do not and will not create the life you desire. You are now ready to personalize your productivity.

3

—

What's Your Productivity Style?

OVER THE PAST THIRTY YEARS, SCIENCE HAS UNCOVERED A number of basic truths about how our brains function that are essential to enhancing your productivity. Understanding and applying these discoveries can go a long way in helping you escape the busyness trap and making your days less stressful as well as more productive, creative, and fun. In the chapters that follow, I will refer to these discoveries as they shed light on the strategies I teach.

One size does not fit all when it comes to productivity. At the same time that neuroscientists have been studying universal patterns regarding brain functioning, they have also been exploring the significant differences among individuals when it comes to thinking and working. These researchers have developed varying definitions of what is often called *cognitive style,* and their findings about how it influences the way a person perceives, thinks, learns, solves problems, and relates to others vary as well.[1]

One way of describing differences in cognitive styles that has captured popular thought is the right brain/left brain dichotomy. Beginning with the work of the Nobel Prize–winning neurobiologist Roger Sperry at the University of Chicago and Harvard in the 1940s and '50s, many scientists have studied the differing functions and activities associated with the right and left hemispheres of the brain. They have found that the right hemisphere is generally responsible for visual and spatial processing, and processes information simultaneously and holistically, while the left hemisphere is responsible for language and speech, and processes information analytically and sequentially. Based on these findings, a broader notion of *hemisphericity* gradually emerged, which suggested that individuals might rely on one hemisphere more than the other. You have probably encountered this concept in popular books, magazine articles, TV commentaries, and workplace seminars. You may have a strong sense as to whether you are mainly a right-brain or a left-brain type, and you may even have developed a tribal sense of "belonging" to one of the two categories.[2]

However, more recent studies suggest that this simple two-sided division between right brain and left brain is overly simplistic and inaccurate. Most scientists now agree that particular brain functions involve *both* hemispheres to varying degrees and that cognitive style is a complex combination of multiple variables. There is no doubt that people differ enormously in their ways of dealing with information, but the differences cannot be categorized simply according to a single two-part dichotomy, left or right brain.

This growing consensus has led most researchers to move toward a *multidimensional model* of cognitive style, one that reflects more accurately the complexity of human thinking and behavior. In particular, one of the most widely used and generally respected multidimensional models is the one developed in 1979 by Ned Herrmann, longtime manager of management education at General Electric. Herrmann's Whole Brain Model is designed to examine how the brain perceives and processes information. The model is represented using four quadrants—A, B, C, and D—each illustrating the unique ways in which we perceive, comprehend, manage, communicate, and use information, all of which impact our productivity at work and in life.[3]

The A quadrant cognitive processes are logical, analytical, quantitative, and fact-based. The B quadrant cognitive processes are planned, organized, detailed, and sequential. The C quadrant cognitive processes are emotional, interpersonal, feeling-based, and kinesthetic. The D quadrant cognitive processes are holistic, intuitive, synthesizing, and integrating.

These four styles are not rigidly defined or mutually exclusive; most individuals have a cognitive style that represents a blend of the quadrants, though one quadrant generally tends to predominate. Thus, although you should not view this four-part typology as a simple, magic formula for diagnosing and treating your personal productivity challenges, it can unlock many mysteries for you. It can help explain why particular productivity strategies that work beautifully for others are actually counterproductive for you, and it can help you identify approaches you may never have considered that can dramatically boost your productivity—and your happiness.

So instead of fighting against your natural thinking, learning, and communicating preferences, work with them. And the first step, of course, is to understand what those natural preferences are.

Originally designed to be studied using EEG measurements of electrical activity in the brain, Herrmann's Whole Brain Model was later adapted to a 120-item pen-and-paper questionnaire, making it suitable for use in a business setting. Herrmann's testing instrument, known as the Herrmann Brain Dominance Instrument (HBDI), has been used by over a million individuals, which means there is a vast pool of data that has served to clarify and codify its accuracy and usefulness. It has also been validated through a number of subsequent studies by other research scientists.

Since the HBDI is not specifically focused on the Productivity Styles of knowledge workers—that is, workers who convert knowledge from one form to another—I have developed a measurement tool called the Productivity Style Assessment inspired by the HBDI. It grew out of my original graduate research on cognitive thinking styles and how they inform an individual's choice of workflow strategies to manage time, projects, and tasks. In that research, I confirmed that there are discernible differences in individuals' cognitive styles and that when you know your own thinking preferences, you can choose and use more effective and sustainable strategies for managing your time, your projects, and your tasks.[4]

I've tested the Productivity Style Assessment with thousands of professionals from many areas of the business world, from CPAs and financial analysts to human resources managers, salespeople, consultants, and physicians. They have confirmed its value and usefulness as a self-assessment and coaching tool, due to both their intuitive sense of its accuracy in describing their own Productivity Style and the effectiveness of the working methods recommended to them based on the assessment's findings.

This twenty-eight-item quiz, the Productivity Style Assessment, is a key part of the courses and seminars I lead at corporations. Now I am making it available to you. It is a self-awareness tool designed to help you identify your preferred Productivity Style.

To take the quiz, read the instructions and complete each item quickly and intuitively. There are no right or wrong answers, and the more honest your responses, the more accurate the assessment is likely to be. The process will take only between ten and fifteen minutes.

THE PRODUCTIVITY STYLE ASSESSMENT

Please read each statement below and rate the statements using the following scale: 1 (Never), 2 (Rarely), 3 (Sometimes), 4 (Very Often), 5 (Always).

	1 Never	2 Rarely	3 Sometimes	4 Very Often	5 Always
1. I use a prioritized list to complete my work.					
2. I complete work quickly.					
3. I am often late.					
4. I have trouble telling my colleagues no.					
5. I plan for the next day.					
6. Daydreaming has allowed me to gain insights and solutions for many of my important problems.					
7. In project meetings, I synthesize disparate ideas into a cohesive whole.					
8. I use step-by-step project plans.					
9. I prefer to work on a team or with another person to get my work done.					

	1 Never	2 Rarely	3 Sometimes	4 Very Often	5 Always
10. I use a deadline as a time frame for completion.					
11. I complete my best work under pressure.					
12. I block time on my calendar to complete my work.					
13. I analyze each project before I start it.					
14. I use established routines and systems to complete tasks.					
15. When I plan a project, I think first about who needs to be involved.					
16. I designate specific time periods for certain tasks.					
17. When I plan a project, I think first about how the project supports the strategic vision.					
18. I eliminate physical clutter in my office.					
19. When I brainstorm, I list my ideas.					
20. It is hard for me to take time to play when there is still work to do.					

	1 Never	2 Rarely	3 Sometimes	4 Very Often	5 Always
21. When I brainstorm, I sketch or draw my ideas.					
22. I accurately complete significant amounts of work.					
23. When I brainstorm, I talk to others about my ideas.					
24. I tend to underestimate how long it takes to complete tasks and projects.					
25. When I plan a project, I think first about what is the outcome or desired result.					
26. I am selective about the tools—pens, paper, folders, etc.—that I use.					
27. I complete project tasks in sequential order.					
28. When I plan a project, I think first about what is the project goal.					

Scoring the quiz: List your scores for the items listed in each column below. For example, if you responded with a 3 (Sometimes) for item 1, write "3" next to item number 1 in the first column. When you have listed all your scores, total the scores in each column. Then write the scores in the appropriate quadrant in the Productivity Style Circle (figure 3.1).

1. = _____	5. = _____	4. = _____	2. = _____
13. = _____	8. = _____	9. = _____	3. = _____
16. = _____	10. = _____	12. = _____	6. = _____
19. = _____	14. = _____	15. = _____	7. = _____
20. = _____	18. = _____	23. = _____	11. = _____
22. = _____	25. = _____	24. = _____	17. = _____
28. = _____	27. = _____	26. = _____	21. = _____
TOTAL: _____	TOTAL: _____	TOTAL: _____	TOTAL: _____
Write this number in the PRIORITIZER quadrant.	Write this number in the PLANNER quadrant.	Write this number in the ARRANGER quadrant.	Write this number in the VISUALIZER quadrant.

Figure 3.1. The Productivity Style Circle. In which quadrant is your highest score? That's your primary Productivity Style.

EXPLORE YOUR PRODUCTIVITY STYLE

Now that you have completed the assessment to identify your primary Productivity Style, what does it all mean? How does it relate to the way you work? Let's begin by considering the characteristics of each of the four Productivity Styles.

WORK SIMPLY: CHARACTERISTICS OF THE FOUR PRODUCTIVITY STYLES

Prioritizer

A Prioritizer prefers logical, analytical, fact-based, critical, and realistic thinking. He or she tends to use time effectively and efficiently, focusing on the highest-value task and on achieving project outcomes. A Prioritizer is generally able to accurately complete significant amounts of work and effectively prioritize tasks.

Strengths:

- Prioritization
- Thorough analysis and logical problem solving
- Goal orientation, consistency, and decisiveness
- Consistency

Pet Peeves:

- Meaningless chatter
- Inaccurate or missing data
- Inefficient use of time
- Vague, ambiguous approaches or instructions
- Overt sharing of personal feelings

Undying Loves:

- Critical analysis
- Robust, fact-based debate
- Spending time wisely and efficiently

Famous Prioritizers:

Philosophers Aristotle and Kant, scientist Sir Isaac Newton, executives Sheryl Sandberg and Marissa Mayer

Classic Quote:

"Being busy is a form of laziness—lazy thinking and indiscriminate action. Being selective—doing less—is the path of the productive. Lack of time is actually a lack of priorities." —Tim Ferriss, author of *The 4-Hour Workweek*

Communication Style:

If you listen closely, you can detect discernible patterns of speech used by Prioritizers. Prioritizers often use facts to illustrate points, speak in a matter-of-fact tone of voice, and frequently use technical jargon, acronyms, and buzzwords. They speak clearly and logically and will ask direct questions about the value and function of products. For example, a Prioritizer might say, "Give me the bottom line. How well does this product work?" Or they might say, "I only want to hear the most relevant data."

A Prioritizer prefers to have information presented in a form that is brief, precise, clear, and technically accurate. For example, Steve Yankovich, vice president of innovation and new ventures at eBay, describes how he prefers communication this way: "I want constant, real-time communication. I want people to be concise. A small screen and less efficient keyboard force people to get the point across. You're not going to type four paragraphs on a phone. Hours matter."

Prioritizers do not like assumptions and fluff—they follow the motto, "Just the facts, ma'am." Prioritizers typically ask "What" questions when they're making decisions: "What does this product or service do?" "What are the problems?" "What are the results?" A Prioritizer will react unemotionally to feedback and wants precise facts when receiving it.

Use of Space:

A Prioritizer's office environment and personal workspace is typically very businesslike, with a professional look and feel. There are clean, functional lines and no excess artwork or decorations. The desktop is clean and orderly, containing just a few professional items.

Decision-Making Style:

A Prioritizer makes decisions by gathering all of the facts, analyzing the issues, and developing theories. Prioritizers argue rationally and solve problems logically. They work precisely with numbers, statistics, and data.

Preferred Productivity Tools:

Productivity tools that appeal to Prioritizers include the iPad (which they can customize to streamline their workflow), productivity apps like Evernote, Noteshelf, To Do, LogMeIn Ignition (which allows them to log in to their PCs and complete work remotely), and ScanBizCards (which lets them scan business cards on the run), as well as classic low-tech tools like legal pads and a label maker.

Planner

A Planner prefers organized, sequential, planned, and detailed thinking. A Planner budgets the time required to complete tasks, sequentially organizes tasks, and prepares accurate, detailed project plans. He or she doesn't waste time on tasks and projects that are unproductive or unimportant, and creates project plans that are sequential, detailed, and concise. A Planner is usually careful about consulting and complying with laws, policies, regulations, and/or quality and safety criteria when planning projects. A Planner maintains detailed lists and frequently completes work in advance of deadlines.

Strengths:

- Action orientation, consistency, and practicality
- Finding overlooked flaws in plans or processes
- Organizing and maintaining data
- Developing detailed processes and plans

Pet Peeves:

- Lack of a clear agenda; disorganization and topic hopping
- Late or last-minute work
- Lack of closure or follow-through and indecisiveness
- Unclear instructions, ambiguous language, typos, and other errors

Undying Loves:

- A schedule and action plan
- Thorough, timely follow-up
- Scheduled appointments and timely arrivals
- Getting to the point

Famous Planners:

Philosopher Plato, FBI director J. Edgar Hoover, British politician Margaret Thatcher

Classic Quote:

"When I am in a situation where there are lots of things to do, I am very organized. I relentlessly check and double-check that all of the little pieces are moving the way they're supposed to be moving. Holding it together is clearly part of my pathology. I like to be in control. Even on summer vacation I write a menu of what I'm going to be cooking for dinner." —Celebrity chef Anthony Bourdain

Communication Style:

A Planner's pattern of speech is characterized by the use of precise, detailed words. A Planner speaks in complete sentences or paragraphs and frequently expresses skepticism and concern for quality, asking precise questions that require concrete answers. You can expect to hear Planners say things like, "I believe in using proven products that have passed the test of time," or "I'm a creature of habit, and I don't easily change how I do things." A Planner prefers to have information presented in a concise, consistent, detailed, and step-by-step format—and he or she expects it to be delivered on time, in writing, and with ample references. A Planner also prefers detailed action plans (including contingency plans) and expects to follow those plans precisely, with few deviations. Planners typically ask "How" questions: "How frequently do problems occur?" "How do you want to approach this project?"

A Planner will react cautiously when receiving feedback and requires neatness and punctuality.

Use of Space:

A Planner's office environment and personal workspace typically have a traditional look and feel, with no impractical or unnecessary items. The layout and the decorations are very practical. The work area is very neat, orderly, and organized, with few personal items cluttering the space. Professional credentials, plaques, and company-issued items are often on display.

Decision-Making Style:

A Planner approaches decision making in a spirit of practicality. He or she often finds overlooked flaws by reading the fine print in documents and contracts. Once a Planner has made a decision, he or she will stand firm, providing stable leadership and articulating plans and ideas in an orderly, consistent fashion. You can count on a Planner to organize and keep track of data, maintain accurate financial records, and develop detailed plans and procedures.

Preferred Productivity Tools:

Productivity tools that appeal to Planners include digital lists and project planning apps like Tom's Planner and Omnifocus (which lets them create and track by project, place, person, or date), Agendas (which lets them create interactive agendas and broadcast them to iPad users), and ZipList (which creates both personal and shared family shopping lists, organizing items both by category and by the store that carries them). Planners also like low-tech tools like label makers, file folders, filing cabinets, drawer organizers, pen holders, and other office organizational supplies. It is fun to turn Planners loose in a Staples or Office Depot store and watch them stock up on all of their favorite productivity toys!

Arranger

An Arranger prefers supportive, expressive, and emotional thinking. He or she encourages teamwork to maximize work output and makes decisions intuitively, in real time, as events unfold, blocking out time to complete work. An Arranger excels at partnering with people to get work done and is an effective communicator with project teams. He or she likes to maintain visual lists, often using color, and intuitively knows what tasks must be completed.

Strengths:

- Anticipating how others will feel and understanding their underlying emotions
- Intuition
- Persuasion
- Teaching

Pet Peeves:

- Lack of eye contact and other personal interaction
- Impersonal approach or examples, relying solely on data and facts
- Tone of urgency or demand

Undying Loves:

- Interactive conversation and approach
- Opportunity to process feelings and emotions
- Acknowledgment and appreciation
- Opportunity to discuss questions and concerns

Famous Arrangers:

Composer Chopin, nonviolence advocate Mohandas K. Gandhi, humanitarian Mother Teresa, media mogul Oprah Winfrey, musician and activist Bono

Classic Quote:

"Listen to your gut, no matter how good something sounds on paper. Instincts play a special role in any kind of business you engage in. They are your guide in the decision-making process and the backbone of your thoughts. Following your instincts is as simple as giving them a voice, challenging yourself to look at things differently, and learning to look before you leap." —Real estate entrepreneur and author Donald Trump

Communication Style:

The typical Arranger tends to be talkative, often using stories about people to illustrate points and speaking with warmth about personal issues. An Arranger expresses concern about people and will frequently ask questions about the way a particular project or task will benefit others.

An Arranger prefers to have information presented through an open, informal discussion. Arrangers prefer eye-to-eye contact; they generally listen actively and appear devoid of hidden agendas, using expressive body language and tone of voice to engage and connect with others. Arrangers typically ask "Who" questions: "Who are the primary stakeholders in this project?" "Who will benefit most from this process?" "Who else is involved?"

An Arranger will react with emotion when receiving feedback and needs to feel enthusiasm.

Use of Space:

An Arranger's office environment and personal workspace is typically welcoming and inviting. It often includes photos, personal objects, or mementos, and has music playing. When you walk into an Arranger's office you can get a sense of who they are from the personal memorabilia, pictures, and tchotchkes that surround you.

Decision-Making Style:

An Arranger tends to approach decision making by intuitively sensing how others will feel. An Arranger recognizes interpersonal difficulties and picks up on nonverbal cues of stress. He or she is skilled at using an understanding of the emotional elements of a situation in persuading and teaching others.

Preferred Productivity Tools:

Productivity tools that appeal to Arrangers include voice-translation dictation apps like Dragon NaturallySpeaking and Dragon Dictation or the Web-based application Copytalk, collaboration tools like GoToMeeting, WebEx, SharePlus Office Mobile Client (an app that enables them to collaborate with their team from anywhere and sync their SharePoint files automatically), and join.me (an app with a mobile viewer that lets them quickly and easily attend meetings). They also love visually and kinesthetically pleasing office supplies—things like notebooks with unlined pages and pens in a variety of ink colors.

Visualizer

A Visualizer prefers holistic, intuitive, integrating, and synthesizing thinking. He or she sees the big picture and has the ability to work very quickly. A Visualizer adroitly manages and juggles multiple tasks and projects. A Visualizer is also able to synthesize disparate ideas into a cohesive whole, generating creative, innovative project ideas. A Visualizer thinks strategically about projects, effectively managing multiple ideas simultaneously while being efficient in task execution. A Visualizer maintains visual lists, often using color.

Strengths:

- Open-mindedness
- Ability to see the big picture, recognizing new opportunities, and integrating ideas and concepts
- Innovation; willingness to challenge the status quo
- Creative problem solving

Pet Peeves:

- Repetition, slow pace
- Rigid, highly structured project plans with no flexibility
- Excessive detail; too many numbers
- Being told "You can't" or "We've always done it this way"

Undying Loves:

- Spending minimal time on details
- Broad conceptual frameworks
- Connections to other approaches

Famous Visualizers:

Scientist Albert Einstein, artists Pablo Picasso and Leonardo da Vinci, entrepreneurs Steve Jobs, Richard Branson, and Larry Page

Classic Quote:

"Some look at things that are, and ask why. I dream of things that never were and ask why not?" —Playwright George Bernard Shaw

Communication Style:

A Visualizer uses visual language when speaking—words and phrases like *see, look, envision, imagine,* and *the big picture.* They typically speak in abstract phrases and frequently use metaphors. They also tend to ask general, broad-based questions about concepts and innovative aspects of a particular task or project.

A Visualizer prefers to have information presented using metaphors or visual aids that place specific details within a big-picture overview or conceptual framework, often aligned to the organization's long-term strategy. Visualizers value the flexibility to move away from a planned agenda in search of new, fun, and imaginative approaches. Visualizers typically ask "Why" questions: "Why is this process better?" "Why do we do things this way?"

A Visualizer will react spontaneously to feedback and prefers concepts.

Use of Space:

A Visualizer's office environment and personal workspace are typically informal, casual, and nontraditional, with an emphasis on space and light and a decorative scheme that is typically colorful, varied, and aesthetically pleasing. A Visualizer prefers original art and playful objects and toys. The space is typically cluttered with piles of paper, personal memorabilia, and collectibles.

Decision-Making Style:

Visualizers make decisions by inventing imaginative, intuitive solutions to problems. They are perceptive and skilled at reading signs of coming change, which sometimes leads them to challenge established policies. They tend to recognize and seek out new possibilities, embrace ambiguity, and integrate ideas and concepts that others may consider incompatible or unrelated.

Preferred Productivity Tools:

Productivity tools that appeal to Visualizers include digital whiteboard apps, Sketchbook Pro (an app that lets them capture ideas while working with a complete set of sketching and painting tools), iThoughts HD (a digital mind-mapping tool), Concur (an app used to photograph and save expense receipts and create expense reports), and Noteshelf (a digital notebook tool). They also love visually vibrant low-tech tools—multicolored Post-it Notes, colored folders, notebooks with unlined pages, pens in a variety of ink colors, large whiteboards, baskets, folders, and bags and clipboards for keeping papers visible and organized. A classic Visualizer would enjoy nothing more than an afternoon in an art supply store with an unlimited budget to spend!

WHICH STYLE IS YOURS?

When you read the description that matched your primary Productivity Style (that is, the style on which you earned the highest score), did it resonate with you? Were there any surprises? Have you seen examples of this style showing up in your work and personal life?

The majority of people who have taken the quiz report a strong sense of affinity with the Productivity Style identified as their primary preference. However, some have another score or scores that were close in value to their highest score. This is to be expected; it indicates a secondary Productivity Style preference. The secondary preference is the style you often use or go to under stress.

The remaining chapters in this book will build on what you have learned here. Each chapter will examine a particular aspect of productivity or a particular busyness challenge through the lens of the four Productivity Styles. As you read, pay particular attention to the strategies, tactics, and tools recommended for your primary Productivity Style preference. Also look at the strategies, tactics, and tools for your secondary Productivity Style preference, noting what modifications or adjustments you might want to make when you are working under stress.

At the same time, I urge you to use your own judgment and experiences to filter the strategies. Review the strategies, tactics, and tools recommended for Productivity Styles other than your own. It is quite possible that one or more of these may jump out at you and prove to be extremely valuable for you. After all, each of us is whole-brained, not merely a one-sided fragment! Even an individual with a strong bent toward the Planner style has a bit of the Visualizer insider her; even an Arranger can find value in the methods that appeal to the Prioritizer.

Do not pigeonhole yourself. Having seen so many working men and women frustrated and confused by productivity systems designed for other people and imposed upon them arbitrarily, the last thing I want to do is create yet another arbitrary set of rules to serve as a straitjacket for you! Instead, pick and choose freely from the array of ideas I'll present in the coming chapters. The goal is to create a personalized productivity toolkit that is in alignment with the way you think and fully supports you as you move beyond busy to reignite purpose and meaning in your life.

MY STORY

Clients and workshop participants often ask me my Productivity Style. Before answering, I ask them to try to guess the answer using the clues and cues I have left behind through my words and behaviors—and many are able to use these clues to correctly identify my style. It may come as no surprise to you that my primary style is that of a Planner and my secondary style is that of an Arranger.

As a Planner, I am an avid list maker and occasionally—okay, frequently—have been known to write tasks on my to-do list that I have already completed just so I can mark them off. I have never met an office supply or organizational tool that I did not like; visits to the Container

Store and Office Depot are delightful, time-consuming, and expensive endeavors for me. My makeup drawer is organized by type, color, and frequency of use, as are the other drawers in the rest of my office and home. When family trips and girls' nights out are on the calendar, I am often the one who plans the trip or night out. My mom told me recently that even when I was a little girl of two or three, I would line up my toys in a particular order and organize my baby dolls' clothing—shirts in one stack, dresses in another stack, and shoes in a third. Who knew that my career path would reveal itself at such a young age?

My calendar is my brain on paper. I use it to keep me aligned to my goals as well as to ensure that I meet all of my commitments and deadlines. When my book editor, Niki, gave me a deadline for the outline, she said, "I put these deadlines on my calendar and I expect you to meet them." I immediately thought—and promptly blurted out—"It is a deadline. Why would I miss a deadline?" (I have since learned that not every author takes book deadlines with equal seriousness. Douglas Adams, author of the classic *Hitchhiker's Guide to the Galaxy,* spoke for the majority of writers when he joked, "I love deadlines. I love the whooshing noise they make as they go by.") But for me, deadlines are absolute, and I will do whatever it takes to meet them.

The Arranger in me is simply unable to stop beginning my e-mails with at least a "Good morning" or "Good afternoon"—despite the fact that I know this bothers Visualizers and especially Prioritizers, who really just want me to get to the point. In writing this book, I dictated concepts and chapters because it is often easier for me to think while talking. This is a typical Arranger behavior, one that I have to frequently warn my colleagues about; otherwise they would be off in a million different directions working on projects and initiatives I was only considering. The desk in my office has numerous photos of family and friends on it. All of my beloved books are organized by subject (of course), and my collection of the three specific types of pens I like to use are displayed in a bright red glass container that I bought at an art show.

My primary preference as a Planner provides the basic structure and organization of my work and personal life. If I am feeling overwhelmed, stressed out, and generally frazzled, it is usually because I have not taken the time to think through my projects and commitments and to update my calendar and to-do list accordingly. Once I do, a sense of calm comes over me and I am able to efficiently execute my work.

My secondary preference as an Arranger helps me to know intuitively what work needs to be done first and how to work best with my clients, colleagues, and partners. My Arranger preference also makes me very sensitive to my work environment and the tools I use. I need natural light, my notebooks, my pens, and a large table to spread out on. So when I am traveling, I pack what I need to create a conducive working environment regardless of where I am—even the floor of an airport terminal; and yes, I do get some strange looks.

It may be that the way I work sounds very restrictive, boring, and way too structured for you. That's fine! Embrace those thoughts and feelings. The way I work is not the way you work, nor should it be. Each of us is unique, and we need to align our workdays and lives to the way we think. When my clients try to use the same notebook system I use or to structure their calendar exactly like mine, unless their primary preference is that of Planner, they become frustrated and inefficient. I then have to bite my tongue to keep myself from saying, "I told you it wouldn't work! My system is not in alignment with your Productivity Style."

So embrace your Productivity Style! Remember, one size does not fit all. When you begin organizing your life and work according to the natural preferences of your style, you are likely to find yourself relaxing and enjoying the sensation of truly being in the driver's seat of your life rather than struggling with the tension that arises from fighting against your preferred thinking style. The feeling of having entered your comfort zone is a sign that you've latched on to the right style *for you*—and it doesn't matter whether anyone else you know understands it or shares it.

In the rest of the book, we will explore how to leverage your Productivity Style to create a personalized path to working simply.

4

—

Manage Your Attention

PING, BUZZ, RING. "DO YOU HAVE A MINUTE?" "THIS IS AN emergency!" Sound familiar? Throughout our workdays, we are consistently and constantly interrupted. Technology, colleagues, meetings, emergencies, and even boredom all contribute to the incessant demands on our attention.

According to a 2005 study by the productivity research firm Basex, interruptions, distractions, and recovery time consume 28 percent of the average knowledge worker's day. That translates into twenty-eight billion man-hours per year lost to U.S. companies.[1] Gloria Mark, a professor who studies digital distraction at the University of California at Irvine, has found that between digital and human factors, there's typically only three minutes of consistent focus before an employee gets interrupted or self-interrupts. (Three minutes! I can barely brush my teeth in three minutes.) Mark also calculates that it may take twenty-three minutes before a worker gets back to whatever task he was completing before the interruption occurred.[2] And in a 2011 survey of U.S. employees by harmon.ie, a social e-mail software provider, almost half of the employees in the study said they usually worked just fifteen minutes or less without getting interrupted or distracted.[3]

It is clear, then, that distractions cost significant amounts of time. But they also cost companies substantial money. The Basex study found that the cost of managing distractions for U.S. businesses is $588 billion, while the harmon.ie study found that a typical company with more than a thousand employees can waste more than $10 million per year as a result of digital distractions.

Distractions and interruptions are significantly undermining our ability to focus, engage, and be productive. Yet we have come to accept workdays filled with distractions and interruptions as normal; many of us complete our work in the "margins" of our days, early in the morning and late at night, due to the pressing demands on our time and attention. Many organizations foster a culture in which being distracted is viewed as necessary or beneficial. They encourage managers to declare, "My door is *always* open," they expect employees to respond to e-mails and text messages within minutes or even seconds, and they lionize workers who somehow manage to do two or three or five things at once, as if "multitasking" is the key to success. In this kind of corporate climate, culturally driven busyness becomes inevitable and is rarely questioned, despite the high toll it takes on our productivity and effectiveness.

It is time for us to push back against the plague of distractions and interruptions. But before we can do this, we need to understand the finite and fleeting nature of our attention and how this affects our productivity.

ATTENTION: A FINITE, PRECIOUS RESOURCE

Human brains come equipped with two kinds of attention: involuntary and voluntary. Involuntary attention is designed to be on the watch for threats to survival and is triggered by outside stimuli—what grabs you. Today, we do not face the same kinds of survival threats our ancestors faced—rampaging predators, attacks by rival tribes. Our biggest threat is an irate client, a demanding boss, or a surly coworker, hardly the same as a charging tiger. However, our brains have not evolved to distinguish between the ping of a new text message and a roar of a wild animal; though at times you might feel as if your e-mail were a predatory animal, in fact it is not. So throughout the average workday our involuntary attention works on overdrive, automatically rattled by the workday cacophony of rings, pings, and buzzes.

As our involuntary attention works on overdrive, we are also battling a neurochemical, dopamine, which unconsciously causes us to want, seek out, and be curious about ideas, thus fueling our desire for information. So if you have ever felt as if you were addicted to e-mail, Twitter, or texting, you were right—and dopamine is the physiological cause.[4]

The addictive power of dopamine is surprisingly strong. As I am typing this, I feel myself wanting to know more about dopamine, a desire I can easily satisfy with a Google search. At the same time, I am wondering whether I've received any e-mails in the last twenty minutes, I'm curious about what the weather will be like for the rest of the week, and I want to see who can meet me for lunch this afternoon. Click, swipe, ping—I am now in a dopamine-induced loop, circling through the Internet rather than accomplishing the task I set out to perform. The dopamine got me seeking, I got chemically rewarded for seeking, and now I want to seek some more. And over time, it becomes harder and harder to stop—checking e-mail, my iPhone, my text messages, Twitter, and LinkedIn . . .

Recently I was working with a colleague, Kathy, on a project in her office. On her desk she had two cell phones—one for personal correspondence and one for business correspondence—as well as her landline and her computer. In the first fifteen minutes of our time together, her personal cell phone rang, she received two text messages on it, her landline rang, her business phone pinged with a new text message, and she received ten new e-mails. At each ping, buzz, and beep, Kathy visibly twitched and looked at one of the four devices. Needless to say, because of all these demands on Kathy's involuntary attention and the resulting dopamine-induced loop, it took us twice as long as it should have to complete our project.

Voluntary attention is the ability to concentrate on a chosen task. It is "voluntary" because you have control over it, whether or not you fully recognize and exercise that control. In her book *Rapt: Attention and the Focused Life,* Winifred Gallagher argues that humans are the sum of what they pay attention to. In effect, what we focus on determines our experience, knowledge, amusement, and fulfillment.[5] So our attention is an enormously powerfully force, one that can profoundly shape our lives and our very being. Yet instead of cultivating this resource with the care it deserves, we generally tend to squander it on "whatever captures our awareness."

My colleague Kathy was clearly squandering this precious resource. So was my client Colin, a lawyer whose goal was to grow his firm by exceeding his clients' expectations, cultivating relationships with strategic partners, and speaking at industry meetings and trade events. (You remember meeting Colin back in chapter 2.) However, when we first began working together, he was focused instead on learning how to use a new dictation service and finding the perfect research software. Colin's primary Productivity Style is that of a Prioritizer, and Prioritizers sometimes get bogged down in finding the latest and greatest technology tools as part of their ongoing quest to improve their efficiency. Colin's attention on these two things was consuming hours of his time—despite the fact that he had an exceptionally competent and talented paralegal who could handle projects like this for him.

Our attention is finite—a precious resource that was hardwired to function a specific way thousands of years ago and that has not changed. So in order to successfully manage our attention, we must fully understand the brain's natural wiring and how this impacts our ability to manage attention.

Unfortunately, managing our attention does not come easy for most people. In part this is because we're simply unaccustomed to thinking about the process in any explicit fashion. But there are also a number of psychological and environmental forces that actively work to sabotage our efforts to focus. These include:

- *Intense emotion.* According to Srini Pillay, an assistant clinical professor of psychiatry at Harvard Medical School, the brain's wiring lends itself to being distracted. The part of the brain devoted to attention is connected to the brain's emotional center. So any strong emotion—frustration with a colleague, problems with your teenager—can disrupt your attention.[6] As you have probably experienced, even working on a challenging project creates anxiety or stress, another strong emotion, which can make you tend to self-interrupt as a way of escaping that intense experience.
- *Physical discomfort.* You are also more vulnerable to distractions when you are uncomfortable, hungry, or tired, asserts Robert Epstein, a research psychologist and founder of the Cambridge Center for Behavioral Studies.[7]
- *Psychological insecurity.* Author Tony Schwartz notes that our responsiveness to distractions is powerfully influenced by our desire for connection. Thus the safer and more secure we feel, the more focused attention we can allocate to our long-term goals.[8]

In order to manage our attention, we must work with nature and with the innate tendencies of our brain to respond to forces like emotion, discomfort, and insecurity rather than trying to struggle against these psychological and physical drives. So what can you do to harness the finite nature of your attention? In the next few pages, we'll offer some suggestions.

MANAGE YOUR VOLUNTARY ATTENTION

As you know from personal experience and now also from research, our brain's wiring lends itself to being distracted. So our first goal is to strengthen our voluntary attention—the attention we have direct control over—in order to improve our focus and our ability to proactively complete our work.

The first step in this process involves *cultivating awareness*. Learning to do this begins with a simple but surprisingly powerful exercise—the *attention awareness exercise.* Select a span of four hours, either during the workweek or on a weekend, as your tracking period for this exercise. Then choose an attention tracking tool that works for you: pen and paper, the notes feature on a smartphone, or a dictation device. Every time your attention wanders, you lose focus, or you are interrupted either by others or yourself, make a note on your attention tracking tool.

You may want to devise different symbols to refer to your own personal "distractors." For example, I have had clients use hash marks to denote the number of times their attention wandered and create abbreviations for the people, things, ideas, and emotions involved—for example, P = person, F = feeling, C = child, E = e-mail, W = Web surfing, and S = social media (Facebook, Twitter, LinkedIn, and so on).

And, yes, the exercise itself is also diverting your attention. However, there is a method to the process. The attention awareness exercise enables you to see, literally in black and white, how often your attention wanders and the triggers that cause this to happen. You have to notice that your attention has wandered in order to do something about it. I suggest that you repeat the attention exercise multiple times during a workweek and at different times of the day. You want to have enough data to thoroughly analyze your attention awareness trends.

Now that you have your attention data, you can start making changes. Review the data and notice any trends or themes:

- Did you find it more difficult to focus right before lunchtime or dinnertime?
- Was it difficult to focus after a long meeting or a difficult conversation with a family member?
- Was it easier to focus after a walk or a workout at the gym?
- Were there specific time periods during the four hours when it was easier to focus?
- Were there specific projects or types of tasks that you were able to focus on for longer periods of time?

Keep notes on the trends and themes that emerge for you.

The second step in strengthening your voluntary attention involves *optimizing the physiological conditions* necessary for ideal attention management. You want to create an environment that supports your unique attention management needs and minimizes the impact of the hardwiring of your brain. If you are tired, hungry, or stressed, you are fighting an uphill battle with your attention. Guess who is always going to win—your brain! If you are up late at night finishing a project, you may not have the ability to focus on a complex task at eight the next morning. If you've just had a very difficult conversation with a colleague or spent an hour consoling an upset friend, be aware and plan accordingly; your voluntary attention muscle is already fatigued due to this interaction.

Plan your self-management activities with all of these factors in mind. Keep packets of nuts, granola bars, or dried fruit in your office drawer, pocketbook, briefcase, and/or the glove compartment of your car to stay properly fueled for maximum focus. Create a playlist of soothing and energizing music to help you relax or recharge after stressful interactions and conversations. Keep comfortable shoes in your desk drawer or in your car or workbag so you can go for a quick walk up and down the halls of your office building or outside. Physical movement is one of the most effective ways to mentally reset and discharge negative energy. And you do not have to walk long to benefit—ten minutes is all it takes.

When TV hostess and media mogul Martha Stewart was asked how she manages to accomplish so much during a day, she responded, "I used to get tired before I started working out on a daily basis. Even a half hour makes a huge difference to the body's energy level over the course of a day. Eating healthy, fresh foods is essential. With nutritious diet and exercise, I can get a lot done in a day."[9]

Optimize the physiological conditions required for you to manage your attention, and you too should be able to boost your sense of focus.

The final step requires that you retrain your brain using a *brain reboot*. Refocusing is hard because we have trained our brains to work on a variety of things at one time. How often have you checked e-mail during a conference call, or fed your child breakfast, unloaded the dishwasher, and packed lunches at the same time? This habit does not improve your productivity; instead, it undermines your ability to focus.

In order to refocus, visualize a reset button in your brain and say, "I need to hit reboot and get back on track." According to Dr. Pillay, this takes the spotlight off the distraction and puts it on the redirection—the refocusing on your task.[10] By frequently rebooting your brain, you are rewiring it for optimal functioning.

Another approach to brain rebooting is the use of breathing to restore your focus. Try taking a deep inhalation breath, pushing out your navel, and then powerfully expelling the air by slightly bringing in your stomach. Repeat this breath five to seven times and observe how the tension and mental chatter in your mind dissipate. Another breath that also short-circuits the mental chatter is to place your tongue on the roof of your mouth and blow out as if you were blowing out candles on a birthday cake. As you blow out, count to seven. You can now regain your focus.

The steps outlined above are universal steps that will help most of us strengthen our voluntary attention. However, each of us is unique. Here are some methods to manage your voluntary attention that are specifically tailored to your individual Productivity Style. (Read all the suggestions in the table below, not just those listed under the heading for your primary Productivity Style. Remember that most people have a style that blends elements of two or even more Productivity Styles—which means it's likely you may discover a tool or technique that works brilliantly for you even if it is designed specifically for those with a different primary style.)

WORK SIMPLY:
STRATEGIES BY PRODUCTIVITY STYLE TO
MANAGE YOUR VOLUNTARY ATTENTION

If You're a Prioritizer

Set a timer or an alarm to go off at specific intervals throughout your workday. The alarm serves as a reminder tool to check your focus and concentration. Then eliminate distractions. When Cory Booker, U.S. senator and former mayor of Newark, New Jersey, was asked how he was so productive, he replied, "I think it is important to get rid of distractions and miscellaneous choices. When I get up in the morning, I do not have a million clothing items to choose from. The more you limit your choices, thereby limiting thought, the more you can simplify your life and focus energy elsewhere."

If You're a Planner

Harness your affinity for planning by carefully planning each day around your varying energy levels, changing patterns in the type of work you do and in scheduled or spontaneous interactions with colleagues and friends. When fashion designer Tory Burch was asked how she finds balance and plans her time, she said, "I've found a way to make things more manageable by prioritizing, focusing on time management and setting boundaries. Sometimes that means rescheduling a meeting."[11]

If You're an Arranger

Pace your work by interspersing solitary work with group projects or conversations with colleagues. The interpersonal interaction will serve as a break and be refreshing, enabling you to more effectively manage your attention and maintain your focus. Claire Watts, U.S. CEO of the giant retail and media company QVC, schedules "open-door times" every Tuesday when anyone in the company can visit her to talk, ask a question, or share something they have noticed.

Music of whatever type you prefer (whether classical, soft instrumental, or rock and roll) can also make it easier for you to focus and complete your work.

If You're a Visualizer

Leverage your affinity for spontaneity and variety by mixing up the type of work you do and the amount of time you dedicate to particular projects. Intersperse fun or very stimulating tasks with routine tasks. For example, when Martha Stewart was asked about how she completes her work, she said, "I try to balance things I have to do with things I want to do. I always find I can be more productive with my work when it's broken up with a bit of pleasure."

For you, the less rigid and predictable your schedule is, the better.

We have control over our voluntary attention, and our voluntary attention becomes stronger when we work with rather than against the hard-wiring of our brains, recognize and deal with the triggers that divert our attention, and leverage our individual Productivity Styles.

Now we are ready to tackle involuntary attention, the form of attention that responds automatically to the myriad distractions in our lives today.

AVOID DISTRACTIONS AND CONTROL YOUR INVOLUNTARY ATTENTION

As we've seen, distractions waste time, erode productivity, and interfere with our ability to control our workdays and lives. Cultural drivers often encourage us to accept or even embrace these distractions, despite their destructive impact upon us. Let's take back control by minimizing and avoiding distractions, thereby dramatically increasing our productivity and effectiveness while reducing our stress.

In my work with clients, I have identified four primary distractions: technology, emergencies, interruptions, and meetings. I will explore technology, emergencies, and interruptions in this chapter and explain ways to minimize the impact of each. I will discuss meetings and managing their impact on your attention and time in chapter 14.

CONTROL DISTRACTIONS FROM TECHNOLOGY

In 1987, economist Robert Solow quipped, "You can see the computer age everywhere but in the productivity statistics." Solow wasn't the last expert to note the discrepancy between the vast amount of time and money our society has invested in electronic information management technology and the seemingly scanty benefits we have received in the form of measurable increases in productivity. In fact, Erik Brynjolfsson analyzed this discrepancy in a 1993 article that popularized what has come to be called the *productivity paradox*. In the words of Yaacov Cohen, CEO of harmon.ie, "Information technology that was designed at least in part to save time is actually doing precisely the opposite. The very tools we rely on to do our jobs are also interfering with that mission."[12]

You and I experience the productivity paradox as *technology overload,* a phenomenon that occurs when the addition of new technology reaches the point of diminishing marginal returns.[13] Our lives have become saturated with technological tools to the point of overflow. One new piece of software or one new feature on our smartphones can tip the scale and send us spiraling down, actually decreasing our productivity. Think about the last time you purchased a new phone and how long it took you to learn to use it efficiently. The period of diminished productivity you experienced is a classic case of technology overload.

It is important to remember that each of us experiences technology overload in a highly personal way. You and your colleague working in the exact same environment can experience technology quite differently. That means it is important to consider your own Productivity Style when deciding on strategies to minimize distractions.

But first, let's look at some data on the biggest digital distractors. Here's how they were ranked in one survey:[14]

- E-mail processing—23 percent
- Switching windows to complete tasks—10 percent

- Personal online activities such as Facebook—9 percent
- Instant messaging—6 percent
- Texting—5 percent
- Web search—3 percent

How would you rank *your* biggest digital distractors? For my client Yvette, the greatest culprit was definitely e-mail. As an Arranger, Yvette prefers to get her work done with and through people. As a result, e-mail is like chocolate for her. It is a connection to her colleagues and a very efficient way to communicate with large numbers of people. So she loved the sound of the e-mail notification alarm—it meant she had a new connection. But constantly responding to the distraction of new e-mail was eroding her productivity. You may have the same problem as Yvette—or perhaps you find that the allure of Facebook or the flow of text messages from your friends and work colleagues is the distraction that shatters your ability to focus.

Thankfully, we aren't helpless in the face of technology overload. There are a number of strategies you can use to take control of the technology that surrounds you and make it work to your advantage. The following table offers a number of ideas about how you can personalize your effort to reduce the amount of technology-driven distraction you experience during the workday.

WORK SIMPLY:
STRATEGIES BY PRODUCTIVITY STYLE TO KEEP TECHNOLOGY FROM DISTRACTING YOU

If You're a Prioritizer

Technology Tips:

- Check and respond to e-mail at "low productivity" times. Follow the natural rhythm of your day, and avoid your e-mail inbox during those periods when you tend to do your highest-quality work.
- Cut the tether to technology: Leave your cell phone, your laptop, and/or your tablet in your office, your briefcase, or your purse rather than carrying them with you everywhere.

Tools to Try:

- Use RescueTime, an application for both your computer and mobile devices. It lets you temporarily block Web sites you deem distracting, tracks time spent on tasks, and alerts you if you are spending too much time on a specific task.

If You're a Planner

Technology Tips:

- Plan and designate specific time(s) to check and respond to e-mail. For example, you could decide to check e-mail in the morning, before lunch, after lunch, at midafternoon, before you leave the office, and once in the evening.
- Communicate the time(s) you check e-mail with colleagues, managers, and direct reports, so they will know when—and when not—to expect a prompt response.

Tools to Try:

- Use AwayFind, an application that works across e-mail platforms and will halt your daily barrage of e-mail notifications, except for the ones that include senders and keywords you designate as urgent.

If You're an Arranger

Technology Tips:

- Turn off the sound on all of your technology tools. Free of beeps, pings, and buzzes, you can scrutinize and respond to new messages according to your own schedule and preferences rather than feeling you must jump every time a machine demands your attention.
- Designate an e-mail-free day once a week—for example, you might declare that you will observe "e-mail-free Friday" every week. On that day, instead of e-mailing your colleagues, pick up the phone and enjoy actually connecting with them.

Tools to Try:

- Use WriteRoom, an app for Macs that runs in full-screen mode and blocks out all other distractions on the computer, leaving you with only the text.
- If you are not a Mac user, use JDarkRoom. It is a free cross-platform application that imitates the functionality of WriteRoom, allowing you to work in full-screen mode distraction free.
- Use Camouflage (Mac) or Dropcloth (Windows) to hide the clutter on your desktop, thereby minimizing distraction.

If You're a Visualizer

Technology Tips:

- Turn off the computer screen, keep your e-mail program closed, and/or close your Internet browser.
- Turn your phone over so the screen is not visible. Reducing or eliminating visual distractions will make it easier for you to focus on the task at hand without being interrupted by your technology tools.

Tools to Try:

- Use Think, an application for Macs that when launched will ask you which window you want to focus on, bring it to the front, and darken the rest of the screen so you can focus.

- Use Isolator, an application for Macs that can completely hide other windows and blur everything behind your active window.
- If you are a Windows user, use JediConcentrate, which works like Think. When you enter concentrate mode, the window you are working on is illuminated and the rest stays dark.

PREVENT EMERGENCIES FROM DOMINATING YOUR DAY

My client Colin had a meeting scheduled with a couple to review their revised trust documents. Just two hours in advance, he was putting the final touches on these documents when the office server went down, destroying all of his work from the previous four hours.

This was an emergency—all hands on deck! Sandy, Colin's paralegal, quickly contacted the firm's IT department and convinced them to send someone down to figure out what they could possibly retrieve. She then called the clients to reschedule their meeting for the next day. Within a few hours, IT had worked magic, finding copies of the documents, enabling Colin to finish his revisions. However, the emergency diverted everyone on Colin's team as they reshuffled casework, a member of the IT department, and Colin himself from their other work that needed to be completed that afternoon. The crisis was managed and the client soothed, but hours of time were lost.

This scenario is repeated frequently in offices across the country. Unavoidable emergencies like this one do happen. But other emergencies happen because of poor planning, misunderstanding of the time and resources needed to complete a project, or some form of procrastination. Regardless of the type of emergency, the impact is the same—an interruption that costs hours of lost time, diminished productivity, and significant amounts of stress.

So what can you do when an emergency threatens to take over your day? Here's an approach that works for many people.

First, *define the emergency* and clarify whether or not it is truly urgent. What's the nature of the problem? Is there an imminent safety concern? What is the impact of the problem on your clients, the business, and the broader organization? Is the problem one that *must* be dealt with immediately, or can it be handled later in the day or tomorrow morning without significantly inconveniencing anyone? Triage your response to the emergency based on the answers to these questions. Don't fall into the trap of redefining everyday problems as emergencies. Put out the burning fires that are threatening lives or property; for other problems that do not truly rise to the level of emergencies, schedule time to tackle them when it suits you best.

Once the emergency has been diverted or solved, you now have an opportunity to *develop a plan* for dealing more effectively with future emergencies. Conduct a postmortem—a meeting at which all the relevant team members gather to discuss the emergency. Avoid acting judgmental or assigning blame, which will tend to make the postmortem into an ineffective exercise in defensiveness and finger-pointing. Instead, focus on developing objective answers to a few basic questions: What caused the emergency? How could it have been avoided? How quickly did the emergency come to our attention? How effective was our response? Have we done everything we could to minimize or alleviate the damage caused? What will we do differently to prevent this emergency from occurring again?

Use the answers to these questions to shape your team's emergency management plan. If you are the leader of the team, communicate your expectations around identifying, managing, and resolving any future emergency. For example, my client Tania, a managing director at a large financial firm, told her team that an emergency is a situation that could result in the loss of a client account or significant revenue for the firm. Other problems, no matter how unexpected or upsetting, do not rise to the level of emergencies and therefore can be dealt with as time permits.

If you are not the leader of a team but simply a team member, ask your manager to clarify what constitutes an emergency. Once the definition of an emergency is clear, decide on and communicate your expectations around resolving any crisis. Teresa instituted a color-coding system to quantify the nature of any emergency and determine the response. An orange emergency required that the team inform her of the crisis within thirty minutes and then use their skills and relationships to resolve the crisis. A yellow emergency required that she be notified within fifteen minutes; she also had to review and approve the plan to resolve the crisis, and she would be available as an additional resource. A red emergency required that she be notified immediately—interrupted in a meeting, called at home, or otherwise alerted. Teresa would then partner with her team in devising the strategy to address the emergency. She would be the point of contact for the client and the internal organization, and she would work alongside her team to resolve the crisis.

Teresa had established good support systems—trusted internal and external partnerships—with knowledgeable colleagues who helped her system work well. By having a clear system in place, Teresa empowered her team to proactively resolve emergencies, ensuring a quick, thoughtful response with minimal impact on the team's overall productivity.

Finally, *invest time in developing systems and processes* that will enable you and your team to prevent emergencies from arising in the first place. Teresa has used three strategies to make this happen. First, when she and her team are planning a project, they conduct a brainstorming session on risks. Everyone on the project team is expected to share any and all risks that could possibly derail the project, prevent them from achieving their goals, or result in a crisis. These sessions get a little wild and far-fetched at times, but identifying and naming the risks enables her team to develop contingency plans.

Of course, Teresa's team still experiences a few emergencies. They use them as learning opportunities, deconstructing each emergency to identify the warning signs that the project or initiative was beginning to derail. They keep them in mind in their next risk brainstorming session.

Emergencies happen. To minimize their impact on you and your team's productivity, clearly define what constitutes an emergency, establish protocols for responding to and handling an emergency, anticipate risks, develop contingency plans, and foster a culture that is willing to learn from any and all crises. Following this path can help you and your team minimize the burden of culturally driven busyness that causes too many organizations to waste countless hours in dealing with avoidable emergencies.

MINIMIZE THE IMPACT OF INTERRUPTIONS

It does not take an emergency to shatter your work focus. The ordinary conditions of modern work life have made interruptions a routine part of our days. Open-space plans, communal workspaces, and the proliferation of technology devices have resulted in very distracted workers. In an Office Workplace Productivity study conducted by Ask.com, 61 percent of respondents claimed noisy coworkers as the biggest distraction in the workplace. The same survey also found that 40 percent of workers said that impromptu meetings from coworkers stopping by their workspace were a significant office distraction.[15]

These interruptions come at a high price. Excessive interruptions affect human behavior by increasing stress and by negatively impacting recall, accuracy, efficiency, and performance.[16] Interruptions are undermining our ability to effectively and efficiently complete our work. It is time for you to take back control and halt the incessant interruptions.

Since productivity is highly personal, your strategy to manage interruptions should reflect your thinking style as well as the realities of your work environment and office culture. Of course, it should also be tailored to your personal Productivity Style. Take a look at the list below and see how many of the strategies suggested there might help you minimize the impact of interruptions on your own productivity.

WORK SIMPLY:
STRATEGIES BY PRODUCTIVITY STYLE TO MINIMIZE THE IMPACT OF INTERRUPTIONS

If You're a Prioritizer

Try This Strategy:

A productivity strength of yours is your ability to complete significant amounts of work and keep your head down. Leverage this strength by communicating open-door/open-office hours to your colleagues. Let them know when you are available each day. Even if you work in an open office space, you can still establish "interruption hours," leaving other periods when your colleagues know that you need to work without being disturbed.

How It Can Work:

One of our clients, a medical technology company, instituted a "stoplight system" in their office. Each team member hangs a colored square on their cube wall indicating their current level of focus and engagement as well as their willingness to be interrupted. A red square signals that the only reason to be interrupted is if there is an emergency and the building is burning down. A yellow card means you are working on a project that requires a significant amount of focus and concentration, so proceed with caution when interrupting. A green card means you are open and available for impromptu meetings or questions. Consider using the stoplight system to manage the interruption traffic in your office.

If You're a Planner

Try This Strategy:

Use your planning muscle by setting appointments with colleagues instead of accommodating drive-bys or stop-ins. When a colleague comes by and asks whether you have a minute to discuss a project, you might respond, "Right now I don't have time, but we can talk tomorrow at 10 a.m., when I'll be able to be fully present and able to focus on the project." You can also redirect your colleague by suggesting that someone else might be able to help them.

How It Can Work:

My client Jeremy is known as the problem solver in his office. He is calm and cool in a crisis and always willing to provide additional information or tools to solve a problem. As a result, Jeremy was consistently interrupted throughout his workday. To take back control of his calendar, he worked with the IT department in his firm to make his calendar viewable by everyone in the office. He meticulously kept his calendar current, indicating when he was available and when he was engaged in project work, and printed it out for posting next to his office door. Now Jeremy's colleagues make an appointment when they need his help. Sometimes they roll their eyes over his carefully planned days, but they now receive the answers and ideas they need to tackle their latest crises without disrupting Jeremy's workday.

If You're an Arranger

Try This Strategy:

Leverage your interpersonal skills by reframing how you approach interruptions. Institute a personal chat budget and let your colleagues know when you are coming close to exceeding your budget.

How It Can Work:

My client Sandy is a warm, gracious, smart, savvy woman who has become the go-to person in her office for training and instructional design questions. Sandy enjoys being a resource for her colleagues and has cultivated personal relationships with most of them. However, her office looks like a train station at rush hour with all of the comings and goings. Sandy's productivity was starting to decline and she was staying late to complete her work, encroaching on her family time. So she decided to institute a personal chat budget. Each day she now gives herself thirty minutes a day for personal chatting. When colleagues come to her office for help, she answers their questions, then lets them know that she is about to exceed her chat budget so she is going to have to get back to work.

Sandy's colleagues laugh, honor her chat budget, and still feel supported and valued by her.

If You're a Visualizer

Try This Strategy:

Use your appreciation of novelty to stimulate you by changing the scenery. Find a conference room on another floor, visit the office cafeteria on off-hours, or go to a local coffee shop where you can complete your work uninterrupted. If you must stay in your office environment, minimize external distractions by using headphones (with or without music playing), or physically reorient your body so people cannot catch your eye.

How It Can Work:

My client Carlos is known throughout the office as the guy who has an office but is never in it. When it's time for him to brainstorm new ideas, he works in the cafeteria; when he needs to write or outline ideas, he goes to the Starbucks down the street where he sits in the back corner with his Bose headphones on, listening to the Grateful Dead. And when he really needs to escape, he goes up to the legal department offices on the tenth floor and works in one of the open cubes along the back wall. Of course, when he gets restless, he goes back to the cafeteria where there's always something going on!

We cannot control all the behaviors of our colleagues; in many companies, we cannot put the walls back up in our open-plan offices. (We'll consider ways of dealing with this challenge and other problems with your physical environment in chapter 10.) However, you can use the strengths of your Productivity Style to minimize the impact of interruptions on you and your ability to complete your work.

Once you are able to manage your attention in a way that fully supports the way you think and work, it is time to focus your attention on identifying your professional and personal goals and priorities. That's the topic we will explore in the next chapter.

5

Set Your Priorities

BECOMING AWARE OF WHAT IMPEDES YOUR ABILITY TO FOCUS and eliminating distractions so you can complete your work are essential to enhancing your productivity. However, if what you are focusing on and working on is not connected to a broader purpose or goal, then you are like a boat without a rudder—directionless and unmoored.

Denise Morrison, the CEO of Campbell's Soup, knew from a very young age that she eventually wanted to run a company. She learned that just as you need to set goals to accomplish a business project, you need to set goals in your life, both short-term and long-term, and develop a plan to achieve them. Denise always looked at her career by asking questions like "Where have I been? Where am I now? Where am I going, and what are the right assignments to get there?" When her current company would work with her to deliver those assignments, she was all in. But when it didn't, she knew she needed to move on.[1]

The READY, Aim, Fire methodology will not only assist you in getting very clear on your goals and priorities, but also ensure that you achieve those goals in the most efficient and effective way possible.

READY: DETERMINE YOUR GOALS

To get ready, you have to become very clear on your goals and priorities—and I suggest you start by taking a very broad look at your life and work rather than focusing narrowly on the next few days, weeks, or even months. Then use these long-term goals as guideposts to shape and direct the short-term steps that will take you there.

I write my READY goals at the end of the year or within a day or two of January first each year. I write my goals or intentions in the following four areas of my life:

- Professional
- Personal
- Health
- Spiritual

I try to be very specific about what I want to create this year, using the following questions as a guide.

Professional

- At the end of my career, I will be able to say that I used all the gifts given to me if . . .
- Where do I want to be in ten years?
- What are my team's or division's goals for this year?
- What are my personal goals for this year?
- What is my one stretch professional goal for this year?

Personal

- What do I want more of from the personal relationships in my life?
- What do I want less of from the personal relationships in my life?

- What do I want to give to the personal relationships in my life?
- How do I want to be present for the people in my life?
- What is my one stretch personal goal for this year?

Health

- How do I want to feel physically this year?
- How will I ensure my optimum physical and mental health this year?
- What changes do I need to make to my diet, exercise, and rest routines to support me in achieving my professional and personal goals?
- Do I have any specific physical goals—for example, to run a 5K race or take a weekly yoga class?
- Do I have any specific rest and rejuvenation goals—for example, to take two days each quarter to think and reflect?
- What is my one stretch health goal this year?

Spiritual

- What is the quality of my spiritual life?
- What changes, if any, do I want to make to strengthen it?
- How will I nurture my spiritual life this year?
- What is my one stretch spiritual goal this year?

As you answer each of the questions above, use READY as your goal-drafting guide. Make sure that your goals are:

R—Realistic,

E—Exciting,

A—Action-oriented,

D—Directive (meaning that they will actually point you in the direction you want to go), and

Y—Yours (not simply someone else's goals for you).

Many people find the READY stage daunting. I used to be one of them. That question, "Where do I want to be in ten years?" used to make my toes curl, because I could not see where I wanted to be next month! I was so busy, focused on the work in front of me and reacting to what was coming my way, that I refused to look up and envision the future I wanted to create.

Nonetheless, I forced myself to engage in goal setting, as every respected time management book and self-improvement guru recommended. Each January, I would go through the motions of setting my goals and New Year's resolutions. I dutifully followed what was then the gold standard of goal-setting methodology: I wrote goals that were described by the acronym SMART: Specific, Measurable, Action-oriented, Realistic, and Time-bound. My list of goals looked very impressive, and for a few days or even weeks I felt quite proud of myself.

Unfortunately, by February my resolutions and goals were rapidly fading in the rearview mirror. (You may have experienced the same thing.) Why? Eventually I realized that something was missing for me. My goals represented a lot of *shoulds* in my life; they were not exciting to me nor really my own. There was no real juice or oomph behind them. They were boring and felt more like obligations than a road map to an exciting, meaningful future.

It was only after I woke up that day after Christmas that I realized something had to change in my life. The first place to start was to get very clear on the *true* goals and priorities of my personal and professional life.

So now when I look forward to getting READY, I feel the way I felt when standing on the starting line in college waiting for the gun to go off for a cross-country race. I have butterflies in my stomach, my muscles are tense and primed, my feet are pointed toward the finish line, and I am actually looking forward to the run, even though it is going to take hard work.

I now set my goals and priorities for the year at the end of the year or within a day or two of January first. I remind myself of where I have come from and ring in the New Year centered on what I am going to focus on and achieve in the coming year. I write my goals and priorities down in the crisp new gray notebook I have specially purchased, and I refer back to them frequently throughout the year to ensure I am properly aiming and executing on my goals (more on that in chapters 6 and 7). Having exciting personal and professional goals and devoting my days, weeks, and months to pursuing those goals in a methodical fashion goes a long way toward helping me avoid the all too common danger of spinning my wheels in meaningless activity, another victim of the busyness epidemic. (See figure 5.1 for an example of what one person's goals for the year might look like. Yours may look very different—and they should!)

Figure 5.1. One year's worth of goals, organized into professional, personal, health, and spiritual goals.

USE THE READY FRAMEWORK TO SET YOUR PRIORITIES

Getting READY, determining your goals and priorities, can be universally applied to all Productivity Styles. Regardless of your thinking style, setting goals that are realistic, exciting, action-oriented, directive, and your own is the essential first step to experiencing true productivity—a clear, focused mind uncluttered by indecisiveness. However, there are some differences in how each Productivity Style thinks that make the process of applying the READY framework unique for each of us. The following table will walk you through some options.

WORK SIMPLY: STRATEGIES FOR GOAL SETTING BY PRODUCTIVITY STYLE

If You're a Prioritizer

The Prioritizer is naturally goal- and outcome-focused, so setting goals feels very natural to you and is at times done without conscious thought. However, the Prioritizer tends to be myopic at times and can become focused on very short-term, immediate goals. If you are a Prioritizer, stretch yourself and challenge yourself to think about the next six months instead of the next six weeks when setting your goals. Be aware of your natural tendency to focus solely on the *what* (the end result you are trying to achieve). It is also very important for you to think about the *how* (the actions you need to take to achieve your goals), the *who* (the other people who need to be involved), and the *why* (the reasons your goals matter to you and your organization).

If You're a Planner

Planning and goal setting come very naturally for the Planner. Like the Prioritizer, the Planner at times tends to get so detailed and sequential in their thinking that the goals and priorities are really next action steps rather than broad strategic goals. If you are a Planner, remember to ask yourself *why* when setting your goals: Why does this goal matter to me, my team, and/or my organization? It is also important to remember to be clear on the *what* (the outcome you want to achieve) and the *who* (the other people who need to be involved in achieving your goal).

If You're an Arranger

The Arranger's natural inclination in goal setting is to think about who will be impacted by their goals and who can support them in achieving their goals. If you are an Arranger, remember to ask yourself about the *what* (the desired outcome you want to achieve), the *how* (the action steps necessary to achieve the goal), and the *why* (the reason the goal matters to you personally, your team, and/or your organization).

If You're a Visualizer

If you are a Visualizer, strategic, big-picture thinking is the norm for you. You see the future and understand how actions today can and will impact the future state of your life and the organization's life. Harness your big-picture thinking by staying focused on the *why* of your goals, but remember to get very clear about the *what* (a specific outcome or goal you want to achieve, making sure that it is quantifiable). Also remember to think about the *how* (ensure that the goal is action-oriented and that you can see how you will achieve it) and the *who* (the other people who need to be involved in achieving the goal).

READY is just the first step in the three-part READY, Aim, Fire system for setting and achieving your personal goals. In the next chapter, we'll move on to the second and third steps, Aim and Fire—and we will do that in the broader context of learning how to wisely invest the most precious and limited commodity you possess: your time.

6

Invest Your Time Wisely

A FEW YEARS AGO, A FRIEND RECOMMENDED THAT I READ THE book *The Last Lecture* by Randy Pausch, saying, "Since you're in the time management business, you might like it."

My friend did not notice me cringe. She did not know that I try to keep my distance from "the time management business," since I think the standard prescriptions of that school of thinking have proven to be inadequate for dealing with the *real* problems caused by today's busyness epidemic. The truth is that, unlike an employee or a team of workers, time cannot be managed. You can't call "Time" into your office and give him a dressing-down: "Time, your performance last week did not meet my expectations. I need another six hours out of you this week." I started Working Simply in order to pioneer a very different approach to the productivity challenges we all face . . . an approach you are already beginning to learn.

However, my friend's book recommendation was well intentioned, and I made a point of picking up a copy of *The Last Lecture* as soon as I could.[1] Unfortunately, I was in the middle of a large project at the time, so it sat on my bookshelf for a few months until one evening when I pulled it down, saying, "I have a few minutes to spend—maybe I'll read a few pages." When I next looked at the clock, several hours had passed—I'd finished the book in one sitting. It was funny and entertaining, but more important, it challenged my perception of time.

Randy Pausch was a professor of computer science and human-computer interaction and design at Carnegie Mellon University. When he was asked to give his "last lecture," as many professors are asked to do, he did not realize that it would truly be his last. In August 2007, Pausch had been diagnosed with terminal pancreatic cancer. But *The Last Lecture* is not morbid or depressing, nor is it about dying. It is about achieving your childhood dreams, overcoming obstacles, enabling the dreams of others, and seizing the moment. It is about living—fully living.

Pausch's cancer diagnosis completely changed his perception of time. He realized that time was all he had. It is an insight that applies to all of us. Time is what we all have, and we all have the same amount—24 hours a day, 168 hours a week. What I learned in reading Pausch's book is that life and happiness are not about having more hours in a day—they are about more purposefully and intentionally using the hours we do have.

After I finished reading Pausch's book, I was curious and wanted to actually see him delivering his "last lecture." I found the video on YouTube and watched it, then watched it again and watched it a third time. I kept coming back to one line in the video when Pausch says, "Do you know what your household time budget is? Probably not. See, you can go and earn more money, but you cannot ever get time back."[2]

I had never thought about my time as a commodity, like the dollars in my wallet. This was thought-provoking enough—to realize that time is a rare and precious thing, a resource that we must never squander but instead must spend with care, planning, and intention, just as we spend the money in our bank account. But Pausch's comparison also emphasizes the *difference* between time and money. Unlike money, time is not a renewable resource. By working harder, building a business, or buying a fast-growth stock, we can earn more money. But once today's twenty-four hours are gone, they will never come back, no matter what we do.

Like many young people, I had always assumed that I would always have more time—a seemingly infinite procession of tomorrows, as free and limitless as the air we breathe or the water that flows from the tap in the kitchen. Pausch's video brought home to me the fact that in reality, of course, that's simply not true. Time is limited and therefore even more precious than money.

What does this mean to you?

The challenge is to shift the way you think about time. The goal is to start thinking about time as a commodity, and in particular as an infinitely valuable, nonrenewable resource.

In my work with clients, in order to make time more tangible and to help them embrace this paradigm shift, I ask them to calculate the monetary value of their professional time. They divide their annual salary by 2,080 hours (52 weeks × 40 hours a week), and the resulting number is the value of one hour of their professional time. They now can quantify their professional time using a numeric, monetary value.

Do you know the monetary value of one hour of your time at work? If so, excellent! If not, determine your hourly rate. Once you know your hourly rate, you can quantify time—its value is no longer nebulous. The objective is to understand and use your time the same way you think about and use your money—only with even greater thoughtfulness and care, if possible.

More important, think about the various ways you use your money—and then begin to apply some of the same thinking to your time. For example, you spend some of your money on daily necessities and luxuries; you give away some of your money to support organizations and causes you believe in; and you save and invest some of your money in order to produce greater value for the future.

In the same way, you can use your time in a variety of ways. You can spend some of your time on activities that are necessary (like driving to work or cleaning your house) or enjoyable (chatting with a friend, watching a movie); you can give away some of your time to help others and make the world a better place (for example, by volunteering at a local nonprofit, caring for someone who is ill, or mentoring a young person); and you can invest some of it in activities that will give you greater value in the long run (taking a class, exercising to improve your health, or attending an event to expand your professional network).

We don't often think or talk about this last use of time. But since time is so limited and precious, this is probably the most important thing we can do with time—invest it wisely so it produces the highest possible long-term return.

"Time is money," the old saying has it. But that's wrong. Time is *more valuable* than money. You need to start treating it that way.

STOP GIVING AWAY YOUR MOST VALUABLE RESOURCE

You remember Andi from chapter 1, whose primary Productivity Style is Visualizer. Andi always said yes. She had a psychological drive to feel needed and valued, and culturally her organization espoused an open-door, collaborative work environment. As a result, the chairs in Andi's cubicle always had people in them, her calendar was overflowing with meetings, and she completed her work between 9 p.m. and midnight or on Saturdays and Sundays. A conscientious team player, Andi was usually working on numerous projects that were not hers and was always available to her team and colleagues. It had been months since she'd watched an episode of *Scandal* without simultaneously tackling work on her laptop, and she could not remember the last time she'd attended her crossfit class.

This pace was starting to wear on Andi, but she kept pushing because she knew the organization needed her. However, she was consistently missing deadlines, her senior manager said she was unresponsive, and the quality of her work was poor. When George, Andi's boss, gave her the bad news in her midyear review, she was stunned. She had been giving away her most valuable resource—time—and the return on her investment was very low. Andi felt as if she had just been punched in the stomach.

When I met with Andi a few weeks later, she was still reeling from the feedback. Her passion and commitment to her work and the organization were clearly fading. From my due diligence, I knew that Andi was a highly respected leader and member of the team, exceptionally bright, talented, and valued by the organization. They wanted her to succeed, but she simply had to complete her financial reviews accurately and on time.

During my first in-person meeting with Andi, it became apparent that our first step would be to reframe how she thought about time. Andi is a very fashionable person who is always impeccably dressed in the latest style. She adores shoes, and I always look forward to seeing her latest purchase and talking fashion with her. So I knew exactly how to help her reframe time.

As Andi sat down for our coaching session, I told her, "You know, Andi, last night in my hotel room I spent some time doing something I bet you've done—a little online shopping. It's a great activity when I'm on the road and I'm tired."

"I know exactly what you mean!" Andi replied. "I could browse those online shops for hours." She smiled, perhaps wondering where the conversation was going.

"Well, last night I found something just perfect for my wardrobe," I continued. "It was a pair of sandals for spring that can be dressed up or down and that will go with most of my spring clothes."

"They sound great!" Andi said. And she leaned forward, waiting for me to describe the sandals in more detail.

But instead, I replied, "Oh, they *are* great! But they cost sixty dollars more than I am willing to spend right now. So I was wondering if you'd be willing to give me sixty dollars so I can buy them."

Andi looked at me, her eyes got really wide, and she stammered in a high voice, "Uh, uh, uh—no, not really."

We've laughed about it since then, but in that moment, Andi was thinking to herself, "Oh my gosh—this is a brand-new consultant to our organization, we have just met, and she is asking me for money! What is going on here?!"

I just smiled. "I understand," I said to Andi. "I guess I just won't be able to get the sandals today. But I did have another favor to ask you. You and I are scheduled for a two-hour coaching session this morning. I wonder whether you might be available right afterward to brainstorm a few ideas on how I can improve my executive coaching practice. I only need an hour of your time."

Andi looked at me and smiled. Maybe she was relieved I hadn't asked her for money again. "Oh, sure," she replied. "I'd be happy to help!"

"Thanks, Andi," I said. "Actually, I won't be needing any extra time from you today. But did you notice what just happened? You would not give me sixty dollars, but you *would* give me sixty minutes of your time. What does that mean? Is your money more valuable than your time?"

A lightbulb went on over Andi's head. "I never thought about it that way!" she said. And we spent the next hour having an in-depth conversation about the value of time—and about how Andi could do a better job of protecting, preserving, and investing that value.

Time is a nonrenewable resource, and if you are like Andi and like most people, you are probably giving away your time with little or no conscious thought. You would not indiscriminately give away your money; why give away your time?

And remember, every time you say yes to someone or something, you are saying no to someone or something else. That's the nature of time, the limited and nonrenewable resource. Do you know what you are saying yes and no to during your workday and the impact that those decisions are having on you personally and professionally?

Stop giving away your most valuable resource—time.

EXAMINE YOUR INVESTMENT STATEMENT

If time is an even more valuable resource than money, your calendar is your investment statement reflecting the way you use it. What does your calendar reveal about your investment decisions?

Take out your calendar and really look at it. Ask yourself:

- Is there time devoted to working on achieving my goals?
- Is there time for me to complete my project work?
- How many hours a day am I in meetings?
- Do I have time allocated to coach my direct reports?
- Is every minute of the day scheduled, or do I have buffer or open time?
- Is there time for me to read and respond to e-mails? To return phone calls?
- Is there time for me to think and reflect?
- Do I have time to plan and prepare for meetings?
- Do I have time to plan and prepare for the next day, week, and month?
- How much time do I spend commuting to and from work?
- Are there personal events on my calendar—exercise, dinner with friends, my child's baseball game, or quiet, reflective time?

When we looked at Andi's calendar after discussing how she was giving away her time, it became very apparent to her exactly when, where, and how she gave away her time each and every day. She automatically accepted meeting requests without reviewing the agenda to determine whether the meeting was pertinent to her actual work and whether she was needed to make a decision or contribute to the conversation. She consistently took calls, stop-ins, and meetings during time she had blocked on her calendar to complete work, and there was absolutely no Andi time anywhere on the calendar.

"If this was my 401(k) statement I was looking at," Andi remarked with a rueful smile, "I'd probably consider firing my investment adviser—the returns are so poor."

"You're right, Andi," I said. "You can tell what a person really values by looking at their checkbook and their calendar—how they spend their time and money. And looking at your calendar tells me that Andi comes at the bottom of your priority list."

Prior to our first session, I had asked Andi to review her individual development plan, which included her professional goals and objectives for the year. As we reviewed those goals next to her calendar, Andi started shifting uneasily in her seat. The reason was obvious: There was no connection between her goals and how she was investing her time. Zero! If Andi had not been sitting there, I would have assumed that I was looking at another person's calendar. Andi's time spend and her goals were so clearly out of alignment that it was no wonder she was receiving negative feedback about her performance!

Fortunately, Andi wasn't trapped in this negative space. Raising her awareness around her actual time spend gave her the information she needed to make significant changes—which she did.

Examine *your* investment statement. How have you chosen to invest your time? Where have you said yes when you really wanted to say no? Is there time on your calendar for achieving your goals? Are you reacting or responding?

Jeff Weiner, CEO of the professional social media site LinkedIn, is acutely aware of the need to control his calendar. He describes his approach this way:

> Oftentimes people just get caught up in the day-to-day flow, and if challenges are coming at them fast and furious there is going to be a natural tendency to solve one problem after another. It is important to take some time to carve out time to think as opposed to constantly reacting. During your thinking time, not only are you thinking strategically, proactively, and longer-term, but you are literally thinking about what is urgent versus important and trying to strike the right balance.[3]

Let's reimagine your time spend to ensure that you are striking the right balance in order to receive the highest return on your investment.

REIMAGINE YOUR TIME SPEND

In chapter 5, I introduced the READY, Aim, Fire methodology, which assists you in getting clear on your goals and priorities and ensures that you achieve your goals in the most efficient and effective way possible. You wrote your READY goals; now it is time to Aim, or align your time spend to your goals.

Aiming is nothing more than a way to organize time on your calendar to advance your goals. To Aim accurately, match your time spend to your goals. Think carefully about each task or project and why you are going to allocate time on your calendar for it. Ask yourself, "How does this task or project move me a step closer toward achieving my goal?"

When Andi looked at her calendar, she realized that the way she was actually spending her time was unrelated to her goals—in fact, in some instances, it actually opposed her goals. Andi's calendar was out of alignment—which explains why, when she Fired (or executed), she never hit her intended target: She was aiming at a different target.

To Aim effectively, it is essential to work with your Productivity Style rather than against it. For example, the Planner in me loves the idea of getting organized and blocking time on my calendar to move forward on my goals. However, my Visualizer colleagues are probably feeling a little restricted and stifled right now by the idea of blocking time on the calendar to complete work. What works beautifully for me may not work for them—or for you.

Here are a number of concrete suggestions about how to organize your calendar in a way that will take the best possible advantage of the natural inclinations reflected in your personal Productivity Style. Read through them all—you may well find an approach described under a style that is not your own that you nonetheless find intriguing and useful. And check out figures 6.1, 6.2, and 6.3, which illustrate three different ways a calendar might be designed to reflect three different Productivity Styles. You may pick up an idea or two that will work for you!

WORK SIMPLY:
TIME INVESTMENT STRATEGIES
BY PRODUCTIVITY STYLE

If You're a Prioritizer

Block your time in small, precise increments, an approach that appeals to your analytical thinking style. For example, schedule twenty minutes at 10 a.m. to check and respond to e-mail, ten minutes to prep for your 10:30 a.m. marketing meeting, and fifteen minutes of drive time to your lunch meeting.

If You're a Planner

Consider blocking your time in relatively large increments—an hour at a time, or by segment: morning, midmorning, lunch, early afternoon, afternoon, and close of business. This will allow you to construct your calendar more like an organized project plan, which appeals to you, rather than creating a more tactical, linear calendar listing tasks in the style favored by the Prioritizer.

If You're an Arranger *or* a Visualizer

Review your goals, then Aim your time spend to your goals by creating theme days—days organized around a theme, category, or type of work. For example, some typical themes are administration, team development, writing, external prospecting, creation, rejuvenation, and play. To determine your theme days, review your goals, your to-do list, and the core accountabilities of your work and life. Notice the different types of tasks and projects that you do, and your themes will naturally emerge. Once you have identified your themes, select a theme or themes for each day of the week. Indicate the theme for that day on your calendar, and complete tasks and projects aligned to that theme on that day. Theme days will give you the freedom and flexibility you need and crave while ensuring that you are hitting your targets.

Arrangers and Visualizers differ slightly in how they use theme days. Arrangers should consider theme segments rather than theme days. For example, Thursday morning's theme might be administration and Thursday afternoon's theme might be team development. Theme segments will provide more variety, aid in reducing boredom during the day, and provide a little more structure to the workday. Visualizers generally prefer theme days or even theme weeks, which provide the room to innovate and create without imposing rigid time frames.

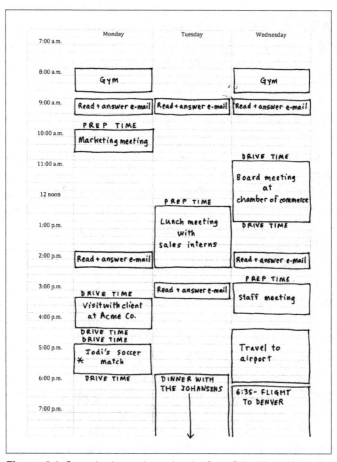

Figure 6.1. Sample three-day calendar for a Prioritizer. Note the small blocks of time set aside for specific activities, including drive time to off-site events.

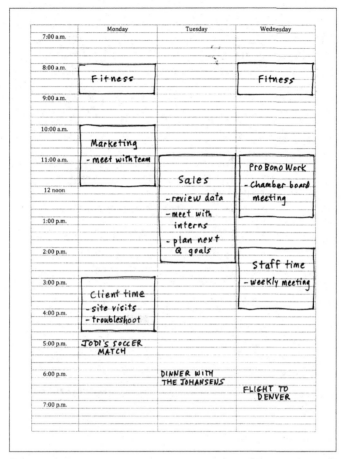

Figure 6.2. Sample three-day calendar for a Planner. Time is blocked off in fairly large increments, resembling a project plan.

Andi has a primary preference as a Visualizer, so she reimagined her time spend using theme days. Because she works for a Fortune 500 company, she does not have the same level of control and freedom that someone who is self-employed or runs her own small company might have. This meant that her designated theme days would not be pristine; a given day would inevitably include some work that was really aligned to another day's theme. Nonetheless, Andi embraced the theme day concept in order to get the variety she needed to keep her work life engaging and interesting.

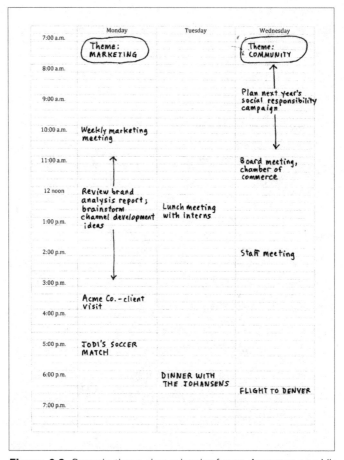

Figure 6.3. Sample three-day calendar for an Arranger or a Visualizer. Note the use of theme days (Monday and Wednesday) to organize and energize activities.

Andi's calendar today is constructed around five themes—client relationship building, analysis and review, risk management, administration, and team—each theme directly aligned to one or more of her goals. Each week, the specific day assigned to a theme may shift; for example, one week, administration may fall on Monday, while in the following week it falls on Friday. However, Andi ensures that each theme is captured on her calendar each week and that to the best of her ability the meetings, calls, and projects for each day are properly aligned to its theme.

Andi has found that thinking and working this way improves her efficiency, but more important, it fuels her creative, innovative thinking by allowing her to focus on one broad topic while freely roaming around in that topic. This has helped her develop an innovative approach to audit reviews and the redesign of one of her company's signature risk management programs.

Brigham is another person we first met back in chapter 1. Like Andi, Brigham has a primary Productivity Style of Visualizer. But unlike Andi, he owns his own business and has complete control of his calendar. Before we began working together, Brigham, like Andi, was giving away his time. He was always available to meet with a friend of a friend's first cousin who was interested in his career of event planning; he attended every networking event in his city, and was always available to his team to troubleshoot and problem-solve. He was exhausted, no longer thinking strategically about growing his business, and becoming disconnected from his team.

After drafting his READY goals and reviewing his to-dos, Brigham identified five themes—administration, team, networking and marketing, strategy, and Brigham day. Here's how he implemented these themes across his calendar.

Monday's theme is team. On Mondays, Brigham meets with each member of his team individually and then is available throughout the day as needed to work on projects, brainstorm, or problem-solve. Brigham's team knows that he will be in the office on Mondays and thus is always on hand to help complete projects—a big difference from the "old days," when his absences often hindered the team's progress.

Tuesdays and Thursdays are networking and marketing theme days. On these days, Brigham may not even come into the office. He has breakfast, lunch, and drinks with clients, prospects, and vendors, and attends networking events.

On Wednesdays, Brigham's themes are administration and strategy. He dreads the administrative aspects of his role, so he completes administrative tasks in the morning, and then as a gift and reward for completing what he calls the "drudgery work," he works on strategy in the afternoon. Brigham is a night owl and starts to get his second wind later in the day, so thinking strategically and dreaming big in the late afternoon aligns to his body's natural rhythm.

Friday is Brigham day. This is his day to use in any way that excites him and moves the business forward. On some Fridays he writes, on others he reads trade publications and brainstorms. As you can imagine, Brigham day is his favorite day of the week.

Andi and Brigham have the same primary preference for Visualizer; however, the realities of their work environment require that they implement their theme days differently.

What if you have a primary preference for two Productivity Styles? Combine strategies and customize. My primary preference is that of a Planner with a very close secondary preference of Arranger. So I have combined both time blocking and theme days to restructure my calendar and make and keep family commitments, thereby enabling me to find the rhythm that feeds my head, heart, and soul. I frequently travel for work and have committed to myself that I will not be away from home more than three consecutive nights. This is blocked on my calendar, so I am visually reminded of this commitment whenever I accept engagements and plan travel.

I have also blocked 5 p.m. on my calendar as the end of every workday. Now, does every day end precisely at 5 p.m.? (Not really.) Do I sometimes work at night and in the early dawn hours? (Yes, I do.) However, as a general rule, I strongly believe in a hard stop to the workday because of the positive impact this practice has both on your productivity and sanity. If late-night hours and predawn work sessions are becoming the norm for you, it's highly likely that your effectiveness is suffering—along with your health and your personal life.

Another practice I recommend: including buffer time throughout your calendar rather than scheduling every minute of every day for meetings or other activities. Buffer time is unscheduled time that can be used to address unforeseen projects, tasks, or emergencies. It can also be used for thinking or reflection. A calendar without buffer time is an invitation for emergencies to take over your day and thoroughly disrupt your plans.

My Mondays and Fridays are reserved for administrative work. Early mornings when it is quiet and serene are blocked for writing, developing content, and designing programs. I am a morning person and love this time of day, when my mind is fresh, clear, and at its most creative. Tuesdays, Wednesdays, and Thursdays are focused on clients and prospecting. Within each of these days, I block time on my calendar to complete work that is aligned to that day's theme.

Does my calendar system work perfectly? Of course not—people are too variable and life is too complicated for any system to work perfectly under all circumstances. However, my system does keep me anchored and focused, and I often make small tweaks and adjustments that help me continue to improve my time investment.

Reimagine your time spend so that your calendar accurately reflects your goals and priorities. Leverage your Productivity Style to determine how best to Aim and align your time spend to your goals. Make your calendar work for you, not against you. Remember, you cannot ever get time back, so make sure that you are investing your time for the highest return for you.

CHOOSE TIME INVESTMENT TACTICS THAT WORK FOR YOU

Michelle Gass, chief customer officer at Kohl's, wakes up at 4:30 a.m. every morning to go running. Avon chairman Andrea Jung wakes up at 5 a.m. *Vogue* editor Anna Wintour is on the tennis court by 6 a.m. every morning before work. For these women, starting early is a key tool for increasing their productivity and effectiveness throughout the day.

Tim Ferriss, author of *The 4-Hour Workweek*, takes a different approach to investing his time. He says that there are "two synergistic approaches for increasing productivity. Limit tasks to the important to shorten work time. Shorten work time to limit tasks to the important."

What is right for *you*? Let's maximize the hours in each day by choosing time investment tactics that work for you. Outlined below are the time investment strengths of each Productivity Style to use and leverage as you invest your time and complete work. Specific tactics you can use to capitalize on the minutes you have each day follow the time investment strengths.

Remember to personalize your tactics. Look first at the tactics for your primary Productivity Style. If you have a primary preference or a very close preference for two styles, look at the tactics listed under each style and combine them in a way that works for you. For a downloadable quick reference guide of the tactics, please go to www.carsontate.com.

WORK SIMPLY:
TIME INVESTMENT STRENGTHS AND
TACTICS BY PRODUCTIVITY STYLE

If You're a Prioritizer

Your Strengths Are:

- Effective, efficient utilization of time
- Maximization of time to increase work output
- Ability to focus on the highest-value task
- Ability to avoid wasting time on tasks and projects that are unproductive or unimportant

So Try These Tactics:

- Time how long it takes you to complete routine tasks so you can plan your days and weeks even more accurately.
- Start your day with your highest-priority project or task.
- Eliminate all clutter—physical and mental. No clutter means no time wasted on maintenance.

- Think about projects that may be completed during downtime or slow time. Without a high volume of work, you become bored, which negatively impacts your effectiveness and efficiency.

A Prioritizer in Action:

When executive Marissa Mayer was at Google, she typically crammed sixty meetings into her workweek. To offset that grueling schedule, she planned a one-week trip roughly every six months, often to a new location. Knowing that she would be out of the office forced her to put systems in place to keep things running smoothly.

If You're a Planner

Your Strengths Are:

- Ability to plan the time needed to complete tasks
- Sequential organization of tasks
- Accurate, complete project plans
- Minimization of risk of rework by following best practice or historical precedent

So Try These Tactics:

- Schedule open or buffer time each week to allow for unexpected opportunities, issues, or problems.
- Build fluidity and flexibility into your plans, allowing for creative insights and the ability to effectively navigate issues or crises.
- Create a structure and plan for the week.
- Include thinking and reflecting time, which is especially valuable to you as a Planner.

A Planner in Action:

Ilene Gordon, CEO of Ingredion, a global ingredient manufacturer that works with food companies like Nestlé, Kraft, and Unilever, said, "I am a big believer in being organized. Every Sunday night was family night. We'd have dinner and lay out a plan for the week and month. Sometimes my daughter would say, 'I have a big paper due, and I'd like your input.' I would copy the chapter she was working on, take it with me, and call her from the road so we could talk about it. Once, I gave her a spelling test from the back of a taxi. It was a lot of energy and you have to be willing to do it, but I never thought for a moment it wasn't possible. You have to have a plan. We had a backup to the backup."

If You're an Arranger

Your Strengths Are:

- Ability to see the big picture
- Ability to encourage teamwork to maximize work output
- Intuitive decision making in real time as events unfold
- Ability to block time to complete work

So Try These Tactics:

- Know your attention span and plan around it.
- Turn off your e-mail notification feature.
- Schedule time in the day to connect and interact with people.
- Align the execution of the task to your energy level.

An Arranger in Action:

Author Keith Ferrazzi is a classic arranger—in fact, his best-selling book is titled *Never Eat Alone,* which is a typical arranger's motto. Keith advises, "If you have fifteen minutes to spare—ping someone—e-mail/connect—use extra time in the day to send an article, make a call or send a text. Taxi time is pinging time. Plane time is pinging time. I reserve those moments for relational curation."

If You're a Visualizer

Your Strengths Are:

- Ability to see the big picture
- Ability to work well under pressure

- Ability to work very quickly
- Ability to effectively manage and juggle multiple tasks and projects

So Try These Tactics:

- Ask yourself, "What is the best use of my time right now?"
- Set firm but realistic deadlines.
- Stay away from boring and repetitive work.
- Keep your calendar visual at all times and stick to simple, basic time frames.

A Visualizer in Action:

Richard Branson, founder of Virgin Group, shared this classic Visualizer advice with entrepreneurs: "Give the rest of your team space to work—in many cases, by moving your office out of the building. Remove yourself from the business's day-to-day functions and find someone to replace you as head of operations so that you will have enough uninterrupted time to look at the big picture and make decisions about the company's future direction."[4]

KEEP YOUR INVESTMENT ON TRACK: PLAN AND PRIORITIZE EVERY MONTH, WEEK, AND DAY

At times, it feels as if our brains are like popcorn machines. "Call Sue." "E-mail Alan." "Pick up the dry cleaning." "Don't forget to buy milk." There is an incessant popping of to-dos, ideas, and errands to run. Not only is popcorn brain annoying, but it also interferes with our ability to prioritize and plan because it takes up significant amounts of mental energy.

Planning and prioritizing have been offered as time-saving tools and as an antidote to the stress caused by overflowing calendars and task lists. Planning and prioritizing are valuable and helpful—but by themselves they will not cure popcorn brain. In fact, the process of prioritizing and planning can *add* to your sense of stress.

Think about the last time you prioritized your task list. The job required you to make decisions among many competing projects, deadlines, and important stakeholders. If you're like most people, you found it difficult. Planning and prioritizing are energy-intensive tasks that become increasingly stressful after your brain has been engaged for a period of time. Our brains require significant amounts of fuel and all of this fuel is used up faster than we realize. As Roy Baumeister of Florida State University explains, "We have a limited bucket of resources for activities like decision making and impulse control, and when we use these up we don't have as much for the next activity." Make one difficult decision—what you need to do first today, for example—and the next one is more difficult. Your best-quality thinking lasts for only a limited time.[5]

So what can you do? How can you conserve your brain's fuel and use it more effectively to prioritize, plan, and ultimately save time? Here are some specific techniques that have been shown to conserve energy and reduce your natural tendency to suffer from popcorn brain.

- Do a "brain dump" by listing everything you need to do in the next several days. Empty onto paper, a whiteboard, or into the computer program of your choice everything and anything that is popping in your mind. Get it all out of your head and into the physical world. Clear the mental decks.
- Brainstorm using mind-mapping tools or paper and Post-it Notes to ensure that the most important ideas are captured and can be easily expanded without additional mental output. This ensures that you are not expending precious mental energy trying to remember project ideas, what you need to do, or whom you need to talk to. Follow the wise advice offered by productivity consultant David Allen, author of *Getting Things Done:* Use your brain to think *about* ideas, not *of* them.[6]

You'll learn more about creating a powerful to-do list and its role in vanquishing popcorn brain in the next chapter. For now, having captured today's serving of popcorn from your brain on a piece of paper, apply the following best practices to your action planning. I have mapped them for you at three time intervals—monthly, weekly, and daily. Get into the habit of using these techniques regularly and you'll find yourself less mentally exhausted. You will be able to turn countless once-wasted hours into productive time.

MONTHLY PLANNING BEST PRACTICES

Monthly planning provides the big-picture view of your goals, commitments, and priorities, ensuring that your calendar is aligned to each of these. Here are the steps I recommend you take once a month, at a routine, preset time—on the first of the month, for example, or on the first Monday of the month if you prefer.

- Review your professional and personal goals for the quarter. Do you have projects and tasks on your to-do list that will move you closer to achieving each of these goals? If not, update your to-do list with the projects and tasks that are required for you to achieve your professional and personal goals. Is there time on your calendar this month to work on these projects and tasks? If not, block or schedule time to work on them.
- Review your calendar for the upcoming month and ask yourself the following questions:
  - Are all of my project milestones and deadlines noted on my calendar?
  - Do I have enough buffer time scheduled this month?
  - How many days this month am I in back-to-back meetings? Where can I shift or eliminate a few meetings to give myself the time I need to digest, think about what happened during the meeting, and develop strategy?
  - Do I have personal time on the calendar this month? Personal time is essential if you want to consistently perform well.
  - If you have a family, a significant other, and/or other special relationships in your life, are their events and needs captured and reflected on your calendar?

- Revise your calendar as needed until you're satisfied with the answers to *all* the questions above.

WEEKLY PLANNING BEST PRACTICES

Weekly planning is designed to prevent your brain from trying to remember and remind you of what you need to do—a task that needlessly consumes precious mental energy. The goal each week is to give yourself the opportunity to review your projects, gather and process the stuff that has accumulated during the week, and ensure that it is collected, processed, and organized. Weekly planning ensures that your brain is clear and prepared for the week.

I recommend you develop the habit of setting aside time for weekly planning on the same day every week—at the end of your workday on Friday or first thing on Monday morning, for example—so that you're ready to hit the ground running when you arrive at the office on Monday. Here are the recommended steps:

- Collect any loose documents, scraps of paper, business cards, and other materials that have accumulated on your desk, in your workbag, and in your pockets. File, trash, or add a task to your to-do list for each item you've collected.
- Review and process your notes. Review meeting notes, notes scribbled on bits of paper, notes in OneNote, and on your computer. Put action items on your to-do list, put project due dates on your calendar, and file any reference notes and meeting materials.
- Review last week's calendar in detail and capture any remaining to-dos and reference information. Transfer to-dos to your task list and file reference information.
- Look at the upcoming week's calendar. Capture any action steps, to-dos about project work, and arrangements or preparations for any upcoming events.

- Review your goals. Evaluate the status of your goals and projects, and ensure that you have at least one action or to-do for each one.

DAILY PLANNING BEST PRACTICES

Daily planning is designed to focus your attention on your top priorities for the day, ensuring that you have a laserlike focus on what you want to accomplish during the day. By deciding what to focus on before the day actually starts, you can minimize the impact of distractions and competing projects that often come up. Ideally, you should plan your day the afternoon or evening before so the next morning you can immediately start working on your priorities. If this is not possible, take just a few minutes for daily planning at the start of your morning, before the floodgates of e-mail, phone calls, and in-person meetings open. Here are the recommended steps:

- Review your current projects and tasks. Before you do any work (including checking e-mail), decide on your top three priorities for the day. Use these to guide and structure your day.
- Start your day by tackling your highest-value task—one that is aligned to your goals and relates to the revenue line, which is where you and your organization make money.
- React to shifting priorities and demands, and decide what to do next during the day by considering the following:
  - Check your required tools. Do you have all the tools necessary to complete a given action on your schedule for today? Many to-dos require a specific location (at the office or a client site, for example) and/or a specific tool (a phone or a computer application). Make sure all the tools you need are in place as you start your day.
  - Check your buffer time. If you have only five minutes between meetings, your action choices are limited. Try to rearrange one or more activities to give yourself some breathing room in the course of your day.

- Check your energy availability. Some projects and tasks require significant amounts of fresh, creative mental energy. If necessary, move one or more activities so that your most demanding projects and tasks are scheduled for the times when your energy is likely to be highest.
- Prioritize your activities. Considering the required tools, time, and energy available, which to-do offers the highest return on time investment?

Each of the monthly, weekly, and daily planning best practices outlined above work for all of the Productivity Styles. However, there are slight differences in each style that need to be considered for optimal planning. Outlined in the table below are questions to consider as you complete your monthly, weekly, and daily planning.

WORK SIMPLY:
PLANNING CONSIDERATIONS
BY PRODUCTIVITY STYLE

If You're a Prioritizer

How You Plan:

You are naturally goal-oriented; planning your months, weeks, and days to achieve your goals is easy for you. At times, however, your focus on the outcome tends to impact your understanding of how the work needs to be completed, who needs to be involved, and why it is important.

Questions to Ask:

- How does the work need to be completed to achieve my goal?
- Who else needs to be involved or know about my work to support me in achieving my goal? Who are the key stakeholders? Who are the constituencies impacted by this work?

- Why is the work important? How does it connect back to my goals and the organization's goals?

If You're a Planner

How You Plan:

Planning is natural for you. At times, however, your focus on how to complete work can create a myopic plan that overlooks or minimizes what actually needs to be accomplished, who needs to be involved, and why the work is important.

Questions to Ask:

- What is the outcome or stated goal for this work?
- Who else needs to be involved or know about my work to support me in achieving my goal? Who are the key stakeholders? Who are the constituencies impacted by this work?
- Why is the work important? How does it connect back to my goals and the organization's goals?

If You're an Arranger

How You Plan:

You intuitively know what work needs to be completed and by when. At times, however, your focus on the people involved in the work or project can overshadow the goal or outcome, how to efficiently complete the work, and why it is important.

Questions to Ask:

- What is the outcome or stated goal for this work?
- What are the specific, tangible action steps I must take to complete the work? How has this work been completed in the past? Is there any historical precedent or prior experience I can draw upon?
- Why is the work important? How does it connect back to my goals and the organization's goals?

If You're a Visualizer

How You Plan:

You are a strategic, big-picture thinker, and long-range planning is in alignment with your natural preferences. At times, however, your big-picture orientation tends to interfere with your determining the shorter-term intermediate goals and action steps needed to realize a broader strategic goal.

Questions to Ask:

- What are the intermediate goals and outcomes needed to achieve my broader goals and those of my organization?
- What specific, tangible action steps must I take to complete the work? Remember to make these action steps small, discrete, and doable.
- Who else needs to be involved or know about my work to support me in achieving my goal? Who are the key stakeholders? Who are the constituencies impacted by this work?

Planning and prioritizing are energy-intensive tasks that use significant mental resources. Harness the productive power of your brain by utilizing the monthly, weekly, and daily planning best practices I've recommended. You'll be glad you did!

7

Free Your Brain with
a Master TASK List

YOU'RE STANDING IN THE SHOWER WITH SHAMPOO IN YOUR hair when you remember to call your sister Caitlin about organizing the anniversary brunch for your parents. Why now? Why can't you think about calling Caitlin when you're near a phone? By the time you towel off and get dressed, six other things have tumbled into your mind, erasing thoughts of Caitlin for the rest of the morning.

Later, at the office, a colleague of yours pokes his head around your open door. "What's the latest on the Callahan project?" he asks. "I'm heading upstairs now, and I know Jim will be asking me about it."

A small shock wave rushes through your body. You meant to speak with the Callahan people the day before, but you never got around to it. "Give me a second!" you plead as you reach for the phone. "Maybe I can reach them right now!"

Later that afternoon, you pull out of the grocery store and merge into the crush of 6 p.m. traffic. Your kids and the babysitter are waiting for you at home. Suddenly you remember that you forgot to buy milk—and with your running late and the traffic lights against you, there's no way you can turn around to buy it now. Why did your brain not remind you that you needed milk when you were in the dairy section picking up those containers of yogurt?

In all three cases, the explanation is the same: *Your brain is a terrible to-do list.*

Scientific findings explain a practical reality about brain functioning: The less you try to hold in your mind at once, the better. Memory starts to degrade whenever you try to hold a group of ideas in mind. Believe it or not, the optimal number of different ideas to hold in mind at one time is no more than three or four—not the seven, ten, or twenty many of us struggle to retain at once.

The implications for busy humans in the twenty-first century are obvious and enormous. Once you consider all the various projects you may be working on at the office—and the separate small but important tasks associated with each project—as well as the urgent or not so urgent connections you need to make with an array of colleagues, employees, managers, clients, suppliers, and other personal stakeholders; and then add to the mix all the things you need to remember from outside the workplace (family obligations, social dates, personal financial chores, housekeeping duties, vacation planning) and the many things you'd simply like to remember to get to because they will enrich your life (that article a friend recommended, that TV show you've been looking forward to, the gallery exhibit you've heard is amazing) . . . add all this together, and it's more than obvious why relying on natural brain functioning is never going to work. We all have to-do lists that overwhelm our brain's memory function. Three or four different ideas? Try three or four hundred!

So what can you do? How can you leverage your brain's natural functioning to improve your productivity and move beyond busy? The solution starts with rebuilding your to-do list.

BUILD A MASTER TASK LIST

Now, I can only imagine what you might be thinking—"I already *have* a to-do list." (Almost everyone does.) "Why do I need to rebuild it? That is extra work, and I am looking to streamline my work and work more simply—not add to my workload!"

If that's your reaction, it's understandable. But the fact is that your to-do list may be holding you back rather than helping you achieve what you want to. Ask yourself:

- Is your to-do list standing up to the rigors of your current workday?
- Does your to-do list accurately and completely reflect *all* of your commitments, tasks, and projects?
- Does it enable you to efficiently use *all* of the minutes in your day to complete work?
- Can you glance at your list between meetings and actually find, select, and complete a task using the few minutes that happen to be available?

If the answer to any of these questions is no, it's probably time to rebuild your to-do list. The inadequacy of the tools you've been using to organize your life and maintain your focus on key goals has been holding you back, making you a victim of technically driven busyness—the kind of busyness we suffer simply because we lack knowledge of the systems that can free us.

The goal is twofold: to stop using your brain to retain and remind yourself of information, and to create a tool that enables you to quickly review what needs to be done and then complete the work.

It is time to build a master TASK list.

Let's re-create your current to-do list using the following four steps: Think, Ask, Sort, and Keep.

We'll start with step one—Think.

Remember the scenario I sketched at the start of this chapter? I described a typical day in which a host of to-dos kept popping up in your brain, usually at the most inopportune times. If that scenario seemed familiar, you need to clear the psychic decks and eliminate popcorn brain once and for all. Remember, your brain is an abysmal to-do list. Do not ask it to do something it does not do well. When you do, you are fighting against nature—and nature always wins. The goal is to use your brain to think *about* things, not *of* things (in the phrase we already cited from author David Allen).

To start rebuilding your to-do list, you have to employ a two-part process.

Part one is the general brain dump. Think about everything you need to do, personal *and* professional. Imagine turning your brain upside down and emptying out its contents onto paper or a whiteboard, or into the computer program of your choice. The tool does not matter. I have had clients fill multiple legal pads or small notebooks, build extensive Excel spreadsheets, or go through so many Post-it Notes that 3M company stock probably rose by a point or two. Choose the tool that works best for you. The goal is to get all the to-dos and ideas out of your head and into the physical world.

Do not worry about the order of the items on your brain dump. There doesn't have to be any logic to the sequence of items on your list—and if you're like most people, there won't be. Personal, professional, social, civic, short-term, and long-term items will all be jumbled together, just as they pop out of your brain. That's perfectly normal.

To help you get clear, listed below is a brain-dump trigger list that will help you think about *everything* that may be lurking in the corners of your brain.

BRAIN-DUMP TRIGGER LIST

- Projects—started, but not complete
- Projects that need to be started
- Commitments/promises to others, including:
  - Colleagues
  - Manager
  - Clients
  - Prospects

- - Other professional contacts/associates
  - Community organizations
  - Significant other
  - Children
  - Parents
  - Friends
- Communications to make or receive from others
- Writing to be finished and submitted, including:
  - Articles
  - Reports
  - Proposals
- Meetings to be set and/or requested
- Errands to run
- Household items:
  - Repairs
  - Maintenance
  - Necessary purchases
- Items to read and/or review
- Administrative items:
  - E-mail
  - Instant messages
  - Social media
  - Voicemail
- Open items or items you are waiting for from others:
  - Delegated items
  - Requests for information
  - Tasks and/or projects to be completed
- Research
- Upcoming personal events, including:
  - Special occasions
  - Birthdays
  - Holidays
  - Travel

- Vacation
- Civic events
- Social events
- Cultural events
- Sports

Completing this brain dump will probably take you anywhere from fifteen minutes to two or more hours, depending on how much popcorn you have been storing in your head. Try to make this exercise fun or at least pleasurable: Drink your favorite beverage, turn on your preferred music, use your favorite pen, light a scented candle—you know what works for you.

A word of caution: During the brain-dump process, you might end up riding an emotional roller coaster. A wild array of feelings may race through your mind, from "Oh my gosh! I am completely overwhelmed! I have three hundred-plus things on my list! I will never get this done! Why am I even considering doing this? How did I let this happen!" to "Wow, I feel good! It's like someone has released the pressure cooker inside my brain. Oh, I feel so much lighter! I feel free!"

Do not let the emotional gyrations you may experience bother you. Ride the roller coaster! I promise the crazy mood swings will stop. Stay focused on the end goal—working simply, efficiently, and effectively. It is almost impossible to prioritize, plan, and efficiently execute when your to-dos are trapped inside your head. Get them out into the physical world—and free your brain to do the productive work it does best.

Now for part two of the Think step. Remember writing your READY goals in chapter 5? In order to realize your goals and create a road map to achieving them, you need to complete a brain dump *for each goal*.

So take out your READY goals, look at the first goal on the list, and think about everything you need to do to achieve that goal—everything. Add any new items that come up to your existing brain-dump document, whiteboard, or computer application. The goal here is the same as part one. Empty your mind of any and all to-dos related to your READY goals.

Figure 7.1. Mark's brain dump (sample).

(Figure 7.1 shows a partial sample of a typical brain dump. Of course, yours will vary—no two brain dumps are at all alike!)

Now that you've finished your brain dump, the internal chatter in your brain is already quieting down. Your mind is free now that it no longer has the responsibility for holding all of your to-dos and ideas. However, what you have poured out on the page or the computer screen is not in an actionable format. All you really have now is a giant disorganized mess that needs to be refined a lot more before it can serve your productivity purposes.

Let's move on to step two—Act.

Review your brain dump. What do you notice?

One of the first things many people discover is that they have listed *projects* rather than actual to-dos. A project is a large-scale task that you have taken on, one that may require many separate action steps and take many days, weeks, or months to complete. For example, a project might be:

- Finalize the PowerPoint deck for the upcoming client meeting.
- Plan my team's off-site leadership retreat.
- Organize the holiday bazaar for our church.
- Clean out the attic.

The problem with a project list is that just *looking* at a list of enormous projects like these is somewhat paralyzing. When confronted with such a list, I often just skip over it in search of something easier to do: I start reading my favorite blogs or perusing online shopping sites, and the familiar downward spiral into procrastination begins.

To avoid this, you need to use the Act step to clearly define *next action steps* for each item from your brain dump. These are the specific actions you need to perform to complete the project. Each action step must be clear enough that you know what must be done, but not so detailed that it is overwhelming and therefore paralyzing. There are two types of action steps: *project actions* and *next actions*. A project action is a desired outcome requiring more than one action step to complete, while a next action is the very next physical, visible action step required to move something forward.

Here is a hint: All action steps start with action verbs. A typical project action might begin with an action verb like *finalize, look into, clarify, resolve, submit, roll out, handle,* or *install.* A typical next action might begin with an action verb like *call, buy, read, purge, e-mail, fill out, draft, review,* or *talk to.*

The goal is to turn each item on the brain-dump list into an action item or a sequence of action items. When you look at your to-do list, you do not want to have to think about your next action step. You want to be able to immediately act or execute on a task.

For example, take a project like "Finalize the PowerPoint deck for the upcoming Jones client meeting." You might turn this into the following sequence of action steps:

- Call Stacy to get updated sales statistics for the PowerPoint slides.
- Schedule an appointment with Gary in IT to help me create animations for the opening and closing slides in the deck.
- Meet with Gary and create the animations for the opening and closing slides.
- Update and revise the PowerPoint slides with the sales statistics and new opening and closing slides.
- Circulate slide deck to Sue, Paul, and Howard for comments and suggestions.
- Implement Sue's, Paul's, and Howard's recommended changes to the deck.
- Send final deck to office services to print eight bound copies.

Notice how I've taken a large, rather daunting project and turned it into a series of manageable, bite-size to-dos, none of which is very intimidating in itself. That's the heart of the Act step.

Complete the Act step by working through each item in your brain dump and determining action steps for each one. Write, type, or dictate the action steps on a clean sheet of paper, a whiteboard, or the computer application of your choice. If possible, try to limit yourself to no more than three or four next action steps for any project. This step might take you thirty minutes to three hours or more, depending on the number of items in your brain dump.

It is possible you might have actually written a lot of your brain dump in the form of action steps—particularly if you are a Prioritizer or a Planner. If so, congratulations. If not, you may find this step laborious and time-consuming. Hang in there—the work will pay off. By determining the next action steps, you develop a list that is highly actionable, specific, and complete—one that will enable you to productively use your time each day to complete the most important work.

At this point in re-creating your to-do list, you have a large, disorganized, probably even chaotic list. It is time to impose some structure. You are ready for step three—Sort.

This is your opportunity to organize and prioritize your action items so that at any given time you can quickly and efficiently execute on the highest-value task based on the time available, the resources available, and your energy level. The Sort step allows you to look at your to-dos and immediately make a decision on what to do next, which is vital in our 24/7, hyperconnected, information-overload culture.

To complete the Sort step, review your action items and think about how you can group them. There are multiple ways to group your action items:

- By tools or resources needed to complete the item (phone, e-mail, computer, a specific computer application like Excel)
- By person (your colleague, your assistant, your spouse)
- By the physical location you must be in to complete the item (office, home, client's location, car, or plane)
- By project
- By due date
- By energy level needed for execution (high, medium, or low)
- By time required for completion (five minutes, fifteen minutes, one hour)

You may find yourself using two or more of these sorting methods, depending on how you work, the kinds of tasks you habitually face, and which sorting techniques appeal to you most. I do recommend that you include at least one set of action items sorted by time required, especially a list of items that can be done in fifteen minutes or less. This is a great list to carry around as a way to convert those odd moments of free time—waiting in the dentist's office, in line at the department of motor vehicles—into productive microsegments of work. This list is also a great go-to when you feel the tug of procrastination. You can quickly complete a task, which gives you a little energy boost, thus helping you transition into working on a more challenging or complex project.

Over time, the categories into which you will sort your action items are likely to vary as your needs, interests, and work methods evolve. Currently, my to-do list is sorted into the following categories: *calls, computer, e-mail, airplane, agendas, project list, errands, fifteen minutes, goals,* and *at home.*

There are two additional sorts that I also use and recommend to others: *waiting-for* and *someday.*

The *waiting-for* sort consists of items for which I am waiting for something from someone. Maintaining a list of these items enables me to keep track of all of my open loops without trying to remember them—something, you recall, that our brains are abysmal at doing.

The *someday* sort includes all the items that I want to do someday. My current someday list includes trips I want to take, books I want to read, and special items I want to purchase when the time is right—for example, a very expensive hair dryer that I've had my eye on (with my hair, a specific hair dryer is very important). My someday list is fun and inspirational; maintaining it frees my mind and allows me to dream big.

I encourage you to always keep a list of your READY goals and projects in the same place as your action steps. Having them together enables you to clearly see the big picture of what must be accomplished as well as the discrete next action steps needed to achieve your goals.

The final step—step four—is called Keep, which is short for Keep Only One List. The step begins when you decide on the type of physical container, computer application, or app that you want to use for your TASK list. It is very important that you keep one and only one list. The objective is to have complete and total line of sight of everything that you need to do so you can make accurate decisions on what work to complete next. Keeping multiple lists thwarts this goal; it creates unnecessary chaos, stress, and wasted time.

CREATE A TASK LIST TAILORED TO YOUR PRODUCTIVITY STYLE

When I first met my new client Ben in his office, the sheer number of task lists he maintained impressed me. Legal pads were stacked on the bookcase behind his desk, notebooks were piled high on the floor, the surface of his desk was awash in a sea of Post-it Notes, and his computer monitor was framed in still more yellow Post-it Notes.

"This is quite an assortment of to-do lists," I ventured.

"You don't know the half of it," Ben admitted, looking a bit embarrassed. "I've got four legal pads with to-do lists on the front seat of my car and two more legal pads in my briefcase. Oh, and look at my wallet!" He pulled it from his back pocket so I could see the array of yellow Post-it Notes bristling from it. Ben was exploding with to-do lists!

Of course, having multiple to-do lists defeats the whole purpose of having a list in the first place. Whenever Ben looked at a legal pad or Post-it Note, he knew he was missing information. When he had time to actually complete work, he would spend precious minutes hunting for what he needed to do next by frantically flipping through legal pads. Ben was in desperate need of one master TASK list.

So what form should *your* list take? It depends on you and your Productivity Style. Tailoring your TASK list to match your Productivity Style is a unique process that pioneers of productivity management like David Allen have not addressed—and one that my clients and I have found to be particularly effective.

Aaron Levie, CEO of Box, uses one sheet of paper, saying that this extreme simplicity is required by a mild case of attention deficit disorder. "I'm a little ADD, so I have one sheet of paper called '50 Things.' It's a list of all the important initiatives, tasks, and projects at the company.

Once every day or two, I run through it and make sure that every one of those things is on track. So now it's just a piece of paper. . . . Ninety-nine percent of my life is digital, but this is my low-tech way of staying focused."[1]

Jan, the vice president of human resources for an NBA franchise team, has a primary preference as a Visualizer. Mounted on the wall to the right of her office door is a six-by-six-foot whiteboard that serves as her master TASK list. All of her to-dos are organized by project and color-coded. In a black box on the far right of the whiteboard, Jan has listed all of her projects in red (one of her team's colors). When she sits at her desk, she can see her list and quickly make a decision on what to do next.

My freelance editor, Karl, has a primary preference for a Prioritizer. He uses a simple ruled pad for his task list. A writer at heart, Karl likes to write his to-dos by hand rather than relying on a technology tool. His to-dos are organized by date, each task occupying a single line on the pad. He takes the pad with him to meetings and appointments, consulting it several times a day to make sure he hasn't forgotten any urgent task.

My task list is actually a small tabbed notebook that I carry with me wherever I go. Yes, I am still very old-school—I use paper rather than a digital app. "What happens if you lose it?" people often ask me.

"I'll have a panic attack, of course," I reply. "But I hope that whoever finds my list will complete all of my work for me!"

Listed below are some additional suggestions on task and execution management tools by Productivity Style. Scan the table—you're sure to find some ideas that will resonate with you as you work on your own master TASK list.

WORK SIMPLY:
TASK AND EXECUTION MANAGEMENT TOOLS
BY PRODUCTIVITY STYLE

If You're a Prioritizer

Tools to Try:

- Ruled or lined paper.
- iDoneThis, an app that will send you an e-mail reminder asking you what you accomplished.
- IFTTT (If This Then That), an app that allows you to define how information moves between apps. It can automate tasks by combining one app's action with another app.
- Zippy, an app for the iPhone that gives you feedback on how you manage your to-do list.
- PhraseExpress, a free text expansion tool to save keystrokes and time. It works by monitoring your typing: When you type a predetermined word or phrase, it triggers a rule that removes your short version and replaces it with the longer phrase.
- Summly, an app for faster news browsing.
- Bump—Use it to share contact information and photos by simply bumping two phones together. It works for Android and iPhone. Talk about efficient!
- Boxer, an e-mail app that helps you manage your inbox using triage tools to help you reply to, organize, and prioritize your e-mail. You can "like" incoming messages, send a reply with auto-responses, or add e-mails to a to-do list. It also integrates with Dropbox for file sharing and syncs up with LinkedIn and Facebook to create profile cards of your contacts. It supports Exchange, Gmail and Google Apps, Yahoo Mail, iCloud, AOL, and Outlook/Hotmail.

If You're a Planner

Tools to Try:

- Notebooks.

- Printable Paper, a Web-based application that lets you download 1,231 styles and types of papers for free, including graph paper and a wide variety of lined papers.
- D*I*Y Planner, a Web-based application that lets you create your own highly customized paper planner system using their templates, covers, and documents.
- Outlook task manager.
- Calendars.
- Wunderlist, an app that lets you create limitless lists of tasks.
- Feedly, a news aggregator application for Web browsers and mobile devices running iOS and Android. It is also available as a cloud-based application. It creates a single place for everything you want to read.
- Cue, a personal assistant app that aggregates information from e-mail, contacts, and calendars into a daily snapshot.
- Doit.im, a free application for all platforms (Windows, Mac, iPhone, and iPad) that lets you set up projects, next actions, tags, due dates, and notes, syncing them all using Doit.im's server.
- Rapportive, a Gmail tool that shows you everything about your contacts from inside your inbox. It combines what you know, what your organization knows, and what the Web knows.
- Pocket, a Web-based application that allows you to collate and organize articles, videos, and any other content you find on the Web. You save it to Pocket from the computer and view it on any device without an Internet connection. It is integrated in three hundred-plus apps, so your reading material is always at your fingertips.

If You're an Arranger

Tools to Try:

- Post-it Digital Notes.
- Stickies.
- Any.do, a to-do list app with a sleek design and innovative approach to managing your life.
- Moleskine, an online store where all of their luxurious notebooks are at your fingertips. There is also an app for your iPad that you can download.

- Ommwriter, a full-screen text editor for both Windows and Mac that adds relaxing backgrounds and peaceful music or ambient noise to not only keep you focused on your writing but help you stay relaxed and productive.
- Evernote Hello, a robust contact management system app that lets you create detailed profiles for each contact, scan information from business cards, and pull in relevant information from e-mails, and of course Evernote to help jog your memory when you see someone again.
- Sunrise, an app that ensures you do not miss another social event. You can RSVP to Facebook events and even wish friends happy birthday, all from the app.
- Pling, a push-to-talk voice messenger that helps teams and individuals communicate quickly and naturally. Send messages to individuals or groups with the speed and brevity of a text message and the personality and ease of a human voice.
- Yammer, a private social network that helps employees collaborate across departments, locations, and business apps. Think of this as your company's own Facebook.
- Carrot, a to-do list app with attitude and "gamification." Earn points for completing tasks and receive praise or shame based on how many tasks you complete. Be prepared to both laugh and gasp!

If You're a Visualizer

Tools to Try:

- Notebooks with unlined pages.
- Whiteboards.
- Reminders, Apple's foray into the task management world of apps. It is a powerful task list that can be synced across iOS devices, although the process is not intuitive. However, what makes this app unique and powerful is its location-based notification triggers. Once you enter a task you set a reminder date or a location trigger. Gone are the days when you are driving by the grocery and you need to buy milk but forget to stop. The Reminders app will not let that happen.
- View Your Mind, a mind-mapping tool for both PCs and Macs that allows you to generate and manipulate graphical and colorful maps.

- Personal Brain, a mind-mapping tool for both PCs and Macs that is dynamic and highly intuitive. It allows you to link ideas, files, and Web pages the way you think. It is hierarchical and associative, animated, nonlinear, and infinitely scalable.
- SwiftKey Note, the fastest way to take notes on an iPhone or iPad. Using prediction technology, it advances the keyboard by learning how you write to provide better autocorrect and smart next-word predictions.

It doesn't matter what *form* your list takes, as long as there is one place you go for all of your to-dos. The key is simple: Make your list work for you, not against you. If the productivity tools you try do not seem to be working well, experiment with another set. Over time, you will find a system that makes it easy—even fun—to keep track of all your tasks.

8

—

Get More Done: Complete Tasks and Projects with Ease

YOU HAVE REIMAGINED YOUR TO-DO LIST, SELECTED AND implemented the best list-making tool, and now have one master TASK list. Now it is time to Fire—to execute on your tasks. It's the final, crucial step in the READY, Aim, Fire system.

There are two simple steps to tackling tasks and projects more easily and quickly: Determine what to do next, and then efficiently complete the work. Simple, yes—but as always, there are more effective and less effective ways to carry out these steps and to personalize them to fit your own Productivity Style.

I recommend you determine what to do next by considering three variables: your time, the resources and tools available, and your energy level. For example, suppose you have fifteen minutes before your next conference call, you are sitting at your desk in front of your computer, and it is 3 p.m. on a weekday afternoon, which means that your energy level is beginning to wane. Based on these variables, what task or project should you work on next?

First, let's consider the time available to you—fifteen minutes—and the main resource or tool you have available at this time: your computer.

The default response that I often see from my clients when faced with this scenario is to just check e-mail. However, I strongly encourage you to avoid the magnetic pull of e-mail, *unless* responding to e-mail happens to be the highest and best use of your time at that particular moment. Instead of defaulting to e-mail, look at your task list and determine which task you can work on that will move you one step closer to your READY goals, using your computer for fifteen minutes.

You may have grouped your TASK list by time and/or tool, in which case identifying an appropriate task might take only a few seconds. If you did not choose to group your TASK list this way, it could take a minute or so.

Let's say you find on your TASK list the following four tasks that could be completed in this time frame using your computer:

- Scan a document from your colleague Tad describing problems with an important client, and send a reply recommending corrective steps.
- Compare the catering menus of three restaurants being considered for next month's off-site meeting, and e-mail your assistant to let him know which one you prefer.
- Proofread the slide deck for a presentation you'll be making in six days at an industry association conference.
- Review the profit and loss statement for your department in preparation for next week's quarterly review meeting with your division vice president.

Now consider the final variable—your flagging energy level. Looking at the four tasks, which can you best complete with a minimal amount of energy?

The first task—advising Tad about how to deal with a possibly tricky problem related to an important client—may require some subtle, even creative judgment on your part. Unless this is an urgent emergency, it may be better to defer this task until the morning, when your mind is fresh.

The third and fourth tasks are both highly detail-oriented—and in both cases, overlooking a single key detail could be quite embarrassing. (Imagine if the title slide in your deck reads, WELCOM TO THE ASSOCIATION CON-FERNCE, or if your departmental P&L contains a sizable red-ink item you are not prepared to explain to your boss.) Since you have several more days to tackle those two tasks, save them for a time when your energy level is higher—and perhaps ask a colleague to double-check your work.

That leaves the important but fairly mundane task of selecting a good restaurant for next month's meeting. Go for it, and check that item off your TASK list.

By considering each of these three variables when determining what to do next, you will be able to capitalize on all of the minutes in your day, leverage your energy, and complete more high-value, meaningful work.

Now, step two: Efficiently complete the work. There are two sets of best practices you can apply that will help you boost your efficiency no matter what Productivity Style you favor. I call these *task execution* best practices and *project management* best practices. They are outlined in the two tables that follow.

WORK SIMPLY:
STRENGTHS AND TACTICS FOR TASK EXECUTION BY PRODUCTIVITY STYLE

If You're a Prioritizer

Your Strengths Are:

- Your ability to accurately complete significant amounts of work
- Your highly effective prioritization of tasks

So Try These Tactics:

- Evaluate your own successes based on the quality of the work versus the quantity of work. What might you need to shift so that you can rate yourself highly on both?
- Batch or group similar tasks to further increase your output and efficiency.

If You're a Planner

Your Strengths Are:

- Your gift for maintaining accurate, detailed lists
- Your ability to frequently complete work in advance of deadlines

So Try These Tactics:

- Effectively use the reminder systems that are available in your technology tools and apps to keep you focused on the most urgent and important tasks in your list.
- Decide in advance how much time and effort you are willing to spend on a task—then stick to the allotted budget.

If You're an Arranger

Your Strengths Are:

- Your ability to craft and use visual, kinesthetic lists
- Your strong intuitive sense for which tasks must be completed at any given time

So Try These Tactics:

- Improve your concentration and tune in to your work by listening to music without lyrics.
- Guard against interruptions in your train of thought from visiting colleagues, e-mails, and phone calls.

If You're a Visualizer

Your Strengths Are:

- Your ability to effectively manage multiple tasks at one time
- Your skill at efficient execution of tasks

So Try These Tactics:

- Just do it! Start by completing the quick tasks that require more speed than perfection to ensure you avoid the black hole of procrastination.
- Stay focused on the task at hand by clearing your desktop of distractions.

WORK SIMPLY:
STRENGTHS, TACTICS, AND TOOLS FOR PROJECT MANAGEMENT BY PRODUCTIVITY STYLE

If You're a Prioritizer

Your Strengths Are:

- Your focus on achieving the project outcome
- Your gift for analytical, logical analysis of the project goal
- Your skill at quick, accurate decision making

So Try These Tactics:

- Remember to consider the emotional needs of the project team members and how they may affect the project.
- Invest time in building relationships that will support project execution and adoption as well as customer and community relations.
- Learn to value feelings and take a more relaxed attitude in regard to "proof" for facts that may be in dispute.

And Try These Tools:

- Todoist is a Web-based free to-do and project management tool ideally suited for personal project management. It is easy to sort your tasks into project and subprojects, manage the tasks within the project with further sublists, and assign due dates to everything. As an added bonus, it integrates with Gmail for seamless movement between your inbox and your project management inbox.
- Basecamp is a Web-based project management tool. It is simple, easy to use, integrates with e-mail, and is available for the iPhone, iPad, and Android. Track tasks within projects, upload project files, and view calendars and timelines, all with a few simple clicks.

If You're a Planner

Your Strengths Are:

- Your ability to craft detailed, sequential project plans
- Your skills at consulting and complying with laws, policies, regulations, and quality and safety criteria when planning projects
- Your strong focus on achieving the project outcome

So Try These Tactics:

- Think about how the project supports the strategic vision; focus on the big picture, the *why* rationale, and the broad organizational context.
- Learn to value spontaneity and take a more relaxed attitude in regard to tightness of form and structure.
- Consider the length of time that it may take other project team members to complete tasks.

And Try These Tools:

- Tom's Planner is an intuitive free Web-based Gantt chart tool that works well as a personal project management tool. It is easy to use and you can tweak your charts on the fly.

- OpenProj is a free open-source desktop alternative to Microsoft Project. It is ideal for desktop project management and even opens existing native Microsoft Project files. It has a robust scheduling engine, as well as Gantt charts, network diagrams (PERT charts), WBS and RBS charts, earned value costing, and more.

If You're an Arranger

Your Strengths Are:

- Your ability to lead a team
- Your skill at partnering with people
- Your intuitive awareness of the next step in a project

So Try These Tactics:

- Be careful not to overlook numbers/data, financial/quantitative aspects, or technical requirements/feasibility analysis that may be crucial to the success of the project.
- Avoid being overly optimistic about how long it will actually take to complete tasks; make sure the time frames you allot are realistic.
- Avoid overcommunicating during the project, which may slow down project execution.

And Try These Tools:

- Collabtive is a free Web application that allows teams to collaborate on projects; manage tasks, milestones, and files; and send instant messages to each other. Receive e-mail notifications on projects and synchronize calendars via iCal task export.
- Asana is a project management, task management, and collaboration tool in one. Conversations, tasks, and files are all in one place, ensuring that you never lose something again. Conversations and tasks are grouped together so you do not get bogged down in e-mails.

If You're a Visualizer

Your Strengths Are:

- Your ability to think strategically
- Your ability to develop creative, innovative project ideas
- Your ability to see and connect disparate project aspects into a cohesive whole

So Try These Tactics:

- Be sure your project plans are specific and clear; plans that are too flexible may put team members in positions that are stressful, unrealistic, and unmanageable.
- Consider focusing on one aspect of a project at a time.
- Be aware of your tendency to avoid tasks that you find uninteresting or unappealing; combat it by interspersing boring tasks with more interesting ones.

And Try These Tools:

- Things is a Mac OS X and iOS to-do and project management tool. The interface is simple, clean, and easy to navigate. It is well integrated into the core applications of Mac like iCal. It is easy to move tasks, organize them into projects, and link them to the calendar. And it all syncs with your iPhone.
- LiquidPlanner is a robust Web-based project management application. It is flexible, allowing you to handle task management, project scheduling, and team collaboration all in one central place. There is a shared inbox to manage incoming project requests, it integrates with calendar and e-mail applications, and it has integrated documents and comments for quick and easy retrieval.

For a downloadable quick reference guide of task and project management strategies, please go to www.carsontate.com.

PACE YOURSELF FOR LONG-TERM SUCCESS

Emily is one of the clients we first met back in chapter 2. Her Productivity Style is Visualizer, and when I began working with her she had been working eighty to ninety hours a week for months. She was exhausted, and the quality of her work was on a downhill slide. Her manager had recently given her feedback that she was unresponsive, too bogged down in the daily minutiae, and failing to communicate effectively with her team.

Ouch! How could this be true? Emily was working *so* hard!

That was exactly the problem. Emily was mentally drained, sleep-deprived, and attempting to overcome her mental and physical depletion by working more and more hours. It clearly was not working. She needed to learn how to pace herself for long-term success.

I first learned pacing from my college cross-country coach, Jim Phemister. Coach Phemister was a wise, thoughtful, kind man who enjoyed a vibrant legal career as a prosecutor before moving to Lexington, Virginia, to teach future litigators at Washington and Lee University School of Law.

During my four years running for Coach, he taught us many life lessons disguised as running and racing tips. For example, we trained in the Blue Ridge Mountains, so we ran hills *all* the time. When running up a hill, Coach taught me to always look two to three steps in front of me rather than at the top of the hill. I discovered that this practice enabled me to stay focused in the present moment and maintain my pace during the hard work of climbing hills. Life lesson: When the going gets tough, stay in the present moment, take the next step that is presented to you, and do not get too fixated on the end goal, because that will only make the run longer and harder.

One of our favorite traditions was a final run with Coach and your teammates on the day of your wedding. On my big day, I woke up feeling a bit worse for wear due to a wonderful party the evening before, but I put on my shorts and shoes and met Coach and my friends Kim,

Josephine, and Natalie for a final run together. I was about to become the last of our group of four to tie the knot.

As we were running through the streets of my hometown of Columbia, South Carolina, Coach told me what he had told Kim, Josephine, and Natalie before me: "Marriage is a marathon, not a sprint. You have to pace yourself so you can finish the race. If you go hard at the beginning, you might not have the reserves to make it through the long climb in the middle."

I have heard this advice echoing in my head for years. I have used it as a metaphor not only for my marriage and personal life, but also for my professional career. When work is tough—when the demands from clients feel unreasonable, when my travel schedule is out of control, when a colleague calls in sick or a computer breaks down—I remind myself of the wisdom of Coach Phemister: "My career is a marathon. I have to pace myself, get water when I am thirsty, and refuel with food and rest." Somehow it helps me get through the day to put the problems I am wrestling with in that kind of bigger, broader context.

Jeff Immelt, CEO of General Electric, offered his perspective on pacing in an interview with Wharton, also using running as a metaphor. "I see all these books for new CEOs about what to do in the first 100 days on the job. It's nonsense. As a CEO, you are running a marathon. If you want to change, if you want to drive stuff that's meaningful in life, it takes persistence. Essentially anything you want to do that is meaningful in life must be done over time. If you want to change big institutions, you've got to have incredible persistence and constancy of purpose."[1]

Today, I approach growing and building my business in the marathon spirit. My projects I've identified to achieve the goals I have set for myself are like individual mile markers. I try hard to stay focused on the work that is currently in front of me, all the while knowing where the finish line is. I have learned the hard way that I need seven hours of sleep to do my best work—just as I needed those same seven hours to run my best time back in my days on Coach Phemister's team. Smart, self-aware pacing has become the secret tool I use to ensure that I am consistently able to perform at my best and not run out of energy before I reach the finish line.

FIND YOUR PERSONAL PACE

Remember Emily, overwhelmed, exhausted, and barely hanging on? She needed to learn how to pace herself for long-term success.

Emily's primary Productivity Style preference is that of a Visualizer, so her pacing strategies were vastly different than the strategies I prefer as a Planner. Like other productivity challenges, pacing is highly individual. It requires that you acknowledge and embrace your Productivity Style preferences. It also requires you to be honest with yourself about your physical needs.

Outlined below are pacing strategies by Productivity Style. As always, read and think about all the strategies listed, not just those recommended for your primary style. You may find that a strategy that belongs to a different style is the perfect one to enhance your own ability to develop and stick to the optimal pacing for life and work.

WORK SIMPLY:
FIND YOUR PERSONAL PACE
BY PRODUCTIVITY STYLE

If You're a Prioritizer

Try These Self-Pacing Techniques:

- Leverage your goal achievement focus by setting mini-goals for each day, week, and month. Then methodically work toward achieving them.
- Time yourself as you complete routine tasks, and then try to beat your time every few weeks. This will keep you focused and engaged.
- Rest and rejuvenation are essential to you, but you tend to overlook or minimize them in your drive to complete your work. Intentionally schedule downtime, vacation, and rest periods on your calendar and stick to them.

If You're a Planner

Try These Self-Pacing Techniques:

- You like crossing things off your list, so make this work for you. Track your progress toward your goals by noting how many items you have crossed off on your list each day, week, and month. And if it helps to write down and cross off tasks that you have already completed, go ahead and do it!
- Structure and form are important to you, so establish a regular structure to your days, weeks, and months that allows you to get into a rhythm or flow of work.
- You frequently complete your work in advance of deadlines, so use the "extra" time for rest and rejuvenation—two precious resources that you tend to undervalue.

If You're an Arranger

Try These Self-Pacing Techniques:

- Laughter is a great energy boost for you, so go ahead and indulge in a few really funny YouTube videos when your spirits are flagging.
- Too much solitary time tends to drain your batteries and reduce your effectiveness. Intentionally intersperse solitary project and task work with pair or group work, which you'll find energizing.
- Use your affinity for music to help you pace yourself. Make separate playlists to energize you, relax you, and sharpen your focus.

If You're a Visualizer

Try These Self-Pacing Techniques:

- Novelty is essential for you to efficiently get your work done. Intersperse "boring" or repetitive projects with projects that are new or at least more interesting to you.
- Spontaneity and fun are the juice that keeps you going. Ensure that there is

room and space during your day for you to be surprised and to just have fun. If not, you'll lose steam and may fall into the trap of procrastination.

• When possible, switch tasks or project types every fifteen to thirty minutes to keep your energy high and stay on pace to complete your work.

In today's business world, we talk and think a lot about the challenges of managing other people, but we tend to overlook the difficulties involved in managing ourselves. These difficulties are real and important. It takes sensitivity, honesty, and self-awareness to recognize and understand the factors that affect your own productivity. And it also takes wisdom and courage to act on that knowledge—to organize and schedule tasks around your unique work patterns, to prioritize activities based on your personal goals, and to say no to tasks that are at the wrong time or place for you. Too often our workplace cultures dictate one way of managing our time and energy—a particular style that may happen to fit a few people while being woefully inadequate for many others. The result is culturally driven busyness that prizes empty symbols (long hours in the office, "face time" with the boss, being seen racing from one meeting to the next, constant e-mailing and texting) rather than real productivity.

Learn to pay attention to the voices inside you—the ones that cry out in distress when you work against your natural Productivity Style, and sigh in satisfaction when you find and follow the structure and pacing that fit your preferences. You'll travel so much further in work and in life—and you'll enjoy the journey!

9
—
Tame Your Inbox

THIRTEEN THOUSAND. 13,000.

That was the number of messages in Emily's e-mail inbox.

No wonder she started each day with a profound sense of dread. What was lurking in her inbox that she had not done? What requests had she overlooked? How far behind was she on her projects? Who had she not responded to?

In an effort to overcome the e-mail monster, she'd expanded her work hours, little by little, until she scarcely had an evening or a weekend completely free. It had been months since Emily had even been able to watch her beloved New England Patriots without trying to work through a stack of e-mail at the same time. But her efforts seemed pointless—after weeks of suffering, the size of her e-mail backlog had scarcely budged.

Emily's inbox was controlling her instead of her controlling it. Increasingly desperate, she knew that something had to be done about it. But what?

Are you in the same boat as Emily—tired of dreading your inbox, sick of the constant sense of low-level anxiety that pervades you when you think about it? If so, you're in good company. The average person spends about 28 percent of their workweek managing e-mail. In 2012, the number of business e-mails sent and received per day totaled eighty-nine billion, and this figure is expected to grow at a rate of 13 percent over the next four years.[1] The ever-increasing volume of e-mail interruptions makes us less productive, less effective, and less creative.

It is time to retake control, halt the assault, and tame your inbox once and for all.

TAKE CONTROL OF YOUR INBOX (AND YOUR DAY)

Most knowledge workers assume that they must start their day with e-mail. Wrong! You do not have to start your day in your inbox—and it is *not* the best way to employ the hour when you are probably at your freshest, most energetic, and most alert. Imagine what would happen if you started your day by tackling your highest-value task? Suppose you began work by preparing a proposal for a new client, drafting your e-newsletter, working on a crucial report requested by your manager, or calling your most important customer to thank them for their business. What would happen to your productivity, your effectiveness, and your sense of control?

Maybe this feels like too radical or risky a change. Maybe you feel you need someone's permission to break with such a deeply ingrained habit. You do not, of course—but if you feel you do, I am hereby giving you permission to stop starting your day with e-mail.

That's exactly what I told Emily when she shared her familiar tale of e-mail woe.

Emily agreed that changing the way she launched her day should be her first step in taking back control of her workday. But she knew it would be hard. She would be swimming upstream, fighting against not only her corporate culture but also the broader work culture in which we all live. After all, everyone starts the day with e-mail. Many people assume that an e-mail they send in the afternoon or evening will be answered, at the latest, early the next morning, during the 8 a.m. e-mail blitz that most people unquestioningly accept as the norm.

A bit nervous about battling this pervasive norm, Emily decided that her goal for the first three weeks would be to start her day with her highest-value task just twice each week. After a few false starts, she noticed that there was something different about the days when she sidestepped her inbox. She felt calmer and more relaxed. What's more, she was actually completing some of her high-value projects—tasks that used to remain one-quarter finished while she tackled yet another inbox barrage. Within six weeks, she no longer had to physically control the urge to open her inbox as soon as her computer flickered to life. Instead, she calmly started her day by addressing her top priorities and began quickly completing high-value work.

"E-mail first" is not the only destructive e-mail norm we need to escape. Many people and organizations live with the expectation that knowledge workers will spend their days on their smartphones and in their inboxes, checking e-mail every five minutes. This practice is a productivity drain and an ineffective use of your most valuable commodity—time.

Heed the advice of Virgin entrepreneur Richard Branson: "You must manage your smartphone; do not let it manage you. Many executives check their smartphones throughout meetings and during off-hours. This is not good for concentration, and has a negative impact on decision making. Use it only in bursts: check emails for an hour or so and then put it away and focus on the task at hand."[2]

Take back control by checking e-mail only at regular intervals at predetermined times of the day—for example, at midmorning, after lunch, and at midafternoon. Then get out of e-mail and get back to productive work.

Remember, we teach people how to treat us. So if you find yourself suffering from culturally driven busyness when it comes to e-mail, establish some new protocols and habits. Let your colleagues, your direct reports, your manager, and all your other e-mail correspondents know that they may have to wait a few hours for a response to a message. If it is an emergency, they can always reach you by phone. Break them of the assumption that every e-mail will receive an instant acknowledgment and response. Will they be upset? It's highly unlikely. After all, the number of e-mail messages that really *demand* an instant response is small. In fact, many of those you exchange messages with are likely to appreciate being released from the tyranny of the instantaneous exchange—and they may begin changing their own e-mail habits to mirror yours.

MAKE A DECISION!

Having altered your work rhythms to regain control over your inbox, the next step is to reduce the amount of time you need to spend processing incoming messages by learning the simple discipline of *making a decision*.

As Emily and I were wading through her thirteen thousand e-mails, I started asking her questions about each message. "Does this message require action by you?" "Do you need to keep this message?" "Have you responded to this message?" In almost every case, Emily had to stop, reread the message, and think about an answer to my question—even with e-mails that had arrived days before and that she had read once, twice, or several times previously. It quickly became apparent that she had been scanning her messages and avoiding making decisions on how to handle them. The result: an uncontrolled, overflowing inbox.

All of the e-mails loitering in Emily's inbox were clutter, simply because she had not decided what to do with them. In the words of organizational expert Barbara Hemphill, "Clutter is postponed decisions." So the key to more effectively and efficiently processing our incoming messages lies in *making faster decisions*. And the best way I know to accomplish that is by using my E-mail Agility Circle. I call it the E-mail Agility Circle because the goal is to become more agile—able to move quickly and easily—in managing your inbox. The faster you can make accurate decisions regarding the content of your inbox, the more time you will have in your day.

USE THE E-MAIL AGILITY CIRCLE

The E-mail Agility Circle is a four-step process—*read, decide, act, contain*—that will help you get into and out of your inbox as quickly as possible, making fast decisions without undermining your accuracy (see figure 9.1).

The first step in the E-mail Agility Circle is to read. Obvious? Maybe—and the fact is that you are probably reading your e-mails already, and (like Emily) rereading them over and over. The problem is that we often open our e-mails when we cannot truly read them and absorb the information they contain—for example, while engaging in conversation, during the last few moments before a meeting, when standing in line for coffee, or while we have one foot out the office door. The result is that we skim them rather than really reading them, understanding and retaining only a fraction of the contents. This forces us to waste precious time rereading the same messages later.

This problem sounds trivial, yet in the real lives of countless knowledge workers it is draining a vast amount of time and energy. For example, let's

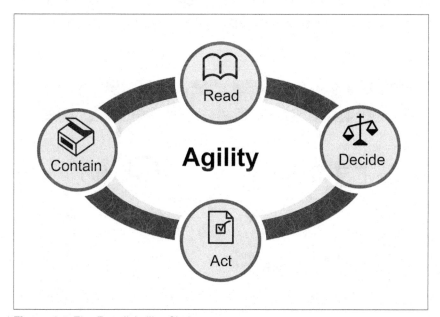

Figure 9.1. The E-mail Agility Circle.

assume you receive a hundred messages per day and that it takes approximately a minute to read each one. That means you've invested one hour and forty minutes reading your messages. But if you were unable to fully read them the first time and therefore need to go back and reread them, the time you've now invested amounts to three hours and twenty minutes.

Do you have an extra hour or more to waste every day? If not, get into the habit of opening your e-mail only when you have the time and energy to really absorb the contents—and then read your messages once.

The second step in the E-mail Agility Circle is to decide. Remember when I pointed out that clutter equals postponed decisions? This is the step in the process where you are actively preventing clutter from building by making a decision about the e-mail message. Ask yourself, "What is this e-mail message? Does it require action?" This is quick and very simple, but very powerful. Do not underestimate the power of making a decision.

The third step in the E-mail Agility Circle is to act. Does the e-mail message require some concrete action by you—for example, to answer a question, send a piece of information to someone else, add a date to your calendar, or recommend a solution to a simple problem? If so, you have three choices (see figure 9.2).

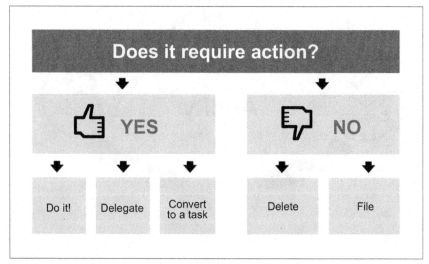

Figure 9.2. E-mail action decision steps.

The first choice is to follow the familiar Nike motto—"Just do it." Take this choice if you can complete the requested task or answer the question in three to five minutes or less. After all, it will take you longer to come back to it later—so just do it now, and get this e-mail out of your inbox and out of your consciousness forever.

The second choice is to delegate the e-mail to someone else. This requires a decision as to whether or not you are the right person to address the issue raised in the message. If not, delegate it, and do so immediately. You can either forward the e-mail to the right person (after adding a few words explaining what you're doing) or write a brief response to the original correspondent recommending the appropriate contact and copying the contact on the message. Either way, your responsibility has been discharged, and once again you can eliminate the e-mail from your inbox with a clear conscience.

The last choice—the one that's probably appropriate for the majority of your e-mail messages—is to convert the e-mail into a task. This simply means reading the message, deciding on your next action step, and converting it into a task. It's as easy as changing the subject line of the e-mail, converting it into a task using the task function in your e-mail program, or creating one or more appointments directly from the e-mail. By converting the e-mail into a task, you've removed it from your inbox and given it a slot in line where you can track and complete the work required at the time that's best for you. (For videos on how to convert an e-mail to a task, go to www.carsontate.com. You will also be able to download quick reference guides outlining the steps in the videos.)

On the other hand, what if the e-mail message doesn't require action by you? In that case, you have two choices: File it or delete it.

How do you decide which to do? I have found that the familiar 80/20 rule applies to e-mail messages: Most people retrieve only 20 percent of the e-mails they file. The other 80 percent remain in the cloud, taking up space while never serving any purpose. So before filing an e-mail message, ask yourself, "When would I *need* to retrieve this information? Do I need it for legal, compliance, or regulatory reasons? Are there specific details about an ongoing project that are available in this e-mail and no-where else?" If not, delete it.

Finally, the fourth step in the E-mail Agility Circle is to contain your e-mail messages. Actually, this is not so much a separate step as a sum-mary of the entire circle. The word *contain* should remind you that your inbox is not an optimal storage container for all of the thousands of mes-sages you receive. So contain those messages by moving them to one of the following locations: your file folders, the trash can, your calendar, or your task list.

Using the E-mail Agility Circle will enable you to keep your inbox clutter-free and dramatically reduce the amount of time you spend pro-cessing your messages.

CRAFT MORE EFFECTIVE E-MAIL MESSAGES

When Emily and I got to this point together, she was starting to feel a lot more relaxed and in control. But her problems with e-mail were still not completely solved. She was still receiving multiple questions and follow-up e-mails about the messages she sent out. All too often, a single e-mail sent to several members of her project team seemed to generate half a dozen questions in response, each requiring still more e-mails in several rounds of communication that might last a week or more.

You may have experienced the same phenomenon—in fact, it may happen so routinely that you've come to assume that this is simply an unavoidable side effect of e-mail. But if you think about it, there is some-thing a bit mysterious about this feedback loop effect. What is going on? Why do you find yourself receiving so many messages in response to your e-mails—especially when you think you've provided all the informa-tion needed in your initial message?

For Emily, this problem was an ongoing source of frustration. It left her feeling increasingly annoyed with her e-mail correspondents, who seemed to be either too stupid to understand the clear and simple mes-sages she had been sending or too lazy to read and absorb them.

However, for Emily—as for most of us—the problem wasn't really that straightforward. Communication between her and her colleagues was indeed suffering a breakdown—but neither ignorance nor laziness was to blame.

The fact is that communicating effectively and clearly is difficult, whether we are using e-mail, writing, speaking, or any other medium. The reason is that we all send and receive information differently. And when you use a delivery channel like e-mail, which excludes the use of nonverbal cues like body language and tone of voice, the challenge of clear communication becomes even more difficult. Then throw in the fact that everyone uses the e-mail medium differently—for example, some people always include a salutation and closing in their e-mail messages, while others never do; some people write only one-line e-mails, while others write short novels. Every distinctive style of e-mail writing demands a unique set of reading and comprehension tools, which only a handful of e-mail users have mastered. As a result, it's really not surprising that information communicated via e-mail often falls through the cracks, setting up the feedback loop problem that Emily found so exasperating.

Emily and I discussed the inherent challenges in crafting effective e-mail messages, pulling out a number of e-mails she had written to examine them with a fresh eye. Rereading her own work after a number of weeks or months had passed, she began to realize that her individual Productivity Style was controlling her approach to writing. Emily was a Visualizer, and her e-mail messages reflected it. In writing an e-mail to outline a project, for example, she was describing the big picture, the strategic objectives, and why it was important to the organization, but she was omitting some of the crucial details that were necessary for the recipients to understand her message—especially those with differing Productivity Styles. Emily was also vague in how she wanted the recipients to respond to and take action on her messages. Even the way in which she addressed her e-mails was potentially confusing—for example, she sometimes included individuals who had the authority to make key decisions about her projects on the cc: line rather than addressing them directly.

The more closely we examined Emily's e-mails, the more she discovered the holes in her messages that were resulting in misunderstandings, extended multiway communication loops, and general frustration.

Fortunately, learning to write more effective e-mails is a lot simpler than becoming a best-selling novelist or a great screenwriter! In fact, it's as simple as getting into the habit of answering four key questions in every single e-mail you write: *who, why, what,* and *how.* Here's how it works:

- *Who?* This breaks down into two subquestions. "Who needs to respond to, take action on, or make a decision about this information?" Put their name(s) on the to: line. "Who needs to know this information?" Put their names on the cc: line.
- *Why?* Look back at the names on the to: line and the cc: line. For each name, ask yourself, "Why is this person involved in the project? Why am I e-mailing them? Why do they need to know? Why does this information matter to them? Why does it matter to the broader organization?" Then think about what you know about those individuals—their interests, needs, backgrounds, and communication styles. Make sure the tone, style, and content of your e-mail matches up—just as you would choose appropriate words, tone, and body language if you were sitting across a table from them and discussing the topic in person.
- *What?* Ask yourself a series of *what* questions to help shape the content of your e-mail. "What is the purpose of the e-mail? What are the main points to be communicated in this e-mail? What are the key facts? What references or research data need to be included? What must everyone know?" Do not hit the send button until you have included every piece of detail required.
- *How?* Ask yourself, "How do I want recipients to respond?" Describe this explicitly in your e-mail. If there's a deadline, say so. If you want an e-mail response, say that. If you need suggested dates for a meeting, names of possible project participants, a list of questions or key ideas to be considered, or any other specific input, describe it. Never

assume that people will understand what you want—tell them as straightforwardly as possible.

Avoid inviting questions and misunderstandings from colleagues. Answer the *Who, Why, What,* and *How* questions every time you write an e-mail message. It's a simple way to ensure that all of your messages will be understood by all recipients, making a host of follow-up e-mails (or phone calls, visits, or other interruptions) unnecessary.

Here are a couple of sample e-mails that illustrate how these questions can add clarity to your messages. First, the sample "before" version—a typical e-mail that may resemble messages you send or receive every day.

Subject: Contract
From: Emily Matthews
To: Sue Anderson
cc: sstevens@business.com; dmengers@business.com;
pstowe@business.com; kmayfield@business.com;
blemming@business.com

The big event is approaching! I hope you're as excited as we are. Now for the purpose of this e-mail. I made the decision to involve our legal department due to the level of leaders we will be working with on this project. As you know, the investment conference includes our top-tier leaders. Contract attached. Thanks for your attention to this. See you soon.

If you find yourself a bit confused by this message, the problem is not with you, it's with the message. What and when is "the big event"? Why, specifically, is a contract attached? What is the recipient of the e-mail being asked to do next? How exactly is she supposed to respond? It seems likely that at least one more exchange of e-mails will be required to clarify these issues before the next steps can be taken. The result: cluttered inboxes and wasted time for at least two people, maybe more.

Now consider the sample revised version:

Subject: Investor Relations Conference—Contract
From: Emily Matthews
To: Sue Anderson
cc: sstevens@business.com; dmengers@business.com; pstowe@business.com; kmayfield@business.com; blemming@business.com

Dear Sue,

We are looking forward to having you speak at our Investor Relations Conference on June 15. Due to the level of leaders participating in the program, I've made the decision to involve our legal department and formally contract for your services, which will protect you and the other top-tier leaders who are appearing at the conference from any unforeseen liability issues that might arise as well as clarifying how expenses and other issues will be handled. To finalize your participation, please review the attached contract, sign it, and e-mail it back to me by May 30. If you have any questions about the contract, you can e-mail me or directly contact Donald Mengers in our legal department at dmengers@business.com.

Thank you,
Emily

Notice how the four-question approach has been used to make the revised e-mail extremely clear. The *Who* question helped determine the names listed on the to: and cc: lines as well as the salutation ("Dear Sue"). The *What* question is answered explicitly in both the subject line and the first sentence of the e-mail ("We are looking forward to having you present . . ."). The next sentence responds to the *Why* question ("Due to the level of leaders participating . . ."), and the last two sentences (beginning "To finalize your participation . . .") answer the *How* question by explaining exactly how the recipient of the e-mail should respond.

Yes, it probably took an extra minute or two to plan and write the revised e-mail. But the amount of time and effort saved by avoiding numerous back-and-forth clarification messages is far greater.

USE THE SUBJECT LINE TO IMPROVE E-MAIL RESPONSE TIME

Mrs. Leech was my fifth-grade teacher and a stickler for paragraphs with topic sentences. We spent the entire year working on writing and writing paragraphs with topic sentences. Even today, when I sit down to write a speech, an article, or a chapter for this book, I can still hear Mrs. Leech in my head asking me, "Carson, where is your topic sentence?" I know that if Mrs. Leech looked at my inbox and read some of the e-mail messages I receive, she would gasp, pull out her red pencil, and write in the margin, "Topic sentence unclear!"

Of course, Mrs. Leech never knew about e-mails. But her wisdom still applies in today's world of electronic communication. Only the format of our written messages has changed slightly. The subject line of your e-mail message is your topic sentence. And a clear subject line is essential if you want to communicate effectively and improve both the quality and the response time on the e-mail messages you send.

So, please, never let yourself hit the send button while the subject line of your e-mail reads "re:re," "fwd:fwd," or some cryptic phrase that relates to a prior e-mail conversation. The topic or purpose of these e-mails is unclear. As a result, your correspondent will waste precious minutes trying to sort, prioritize, and decode incoming messages—and your important communication may get lost and forgotten.

Make sure the subject lines on your e-mail messages reflect the current topic, purpose, or desired outcome. When responding to an e-mail you've received, change the subject line to make it current and clear if necessary. Or consider using one of the following standard e-mail subject lines:

- Action Required—DATE
- FYI—3rd Paragraph Client X Mention
- Update: TOPIC
- Reply by—DATE
- NRN—No response needed
- EOM—End of message

The last subject line above (EOM) is an especially powerful one. Here's how it works: When you have a short, simple message to convey, type the entire e-mail in the subject line of the e-mail, and put EOM at the end. (For example, "Tuesday marketing meeting moved to 2 p.m. EOM.") Now your recipient does not have to open the e-mail message, saving them precious minutes.

When e-mail subject line best practices spread throughout an organization, the savings in time and energy can be significant. A few months ago, the sales team of a consumer products company reached out to me because they were overwhelmed by e-mails. One strategy they implemented was agreeing to specific, standard subject lines that would enable them to prioritize incoming messages and more effectively manage their days. Within three months of making this one adjustment, the sales representatives were spending fewer hours each week on administrative e-mails, and client response times had improved by 20 percent.

Stop neglecting the subject line on your e-mail messages, and watch your productivity soar.

MAKE YOUR E-MAIL TECHNOLOGY WORK FOR YOU

Emily's Productivity Style was hampering her e-mail effectiveness in another way. As a Visualizer, she was very hesitant to file her e-mail messages. Living by the Visualizer's motto, "Out of sight, out of mind," Emily feared that she might forget about any message that was not immediately visible whenever she turned on her computer—and if she forgot about the message, she might also forget about the person who sent it or the project it described.

At the same time, however, Emily realized that she could not effectively complete her work and respond to new messages in a timely fashion with thirteen thousand older messages crowding her inbox.

The problem: technically driven busyness that was causing Emily to waste countless hours scrolling through old and irrelevant e-mail messages. The solution: to make the technology in Emily's e-mail system work for her and her Productivity Style.

Let's look at each Productivity Style and consider how e-mail strategies and tools can be aligned to the specific thinking preferences associated with that style.

WORK SIMPLY: STRATEGIES TO MASTER YOUR E-MAIL BY PRODUCTIVITY STYLE

If You're a Prioritizer

As you recall, the Prioritizer's thinking tends to be logical, analytical, fact-based, critical, and realistic. So if you're a Prioritizer, your e-mail technology strategies should be logical and linear, designed to enable you to gather the necessary facts to make faster decisions. Here are some specific recommendations:

Create and Use Rules to Prioritize Incoming Messages. All of the popular e-mail programs—Outlook, Outlook for Mac, Lotus Notes, and Gmail—have a "rules wizard" or similar feature that makes it easy for you to establish rules for managing the flow of e-mail into your inbox. This is a godsend for the Prioritizer— in fact, you can think about these rules as the *ultimate* prioritizing tool for e-mail.

Here's how these rules work. When you receive an e-mail message, it is first sent to the server that hosts your e-mail service and then directed to your specific inbox. The rules sort or filter all incoming messages as they arrive. The beauty is that, using the rules wizard, you can tailor the rules to meet your specific priorities and preferences precisely. For example, you could write a rule to automatically send all of your monthly trade publications to a specific folder; you could send all of your online shopping receipts to another folder; you can automatically forward and delete messages when you are on vacation; and you can write a rule to automatically track all of your open or pending requests. By writing and using rules, you can make and immediately implement decisions about your priorities—which e-mail messages to read now, which to read later, and how to route messages of various kinds—and then let the technology do the rest.

If you don't know what rules to write, take some time to study the contents of your inbox. What patterns can you detect? What e-mails do you receive daily, weekly, or monthly? Do you need to see this information when it comes in? How might automating some of the filing, sorting, and responding free up some time to work on higher-value tasks? Answering questions like these can help you decide the rules that will work best for you.

Set a Numerical Goal Governing the Number of E-mails in Your Inbox at Any Time. If you're a Prioritizer, you tend to be very goal-focused, with a special preference for quantitative targets. Leverage this preference by setting a goal of no more than a specific number of e-mail messages in your inbox at one time. My client Gene set his limit at twenty. So at the end of each day he reads, processes, and organizes his inbox until he has reduced the backlog to no more than twenty e-mails. The limit keeps his inbox in control, and achieving his goal each day gives him a satisfying feeling of accomplishment.

Limit the Time You Spend Processing E-mail. The Prioritizer is usually able to complete significant amounts of work very quickly. Harness this ability by limiting the time you spend processing e-mail. Give yourself only thirty minutes to read and respond to e-mail, and watch what happens! Working within a strict time limit, you will be amazed at how quickly you can read, process, and organize your e-mail messages.

If You're a Planner

If you're a Planner, your thinking is generally organized, sequential, planned, and detailed. That means you should employ e-mail strategies that will enable you to better organize and plan both your e-mail time investment and e-mail responses. Here are some ideas:

Check Your E-mails on a Schedule. As a Planner, you probably enjoy using schedules and work well with them. Apply this scheduling inclination to e-mail management. Determine the specific times during the day when you want or need to check your e-mail. Your e-mail schedule may vary slightly from day to day or from week to week. The key is that you should impose order and structure on the time you spend processing e-mail. (It's an approach I recommend to almost everyone I work with, but it's especially well suited to the Planner.) You'll watch your effectiveness soar as a result.

When Writing an E-mail, Use the Subject Line to State the Recipient's Next Action Step. As a Planner, ensuring fast and accurate responses to your e-mail messages is very important to you. In pursuit of this goal, use the subject line to state the recipient's next step. Include both the topic of the e-mail and the specific action step you need the recipient to take—for example: *Action Required—Revise Q4 Sales Projections by 5/16*. This technique ensures that the recipients of your messages know exactly what you need and when you need it completed.

Organize your E-mail File Folders Using Numbers and Symbols. A Planner generally loves to organize. You can create your own organizational system for e-mails that customizes the built-in alphabetical organization by using numbers and symbols. Here's how it works: Suppose you have three current projects that are crucially important to you, known as "Henderson," "Frank," and "Bernstein." Rather than letting these files fall into their alphabetical locations under the letters H, F, and B, place a number in front of the file folder name—"1 Henderson," "2 Frank," and "3 Bernstein." These three files will rise to the top of your e-mail archive, with all the other (nonnumbered) files following in traditional alphabetical order. (Notice that once the Henderson project is completed or otherwise drops off your high-priority list, you can simply remove the number and let it return to its conventional location under H.)

If you insert a symbol in front of the name of a file folder, this file folder will move to the top of the list in front of any numbered file folders. For example, you might want to create a "Waiting For" file containing e-mails that describe follow-up steps you need to keep track of. If you label that file "@Waiting For," it will always appear at the front of your archive.

If You're an Arranger

If you're an Arranger, you tend to engage in supportive, expressive, and emotional thinking. To match your style, your e-mail strategies should be engaging, should reduce or minimize distractions, and should be designed to give you back time to connect with colleagues. Here are some ideas you will want to consider:

Think Carefully Before Adding One More Person to the cc: Line. As an Arranger, you prefer to work with people to complete work. Your inclusive style means that you might be prone to overcommunicate with colleagues in an effort to maintain your connections with them. Be aware of this tendency. When drafting an e-mail message, think carefully about who really should appear on the cc: line. Avoid loading up the cc: line with people for whom the information in the e-mail falls into the "nice to know" category. Stick with those for whom it is truly "need to know" information, and you will avoid needlessly cluttering other people's inboxes—as well as your own.

Try Listening to Music While Processing E-mail—It Makes It More Fun! For an Arranger who enjoys connecting with people, e-mail can be a little sterile and dull. Many Arrangers also question the value of e-mail communication because it does not adequately meet their high need for strong interpersonal relationships.

For example, my client Avery—a classic Arranger—was drowning in her inbox and had received feedback from her manager and vendor partners that she was unresponsive and oblivious to essential information. The problem? She considered e-mail cold, impersonal, and a waste of her time. The solution we devised played upon two of Avery's special loves—music and chocolate. Now Avery turns on her favorite music when she processes her e-mail and rewards herself with a tiny square of chocolate when her inbox is clean. It is a simple way of making the process more engaging and enjoyable for her.

Create and Use Templates for Routine Requests and Tasks. Boring and repetitive work can suck the life out of an Arranger. To minimize the problem, create templates by using the auto-signature feature in your e-mail program or by creating and saving them using the template feature available on Outlook and Lotus Notes. (Unfortunately, Gmail users do not currently have this option.) Either way, when you receive a routine e-mail that demands a standard reply, you quickly send out the template rather than having to rewrite a boring and repetitive message. This system allows you to get back to more interesting and engaging work quickly and easily without ignoring an important message that deserves a response.

If You're a Visualizer

If you're a Visualizer, your thinking is characterized as holistic, intuitive, integrating, and synthesizing. Your principal strength is your ability to see the big picture. So you need e-mail strategies that will enable you to see the important messages and synthesize the incoming information quickly and easily. Here are some techniques to try:

Color-Code Your Incoming Messages by Sender or by Subject. Use color to make specific categories or types of messages stand out in your inbox. For example, you might write a rule that color-codes messages from your manager in red, messages from top clients in green, and messages from major suppliers in yellow. (The message itself actually appears in this color when it is viewed in your inbox.) Or you might color-code messages that are sent only to you in blue, thereby differentiating them from the hundreds of messages where you are just another name on the cc: line. Color is your friend. Use it to help you quickly see the messages that require your immediate or timely attention.

Turn Off the E-mail Notification Alarm. Distractions are pervasive and persistent in all offices, and the most insidious distraction of all is the e-mail notification alarm. It is particularly disruptive for a Visualizer who responds to visual cues. Do not let technology hijack your attention. Turn it off, and let the e-mail wait until you are ready to read and respond to e-mail messages. (Again, this is a technique that practically everyone can benefit from, but it is particularly essential for the efficiency of a Visualizer.)

Use Auto Preview so You Can See the First Few Lines of an E-mail Without Opening It. You can minimize the time you spend opening and reviewing messages by customizing the view of your e-mail inbox. Use auto preview so you can see the first few lines of the e-mail without opening it. It's often possible to make a decision about how to process the e-mail based solely on the opening few lines. Let your eyes and the technology work *for* you.

When I checked in with Emily a month later, the difference was palpable. She felt freer, more relaxed, and more productive. The people she worked with noticed the difference too. Colleagues who'd begun to complain about unanswered e-mails and missed deadlines were now thanking Emily for being so responsive and reliable. Best of all, Emily had cut way back on her weekend and evening hours. She'd even gone back to regularly watching her beloved New England Patriots play on Sundays—without having her computer screen open in front of her!

I cannot guarantee that taming your inbox will transform your life the same way it did for Emily. But I promise it will make a difference that you will notice and appreciate—just one step on the road to a freer, more productive, and happier you.

10

Shape Your Space for Mental and Physical Freedom

EVERYONE KNOWS THAT THE LATE STEVE JOBS, FOUNDER OF Apple, was a genius when it came to product design, technological innovation, and marketing. But did you know that he also had unusual insight into the challenges of personal productivity?

When it came time to design a new building to house the headquarters of Pixar, the remarkable computer animation movie studio that Jobs helped to build, he insisted that the space be designed with the bathrooms in the center. Why? Jobs knew that he wanted Pixar to be a place where creativity thrived, and he knew too that creativity is fostered by continual random interactions among people with different talents and interests. So he decided that the center of the building—the crossroads where all departments intersected—would contain the bathrooms, which were the only rooms that everyone would eventually have to visit. In the words of writer Carleen Hawn, "Jobs realized that when people run into each other, when they make eye contact, things happen. So he made it impossible for you not to run into the rest of the company."[1]

The results have been remarkable: Pixar employees have been known to work twelve-hour days without complaint because the "workspace isn't boring."[2] The studio has enjoyed an unequaled track record of commercial and artistic success, producing one blockbuster hit after another and winning a string of Oscars along the way.

Pixar is not the only company that has used the power of smart environmental design to foster creativity, productivity, and success. Motorola engineers left their cubicles and went to an alternate open, creative space to design their phenomenally popular Razr mobile phone. Toy maker Fisher-Price developed a dedicated space, the Cave, where designers, engineers, and marketers meet to build prototypes of toys from foam, cardboard, glue, and acrylic paint.[3] Microsoft's Entertainment and Devices division designed a studio with a transparent, open workspace, adaptable areas, and a central spine where technology stations are docked and easily reconfigurable, enabling individuals to add another monitor for their own use or move their workspace to be in closer proximity to another team member they are collaborating with.[4]

These smart companies know that space matters. Engaged, productive employees do not work in a vacuum. They need workplaces that help them bring out the best in themselves—mosh pits of creativity where energy and inspiration can flow freely.

Of course, corporations hoping to produce the next billion-dollar product aren't the only ones that need to think about the impact of space on productivity. Individual working men and women like you and me should be equally aware of the effect that our surroundings have on our productivity. That is why when I am working with an individual client, I always want to see their physical workspace, either "in the flesh" or at least by studying photographs. I have found that it is virtually impossible to fully support a client in achieving their productivity goals without considering their physical workspace.

MAKE YOUR SPACE REFLECT WHO YOU ARE AND THE WORK YOU DO

Unfortunately, plenty of people—including both those who work for large corporations and those who are entrepreneurs, working alone or with a small team of colleagues—do not feel motivated or empowered to take control of their working spaces. Many simply move into whatever cubicle or office is provided for them, prop up a family photo on the desk, and start working. Others create a workspace in an unused corner of their home, stick in a cast-off piece of furniture or two, plug in a computer and a lamp, and call it a day. The amount of time and energy they devote to customizing the workspace is minimal. And that is a shame—because an investment in rethinking and reshaping your work environment can pay huge dividends in increased productivity and happiness.

A cornerstone of working simply is making your space reflect *you*. The process begins with reflecting on the types of work that you do.

First, think about your role and the core accountabilities of your position. Are you the leader of a large team who spends 90 percent of the day in meetings? Are you an interior designer crafting artful, relaxing spaces in people's homes? Are you the manager of a local coffee shop? Or are you a financial analyst at an investment bank or a brokerage firm? In each of these roles, you are responsible for completing different types of work. The types of work that you do should inform how you design, set up, and work in your space.

For example, my colleague Keira is an executive coach leading a highly successful consulting practice. She does one-on-one executive coaching, seminar design, research and writing, on-site client work (consulting and facilitating), and administrative tasks to support her company. Each of these types of work is slightly different and requires different tools and space requirements.

In order to support her work, Keira has used what we call the kindergarten model to design her space.

My daughter, EC, attends a local preschool where she is in a class with twelve other three-year-olds—an environment that makes my head spin just thinking about it! She has two engaging, loving, kind, and patient teachers who make teaching this many children look effortless. As I have come to discover, one of their secrets is the layout of their classroom space.

When you walk into EC's classroom, there are cubbies along the right-hand wall labeled with the children's names. Each child's school bag, lunchbox, coat, hat, gloves, and other belongings are all placed in their specific cubby. Next to the cubbies is the (play) kitchen including two stoves, a refrigerator, an assortment of plastic food, and a shopping cart. From there you move on to the blocks and puzzles stacked on shelves, then the dress-up area replete with a large crate full of fabulous costumes.

At the center of the room in the back is the reading center. Books are stacked on shelves, there are beanbag chairs for reading, and the bulletin board and circle-time area are located nearby. In the center of the room are tables and chairs used for art projects, snacks, and lunch.

As you can see, the room is organized into zones by type of activity or play, with all the resources and equipment for that specific activity contained in that zone. The books are not kept in the kitchen, and the jewelry used to accessorize the costumes is not kept with the puzzles. Everything in the room has a specific place and is kept in its place. The children know where to find the toys they want to play with and can easily put away their toys when they are finished playing.

This is the kindergarten space model at its best—simple, efficient, and effective.

Of course, a kindergarten classroom is generally a large area with plenty of room for different specialized niches. Most working people do not have quite that much space to work with. However, you do not need to occupy the CEO's corner office to make your space effective for you. At this point, I think I have worked in almost every type of space, and I can testify that any type and size of space can be configured to optimize your work output and support you.

Here's how my colleague Keira has adapted the kindergarten model to her needs. To the right of her desk are two small chairs facing each other that she uses for her in-person coaching clients, along with a small table with a phone that is used for her virtual coaching clients. To the left of the two chairs is a large bookcase with all of her reference materials and books that she often reads while relaxing in one of the chairs. There is a small table behind her desk that serves as the technology zone, where Keira keeps her computer and her printer. Keira keeps the surface of her desk free of any items since this is where she does the majority of her workshop design. There's a place for every activity, and each place is designed and equipped to support that activity.

The kindergarten model does not just apply to physical space. With variations, it can also be used for configuring a mobile office or even your workbag. For example, Jason, a serial entrepreneur who has his fingers in multiple businesses—commercial real estate development, construction management, property management, a bar, and an art gallery/coffee shop—works out of a bag, or as Jason and I call it, The Bag.

Jason spends over 90 percent of his workday in transit, driving from one property site to another and walking through large commercial buildings with clients. He and I collaborated on designing The Bag, which enables him to carry everything he needs to be productive as he travels the region throughout his busy day.

The Bag has specific zones for each type of work in the form of pockets, file folders, and plastic pouches. An outer pocket contains Jason's cell phone (his most important and frequently used tool) as well as pens and pads for taking notes. The phone charger is carefully wrapped using heavy-duty rubber bands.

The center compartment has three divided pockets. In the center pocket, Jason keeps his laptop along with its power cord and accessories in a small plastic pouch. In the pocket on the left, he keeps his master TASK notebook, extra pens, and a highlighter. In the pocket on the right are plastic file folders labeled by client name, extra file folders, and an additional notebook. Thus each area of The Bag supports a specific type of work and contains only the tools needed for that type of work.

Both Jason and Keira have designed their workspaces to support the types of work they do. In both cases, they followed the basic principle of developing individual work zones that are equipped to support specific types of work. But the solutions they developed are radically different because their work lives are equally divergent. You too need to devise your own workspace solution, one that is customized to fit the ways you work each day.

CUSTOMIZE YOUR SPACE TO FIT YOUR PRODUCTIVITY STYLE

In addition, you need to customize your space based on your Productivity Style.

When you walk into Chris's office and training studio, you feel as if you know Chris—her personality and tastes are reflected throughout the space. Chris is a communications expert and speaking coach whose primary style is that of an Arranger. Her office and training space is in an older part of the city in a beautiful old warehouse with original hardwood floors, exposed brick walls, and high, open ceilings.

When you walk in the door, jazz or soft classical music is always playing, the harsh overhead lights are turned off, and warmly glowing floor and table lamps are turned on. One wall is painted a vibrant shade of blue, and the rest are covered in original artwork and photographs of Chris with friends and colleagues. There is a welcome desk just inside the door on which copies of Chris's most recent book and brochures with information about her firm are displayed. In the studio there is a huge custom-built U-shaped conference table that can easily be reconfigured for small-group work and collaboration. All of the chairs in the office are large, plush, and very comfortable.

Chris's space is not only highly functional and fully supports the work that she does each day, but it is personalized to support her primary Productivity Style.

Let's look at each Productivity Style's strengths and consider how these strengths can inform the personalization of your space.

WORK SIMPLY: WORKSPACE CUSTOMIZATION TIPS BY PRODUCTIVITY STYLE

If You're a Prioritizer

Prioritizers are highly efficient, succinct, analytical, and focused on outcomes. That means you are very businesslike and professional, distilling ideas down to their most salient points while reducing the excess.

Space-Shaping Tips to Try:

- Aim for a professional look and feel.
- Remove all "excess" artwork, decorations, and accessories.
- Create clean, functional lines throughout the space.
- Select simple, sleek, streamlined furniture.
- Install ample, high-wattage lighting.
- Maintain a clean, orderly desktop.
- Minimize visual clutter.

If You're a Planner

Planners are organized, structured, practical, and exceptional problem solvers. That means you are cautious, traditional, and able to proficiently create and implement highly efficient project plans.

Space-Shaping Tips to Try:

- Aim for a traditional look and feel.
- Eliminate all impractical or unnecessary items.
- Design a practical layout with a few simple decorations.
- Maintain a space that is neat, orderly, and organized.
- Minimize personal items that may contribute to visual clutter.
- Select furniture that emphasizes functionality rather than aesthetic appeal.

If You're an Arranger

Arrangers are supportive, expressive, and emotional. That means you have never met a stranger—only newfound friends; you encourage teamwork; and you excel at partnering with people to get your work completed.

Space-Shaping Tips to Try:

- Create a welcoming, inviting atmosphere.
- Use warm colors and soft lighting.
- Fill the space with personal memorabilia and photographs.
- Select accessories that will lend a personal touch to your space.
- Choose furniture that is comfortable and easily configured for conversation and collaboration.
- Play music, light a scented candle, or add other touches to stimulate all five senses.

If You're a Visualizer

Visualizers are visionary, big-picture thinkers, who play with concepts and enjoy synthesizing disparate ideas and data. That means creative, innovative ideas are the norm for you, and you like to explore new horizons and continually ask, "What's next?"

Space-Shaping Tips to Try:

- Design decor that's colorful, varied, and aesthetically pleasing.
- Select furniture that is informal or casual, loosely structured, and nontraditional.
- Display original art or objects.
- Emphasize space and light.
- Ensure that there is room to spread out, draw, dream, and create.
- Include playful objects and toys.
- Fill the space with personal memorabilia and unique collectibles.

Of course, as we've discussed throughout this book, many people blend two or more Productivity Styles into a unique, compatible whole. You may find that there are elements from differing styles that you want to combine when designing your personalized workspace. Go for it! The key is to make sure that the space you work in makes you feel comfortable, energized, and productive, no matter what kind of work you may happen to be doing on a particular day.

FIND AND USE PHYSICAL ORGANIZATIONAL TOOLS THAT WORK FOR YOU

Your work environment does not only include such features as lighting, furniture, and decorations. It also includes the organizational tools and office supplies you use—everything from file folders and wall calendars to computer programs and mobile phone apps. Tools like these can have a huge impact on your productivity, either working for you or against you. And just as with office design, too many people fail to think through their choice of tools and customize them to fit their needs. Many simply accept the tools and supplies provided by the company they work for or use the systems they first learned about years ago. In many cases, the result is a severe case of technically driven busyness. They waste countless hours every year struggling to make tools they find dysfunctional work for them—a losing battle at best.

In reality, no one needs to settle for productivity tools that do not fit their needs. There are thousands of different organizational tools and office supplies on the market today, which makes it both hard and easy to select the physical organizational tools that will work for you. The availability of so many choices can be paralyzing and overwhelming. (Who knew that there were hundreds of different shapes, colors, and widths of binder clips?) But the vast array of options also means that no matter how unusual or distinctive your preferences may be, it is extremely likely that you'll be able to find tools that are perfect for you. That means you can create a working system that makes your job easier and more enjoyable rather than frustrating and painful.

In selecting your physical organizational tools, once again you want to personalize them based on your Productivity Style. Each Productivity Style has different needs and preferences when it comes to the types of tools that will optimize their work performance. Let's explore each style and suggest some tools that will fully support you.

WORK SIMPLY:
SELECTING BY PRODUCTIVITY STYLE THE TOOLS THAT WILL WORK FOR YOU

If You're a Prioritizer

How to Think About Your Productivity Tools: Your tools should maximize your output, avoid visual clutter, and be readily accessible at all times. Leverage your affinity for technology by looking at each piece of technology you currently use and asking yourself, "What else can this tool do for me?" For example, take the time to explore and experiment with all of the shortcuts and embedded efficiencies available in your e-mail program, and learn the most efficient keystroke commands that can shortcut tasks in your favorite word processing and spreadsheet programs.

    Some Tips to Try: You like consistency and will be distracted if you do not have the right tool. Avoid the distraction of significant amounts of color by using the same color pens, file folders, binder clips, and Post-it Notes; consider plain, light-colored items, which you may find less distracting. Maintain an ample supply of your favorite lined legal pads and notebooks so you do not run out. Use filing cabinets, bookshelves, and credenzas to store and organize your supplies and work materials so you can maintain an uncluttered work surface.

If You're a Planner

How to Think About Your Productivity Tools: Your tools should support your preference for structure and organization, thereby maximizing your efficiency. Office supply and storage supply stores are a favorite shopping location for you because you love organizational items. Avoid the tendency to overbuy or over-stock on physical organizational tools such as binder clips, pens, file folders, and notebooks, because the excess can clutter your environment and reduce rather than enhance your effectiveness.

Some Tips to Try: Leverage your natural inclination for organization by seek-ing out just the right types of supplies. For example, find just the right size file folder to store your receipts, and spend a little more to buy one made of plastic because it is durable and will withstand the rigors of your workday. Invest in high-quality drawer dividers and containers to streamline and organize your work-space. A label maker may be your best friend—use it to label file folders, contain-ers, and even shelves. The clean lines and uniform font of the labels will appeal to you.

If You're an Arranger

How to Think About Your Productivity Tools: Your tools should appeal to you both kinetically and visually. It is very important that you touch and feel any office supply before you purchase it. For example, the weight, width, and texture of pens matter to you, as does the color and weight of your notebook's cover. (One of my colleagues says her master TASK notebook "feels like silky butter," and she has even been known to caress it.) If you order office supplies online, know the return policy, because once you have the chance to touch and use the item, you may need to return it.

Some Tips to Try: It is also important that your physical organizational tools be visually appealing. If a tool is unattractive to you, you will not use it. Seek out novelty office supplies with unique, visually appealing characteristics. Consider colorful tools—colored file folders, binder clips, baskets, and organizational con-tainers. Then create a color scheme based on type of work, project, or client. The Web site See Jane Work (seejanework.com) is an excellent place to start.

Your physical tools should also support your affinity for collaboration. Use Skype or a GoToMeeting-type program so you can see your colleagues, clients, and vendors as you talk with them. Learn the sharing and collaboration options available to you on all of your technology platforms and enjoy using the ones that appeal to your aesthetic sense.

If You're a Visualizer

How to Think About Your Productivity Tools: Your tools should support you as you play with ideas, explore what is next, and focus on your highest-priority work. Use unlined paper, unlined notebooks, large whiteboards, and colorful pens and markers to ideate and capture to-dos, and maintain an ample stock of multicolored Post-it Notes at all times for display on walls, doors, and whiteboards—they are a great way to physically play with ideas.

Some Tips to Try: Store your project work where you can see it. "Out of sight, out of mind" is very real for you. Try storing your file folders in colorful baskets rather than a filing cabinet, and use transparent plastic containers to store supplies.

The variety of physical organizational tools available today makes it easy to find the tools that are ideally suited for you and will fully support your work. The physical organizational tools you use matter and are essential to improving your efficiency and effectiveness. Do not compromise on them.

FACE THE REALITIES OF YOUR WORKSPACE

At this point, you may be thinking, "All of these strategies to make my space reflect me and support my work are excellent, but I work in a space that is dysfunctional and that I have little control over. What can I do about it?"

Many people, especially those who work in a corporate environment, must deal with restrictions on the space they spend their day in. There may be rules about the size and shape of cubicles and offices, the kinds of furniture and fixtures permitted, and the colors of walls. And even those who work at home or in their own entrepreneurial settings may be limited in their choices due to circumstances that may include the need to share a space with family members or a colleague. However, these limitations need not force you to simply accept a space that is seriously wrong for you. Here are some suggestions for ways to work around the restrictions you may be grappling with.

First, if you are working for a larger company, determine what you really *need* to make your space more functional for you, and then ask your organization to support you. As Carin Warner, a trusted colleague and vendor partner of mine, always says, "If you don't ask, you don't get." Clearly state why you need a specific tool or environmental alteration, how it will improve your productivity and effectiveness, and any accommodations you are willing to make. You may be pleased to find that your organization is more willing to accommodate you than you assume.

Gina, a business developer for a commercial real estate firm, often reviews long, complex legal documents as part of the process of negotiating the lease and purchase of property. She was finding it increasingly difficult to review the legal documents and cross-check them against tax regulations, property guidelines, and prior conversations due to the sheer size and complexity of the papers she needed to access simultaneously. So she asked to have her office equipped with two large computer monitors instead of one.

However, before making this request, Gina made certain that the odds were stacked in her favor. It helped that she is the top producer in her firm, having brought in all of the largest deals in the last five years. Furthermore, she had done her due diligence: She researched how much the monitors would cost and was prepared to quantify the return on investment for the organization if they purchased the monitors for her. So when she asked for the computer monitors, her firm quickly said yes.

If you work for a big company, follow Gina's example. Determine exactly what you need to be successful and productive, be prepared to articulate why it is necessary and how it will benefit the company, and then ask for what you need.

Another way to deal with corporate space restrictions is to get creative and innovate. For example, a few of our clients are in consulting roles that require them to work at their clients' sites, where they have absolutely no control over their workspaces. They are often relegated to unused cubicle space, tables and chairs in the middle of the office, or small, dark rooms.

In response, these resourceful consultants adapt. To combat noise, they bring headphones and plug in when they need quiet to work uninterrupted. For additional light, they bring small clip lights originally designed for reading in bed, now repurposed as laptop attachments. Another client, whose organization would not permit hanging anything on the walls except the company-issued artwork that was already hung when he arrived in his office, repurposed one of the pieces of artwork into his TASK list. He took white butcher paper, cut it to fit the glass on the framed art piece, and affixed the paper to the glass using painter's tape. Then he posted colored Post-it Notes with his to-dos on them on the paper. The display was highly functional, appealed to his Visualizer preference, and stayed within the parameters of his space restrictions.

Of course, there are often limits to the physical changes you can make in your workspace, particularly if you share an office with other colleagues. The standard-issue cubicle many workers are required to occupy imposes severe restrictions on the amount of space you enjoy, the kind of lighting available, and the type of seating, storage, and working surfaces you have. I don't recommend making wholesale changes, especially those that may affect people around you, without first consulting your coworkers. When you do, you may find that they share your dissatisfaction with their surroundings, and improving the environment may even become a joint project.

However, even if you are working within narrow parameters, there may be a number of steps you can take to improve your working environment without impinging on others. For example:

- If you can't alter the colors or textures of the walls or dividers around you, try displaying one or more posters or artwork in your immediate work area to create an ambience you find more appealing. The art you choose needn't be large or obtrusive; framed photos on your desk and a favorite print pinned on a nearby wall can markedly improve your mood. Even choosing a more attractive screen saver for your computer or smartphone can make a meaningful difference.

- If the overhead lighting feels harsh or sterile, try bringing in a small desk lamp like the ones found in college dorm rooms. A glowing circle of light illuminating the papers you're working with can have a surprisingly powerful soothing effect without disturbing those nearby or clashing with the overall office decor.
- If you dislike the color or texture of your work surface, visit an office supply store and buy an inexpensive desk pad in the design of your choice. Changing the appearance of the material you may stare at for several hours a day can definitely affect your attitude.
- If ambient noise or unwanted music is a problem, consider using noise-reducing headphones to create a comfortable zone of silence for yourself. (But be alert to the needs of colleagues or clients and be ready to shed the headphones when others want your attention— otherwise you'll quickly develop a reputation as standoffish.)

Do not let space restrictions impede your productivity and effectiveness. Innovate, get creative, and make the space constraints work for you, not against you.

PUT THE WALLS BACK UP

There is one corporate space trend that frequently impedes productivity and effectiveness: open-space floor plans. These are floor plans that often have no walls at all, just rows of tables and chairs, desks and pods of desks grouped together. Open-space floor plans also include low-walled cubicles where you can see the heads of the workers peeking out from the tops of the cubes.

There are many reasons why companies are opting for open-space floor plans. They save money: Fewer walls and fewer private offices mean less expenditure on architectural design, painting, lighting, and other forms of maintenance. It is possible to squeeze more workers into a given number of square feet when private space is eliminated, further reducing costs.

Open-space plans also mean less "waste" when particular workers are on the road, working at home, or on vacation; rather than leaving private offices empty, individual absences simply free up desk or cubicle areas to be occupied by other workers. (This approach has even been formalized under the name of *hoteling,* a system in which no one is assigned a permanent space and instead everyone who shows up at the office must scramble to find and claim an available desk or cubicle.)

Finally, open-space plans are simply trendy. Thanks to their adoption by some creative and high-tech firms, they are viewed as obvious ways to promote innovation, collaboration, and teamwork. Some managers seem to assume that tearing down the walls at headquarters will instantly transform a staid, boring company into a vibrant innovator.

Unfortunately, the results do not bear out these expectations. The problems I have experienced personally when I worked in a cubicle village and concerns I have heard from my clients have solidified my belief that there is value in walls. I believe it is time to put the walls back up in our office spaces.

This belief is not based simply on my subjective reactions or those of my clients. A growing volume of evidence from surveys and research studies supports it. As author Susan Cain has written:

> Open-plan offices have been found to reduce productivity and impair memory. They're associated with high staff turnover. They make people sick, hostile, unmotivated and insecure. Open-plan workers are more likely to suffer from high blood pressure and elevated stress levels and to get the flu; they argue more with their colleagues; they worry about coworkers eavesdropping on their phone calls and spying on their computer screens. They have fewer personal and confidential conversations with colleagues. They're often subject to loud and uncontrollable noise, which raises heart

rates; releases cortisol, the body's flight or fight "stress" hormone; and makes people socially distant, quick to anger, aggressive, and slow to help others.[5]

Open-space floor plans have been shown to be negatively related to workers' satisfaction with their physical environment and perceived productivity. For example, when employees in one study were relocated from traditional offices to open offices, their satisfaction with the physical environment went down, their physical stress increased, coworker relations declined, and job performance suffered.[6] It is important to note that in this study the employees' negative perceptions did not abate even after an adjustment period of six months. Another study of the corporate offices of a large multinational telecommunications firm confirmed these findings, adding that office workers in open-space plans expressed concerns over reduced privacy, noise, and less personal control of their workstations.[7]

Still another research study by Sara Varlander found that there were often unintended consequences of an open-space design. In the organization she studied, the new office space did promote more spontaneous and frequent interaction, dialogue, and meetings. However, the open plan led to employees being disturbed and interrupted by colleagues speaking to each other. And while the open-space plan was designed to enhance teamwork, it also made it easy for team members to see who violated rules about personal phone calls, work hours, and even the temperature and smell of the workspace, leading to increased disputes among team members.[8]

At this point, you may be wondering whether the *type* of work that is being performed helps to determine whether a particular space plan is effective. For example, it might seem logical that an open-space plan could work at a freewheeling, creative company like Pixar, while a bustling law firm, where privacy and confidentiality are paramount, might require closed workspaces.

This kind of distinction seems very logical—but the research tells us that the type of work being performed does not fundamentally matter. Open-space plans negatively impact workers no matter what kind of work they do. In fact, one study focusing specifically on creative workers found that open-space design actually undermined the kind of creativity that it was intended to foster.[9]

Another study examined knowledge workers at four different job levels (secretarial employees, their supervisors, staff specialists, and managerial employees) who were moved from conventional offices to an open-plan office. The employees at all levels reported decreased satisfaction, including a decrease in confidentiality of conversation.[10]

It is time to put the walls back up in our offices. We can create open space for collaboration and brainstorming without requiring that every team member work in an open space at all times.

I opened this chapter by describing the headquarters at Pixar, a company dedicated to innovation and creativity. Pixar provides plenty of open areas for workers to collaborate and interact. But its workers are given complete freedom in designing their personal spaces, and all of the individual workspaces have walls. Let's put the walls back up—and watch productivity soar.

11

Stop Pushing Papers

"DON'T MISS GET ORGANIZED DAY! THE WINNING TEAM WILL receive iTunes gift cards and a free Get Organized Day T-shirt!" That was the message on the flyer in the corporate break room where I was meeting with the Get Organized Day project team to prepare for this event. I had been asked by a company to kick off the big event, and my team would be providing on-site assistance to the employees throughout the day.

What I found both interesting and ironic is that the company manufactured storage and organizational supplies. The company was a significant player in the $1 billion-a-year storage container market. I wondered: Why did a company that designed and distributed products to help consumers and professionals get organized need a Get Organized Day for their own employees?

Martha, the project manager, told me that there were three reasons for the event. First, it was a great marketing and promotional activity. The company was going to have a great story to tell, replete with before and after photos. These would be posted on their Web site and on all of their social media platforms and sent to print, TV, and radio media outlets in hopes of getting coverage for an event that would highlight the value of the company's products.

Second, the company had realized that its employees were not making good use of the very storage and organizational supplies that it produced. It was time to get the company's people walking their talk, and Get Organized Day would provide the impetus.

Third, the sad fact was that the company's offices were a mess. There were mountains of paper and unused products on desks, in the aisles, and falling out of storage cabinets, impeding work, eroding productivity, and even endangering the employees.

I was convinced. So a few weeks later, on a Friday morning, I kicked off Get Organized Day with a presentation on how to stop pushing papers. The entire organization then fueled up on pizza and went to work organizing and taming their mountains of paper. My team spent the afternoon coaching, building retrieval systems (more on that later), and encouraging team members as they got organized. At the end of the day, offices were gleaming, mountains of unused company products were stacked, sorted, and ready to be donated to charity, and every paper-shredding container— including all the extra containers that had been brought on-site for the event—was overflowing with piles of papers. Get Organized Day had been a tremendous success, and the leaders were thrilled.

Yes, it was ironic that this company should have found itself awash in untamed mountains of paper. But in a larger sense, it is somewhat amazing that this problem should be so widespread in every industry here in the twenty-first century. Many experts—especially those in the electronic information industry—have long been predicting that the need to organize paper will soon become unnecessary. Aren't we in the digital age, where paper files are obsolete and unnecessary?

Electronic information management is here to stay, but that has not reduced the volume of paper in our offices. The average office worker uses a staggering ten thousand sheets of copy paper every year.[1] And with the increase in paper volume goes a steady increase in the complexity of organizing and managing it. The *Wall Street Journal* has calculated that the average American worker wastes six weeks per year searching for lost documents.[2] What's more, all of this paper is expensive! Ernst and Young estimates that it costs about $25,000 to fill a four-drawer filing cabinet and $2,100 a year to maintain it.[3]

So paper management is still important in today's electronic world—in fact, it is vital. Think about how much it must have cost the company to plan, organize, and implement their Get Organized Day, not to mention the employees' time that was spent organizing and purging.

And these are just the immediate monetary costs. The hidden costs are even more significant. One of the primary reasons the company decided to hold the event was because of declining productivity among its teams. The creative department responsible for designing new storage containers had literally run out of space to test and experiment with prototypes. The offices of the marketing team were filled with piles of old ad copy and brochures that were stifling creativity. The teams were wasting their time shuffling and sorting paper. Unused products, old files, and mountains of project binders were getting in the way of the employees doing their work.

Pushing papers is probably the single biggest drain on the American economic system. Fortunately, it's one that can be dramatically reduced by following a few simple principles.

YOU NEED A RETRIEVAL SYSTEM, *NOT* A FILING SYSTEM

The paper shuffle symptoms are obvious: stacks of paper on the desk, floor, and credenza, and the frequent refrain of "I know it is here somewhere, just let me find it." The most common solution to this malady is to build a filing system. The problem is that I have only met *one* person who actually *likes* to file papers. The rest of my clients absolutely abhor it, so of course they avoid it. And that means that creating a filing system simply results in one more task that doesn't get done, while the symptoms of paper pushing continue to worsen.

The reality is that you do not need a filing system—you need a retrieval system. After all, your goal is to quickly and easily access the information contained on that paper at a future date, not simply to get it out of the way.

Building an effective retrieval system starts by asking yourself three essential questions about the information contained on every piece of paper that crosses your desk:

1. Do I need to retain this information for compliance, tax, or legal reasons?
2. When would I need to access this information again?
3. Where else can I find this information?

The answers to these questions will help you decide what paper to keep, what paper to toss, and how to design a retrieval system that will make it easy to access vital information when you need it.

Let's start with the first question: "Do I need to retain this information for compliance, tax, or legal reasons?" There are specific record retention guidelines set by the IRS for personal and business documents, as well as legal guidelines for employment files, termination files, and contracts. You need to understand these rules and apply them consistently.

When we supported Get Organized Day, the company's legal department drafted a comprehensive set of record retention guidelines that were distributed to every employee, posted in all of the common areas, and available on the company's intranet site. All documents on this list were retained. Any documents that were questionable were retained and not shredded until the legal department had approved doing so.

If you are a corporate employee, ask your employer for their record retention guidelines. If none have yet been developed, or if you are self-employed or running a small entrepreneurial firm, go to IRS.gov to access a complete listing of the business and personal documents you are required to retain and for how long. Keep the required compliance, legal, and tax documentation.

If a particular document does not need to be retained for compliance, tax, or legal reasons, proceed to question two: "When would I need to access this information again?" For example, suppose a colleague gives you a printed copy of the presentation she has prepared to make in front of the management team on Friday. When will you need access to this information again? Friday morning.

Suppose you've been given a printed receipt for the hotel room you used during the company sales conference. When will you need access to this information again? At the end of the month when you complete your expense report.

Now, what if a piece of paper arrives in your universe that you do not need to keep for compliance, tax, or legal reasons, and you cannot determine when you would need to access this information again? Do *not* retain the paper. Throw it away.

For example, you receive a copy of the office cafeteria menu for the week. Since you are not eating at the office this week, you do not need to access the menu again, so throw it away.

You may be thinking, "This sounds risky! I may not be able to think of a specific time or reason that I might need to retrieve the information, but something might come up that would make this information essential! Maybe it's better to hold on to the paper—just in case."

This is a common thought—we've all had it. It leads us to keep adding pieces of paper to the growing stacks in our offices—"just in case." But you need to resist this temptation. The Pareto principle, also known as the 80/20 rule, applies to your papers: 80 percent of what we retain we never access again.[4] If a circumstance does arise in the future when you need the information, it is highly probable that you can find the information somewhere else. So if there's no *specific* reason to keep the information, throw it out!

This brings us to the third and final question: "Where else can I find this information?" Here is where new technology plays an important and very positive role. With the proliferation of information available to us with a few keystrokes via the Internet and company intranet sites, practically every kind of useful information is readily available without the need to retain a printed document.

Suppose you receive a printed copy of your company's new vacation policy along with your pay stub one month. You will ask yourself question number two, "When would I need to access this information again?" Your answer is, "When I am submitting my vacation request to my manager for approval." It is tempting at this point to keep the document. But do not make that decision until you've asked yourself question number three, "Where else can I find this information?" A moment's reflection tells you that you can probably find this information on the company's intranet site, in the online employee handbook, or by asking your human resources manager—three different places, each of them probably faster than searching through your personal filing system. So you do *not* need to retain this piece of paper. Remember, time is a commodity—and you do not have six weeks a year to spend searching for documents.

Applying the three-question approach to deciding what to keep and what to toss will ensure that your retrieval system contains only essential documents. You now have a pared-down collection of documents that takes up much less space and is much faster and easier to use—one that enables you to put your hands on essential information in a few moments rather than requiring a lengthy, exhaustive search through an ever-growing pile of papers.

THE FOUR-STEP PAPER MANAGEMENT METHOD: READ, DECIDE, ACT, CONTAIN

It's time to begin maintaining and using your drastically simplified retrieval system. As we've seen, the costs of paper shuffling are time and money, and both are directly related to postponed decisions. So the most effective antidote to the paper shuffle is making decisions *now* to save time and money later. And to make faster and more accurate decisions, use the four-step paper management method as papers cross your desk in the course of an ordinary day. The four steps are *read, decide, act,* and *contain.*

Does this look familiar? These are the same steps in the E-mail Agility Circle, because the malady is the same—postponed decisions. You know how it happens: A piece of paper appears on your desk. You look at it, decide that the action it requires will take too much time, energy, or thought to complete right now, so you set it aside. Then the piles start to build.

Instead, let's start making some decisions so that the piles of paper never develop in the first place. Here's how the four steps work when applied to physical papers.

First, read. Simply read the paper and ask yourself, "What is it?" Is it a report, a magazine, a receipt, an article?

Second, decide. Does this paper require action? Yes or no? If the document does *not* require action, then ask yourself the three questions from building your retrieval system: "Do I need to retain this paper for tax, legal, or compliance reasons?" "When would I need to access this information again?" "Where else can I find this information?" As we've seen, in many cases the answers to these questions will tell you that it is safe and appropriate to recycle, shred, or trash the paper.

Third, act. If the document *does* require action, you have three options—complete the action step, delegate the action step, or create a task.

If you are the right person to compete the task—if you have the knowledge, skills, and resources to do it, *and* if this is the highest and best use of your time—and if the action required by the document can be completed in three to five minutes, just do it! Complete the task. The task will be done, the document will no longer be necessary, and you will have cleared your desk (and your brain) to focus on something else.

If you are *not* the right person to complete the task, then delegate the action step from the document. Send the task on to someone else—and once again the document will no longer be necessary.

If you are the right person to complete the task *but* the action required will take longer than three to five minutes, then create a task to complete the action at a later time. This is the most frequently used step in the act process. Write or type the next action step(s) you are going to take to reach the desired outcome on your master TASK list, using whatever tool you prefer for the purpose—a notebook, a computer program, or a white-board on the office wall.

Converting the document on your desk into a to-do item on your master TASK list is an essential step, because the sheer volume of paper in our world today makes it virtually impossible to use individual pieces of paper as visual cues of what needs to be done. So don't skip this step, thinking, "Oh, I can just hang on to this memo [or letter, report, or maga-zine clipping], and that will remind me of what I'm supposed to do!" That kind of thinking leads you straight back to an office filled with tumbling stacks of papers. Turn the action step into a task, and either file the paper or trash it!

The other reason I am suggesting that you create a task is because you want a TASK list with integrity—one that is whole and provides you with a comprehensive picture of *everything* you have committed to com-pleting.

The fourth and final step, contain, is about quarantining the loose paper that may remain on your desk after you've completed the first three steps. The goal is to eliminate as much visual clutter as possible while continuing to maintain your retrieval system.

The first step in corralling your loose papers is to name file folders, baskets, bags, or other storage containers. To name your file folders, do not overthink it. Look at the piece of paper and name the file or container based on whatever comes to mind first. For example, one of my clients has a red folder with the label "Things My Clients Bitch About"; another client has a green folder labeled "RSVP"; and still another has a folder named "Sally's School Stuff." The name needs to resonate with you and *only* you. This is *your* retrieval system. If you name your file folders and/or paper storage containers this way, then it will be very easy to retrieve your information. You will think, "I need to respond to the invitation for the Women in Business awards luncheon," and immediately open your RSVP file.

You may find it helpful to separate the paper into two categories: reference and action. The reference papers are ones that you use infre-quently, such as documentation you are retaining for tax, legal, or compliance reasons. Keep these papers in their own storage container or filing cabinet.

The second category is for the papers that require actions you have documented on your TASK list. For example, here are files some of my clients create: "Review and Sign," "To Read," "Waiting For," "Open Invoices," "Project XYZ."

Consider using a single file folder or container for the items that require action that you do not want to subdivide into discrete categories like the ones listed above. For example, I have a yellow plastic folder labeled "TASK List Support Materials." At the moment, this file folder contains the draft of an article I am rewriting, the proposal for a client video documentary, and an insurance form to be filed. Each of these to-dos is listed on my TASK list, I have a specific place where these support materials are filed, and, most important, I know where to go to retrieve the materials that I need to complete each to-do.

Ideally, all your action files will be located as close as possible to where you complete your work—for example, a file drawer in your desk, the credenza behind your desk, a crate on the floor next to your worktable, or the bag that is your mobile office. It is essential that these action files be readily accessible because you use them throughout the workday. (At the end of this chapter, I'll offer some personalized tips about how to ensure that your retrieval system is designed to fit your own Productivity Style, which will make your management of information even more powerful and efficient.)

The paper management system I've just outlined has universal application beyond work and can be used for personal papers at home as well. Follow the exact same process.

For example, let's use the process with personal mail. You open your mailbox and a large pile of mail falls at your feet. First, take one piece of mail at a time, read it, and decide what it is—an invitation, a bill, a bank statement, a catalog, a magazine, a charitable solicitation, or other mail. For each item, ask, "Does it require action—yes or no?"

For items that do *not* require action, ask yourself whether you need to keep the item for tax or legal reasons; for example, the letter from Habitat for Humanity thanking you for your donation needs to be retained as supporting documentation for your tax return. If you receive informational or reference material in the mail, then ask yourself, "When would I need to access this information again?" and "Where else can I find this information?" If you do not need to retain the piece of mail, recycle, trash, or shred it. I have personally found that it is most efficient to carry my mail over to our recycling bin and immediately cull all of the catalogs, advertisements, and flyers (except for the few I am actually interested in reading). There is an immediate sense of satisfaction because I dramatically reduce the stack of mail.

If action is required by you—for example, to pay a bill, purchase a birthday present, or read a magazine—you can do it immediately, delegate it, or create a task. For the majority of the actions that arrive via postal service, creating a task is the most frequently used option. Remember to note the next action step on your TASK list and then contain the paper.

At our house, we have a red container for all of the bills. Any bills that come in during the week are placed in this container. On Saturday morning, my husband, Andrew, takes the red container to the kitchen island, opens his laptop, and quickly pays the bills online. The paper bills are then shredded. We also have a basket in our den next to our two chairs where we put all of the newspapers and magazines that we want to read. Every few weeks or so, the basket is purged, and newspapers and magazines are recycled even if we have not read them, because there is only so much room to contain them.

My client Jill used the paper management system to finally get control of her entire family's avalanche of documents. Now she reads, decides, acts, and contains her mail each day so it does not stack up. She has even trained her children to do so as well.

Jill has set up two small containers on the counter near the back door. One is labeled "Signature" and the other is labeled "Check." These are the two most frequent actions required on the papers that are brought home by her children—review and sign a test, sign the permission slip for the field trip to the zoo, or complete the order form for school pictures and include a check for payment. Each afternoon when her children get home from school, they quickly empty their backpacks and put the papers she needs to read and act on in the appropriate container.

If there are papers that do not fall into either of these categories, the children show them to Jill after dinner, and she takes the appropriate next step—either immediately completing the next action step or adding the next action step to her TASK list. Jill has a green file folder for her bills and a red plastic folder for errands that contains all of the supporting documentation for the items she needs to purchase—for example, the specific type of cleats for soccer or the type of posterboard for the school project. She has a small plastic file box for all of the information that needs to be retained for tax and legal reasons; it is kept on a high shelf in the pantry, accessible and near her desk in the kitchen, but not in the way.

As a result, Jill's kitchen and entryway are neat and paper-free. Everyone in the house knows the paper system and what to do with their papers. Jill has reduced the visual clutter in her home and eliminated the "Where is my permission slip?" drama that had a habit of occurring at 6:30 a.m. Most important, she is able to quickly and efficiently complete her to-dos, stress-free.

BUILD YOUR PERSONALIZED RETRIEVAL SYSTEM

The four-step paper management method is a universally applicable process that works with all Productivity Styles. However, the ways you decide to contain your papers should reflect and optimize your Productivity Style.

Let's explore how each style can leverage their Productivity Style to personalize their retrieval system and select tools that will fully support you.

WORK SIMPLY:
TIPS BY PRODUCTIVITY STYLE FOR BUILDING
YOUR PERSONALIZED RETRIEVAL SYSTEM

If You're a Prioritizer

Your Approach to Document Retrieval: Analytical, logical, fact-based, and critical thinking is your preference, so your retrieval system must be clean, crisp, and efficient. Either an alphabetical or a numerical filing system, which appeals to your quantitative orientation, is ideally suited for you. For example, you might want to set up a monthly calendar filing system. Number hanging file folders from 1 to 31, representing the days of the month. In the hanging file numbered 1, place all of the materials you will need to access on the first of the month—boarding passes for a flight you'll be boarding that morning, client presentation books for a meeting that afternoon, tickets to the opera that evening. This system can also be an electronic system—create and use numbered folders on your computer, iPad, or other technology tool.

    Specific Tools to Try: File folders and filing cabinets are your preferred tools, and you may feel it's important that your file folders be the same color, preferably manila, and new or gently used—no frayed, rough edges or stained folders for you. Efficiency is important to you, so consider only one file folder per hanging file for quick retrieval. The labels on the file folders ideally are uniform and typed, so consider investing in a label maker. Since visual clutter is a distraction for you, keep your papers and files in drawers or at least out of your line of sight—for example, on a table or credenza behind your desk so they are still accessible, but not always visible to you.

If You're a Planner

Your Approach to Document Retrieval: Organized, sequential, planned, and detailed thinking is your preference. You have never met an organizational supply or tool you did not like, especially file folders, filing cabinets, and storage containers. An alphabetical filing system is optimal for you, appealing to your sequential thinking preference. Like most Prioritizers, you prefer file folders to be the same

color and new or gently used. Rough edges and stains jump out at you, and il-
legible or sloppy handwriting on filing labels are distractions due to your detail
orientation. Invest in a label maker; you will love the crisp, uniform labels it creates and will probably start labeling everything in your office.

Specific Tools to Try: To leverage your planning orientation, consider setting
up a weekly filing system. Label seven hanging file folders with the days of the
week. As you plan your week, put all of the items you will need for each day in
the appropriate file folder. You could also set up this system using mail sorter
trays or plastic containers on a shelf, labeled with each day of the week, of
course, and placing all of the items you need for each day's work in the mail sorter
tray or container.

If You're an Arranger

Your Approach to Document Retrieval: Supportive, expressive, and emotional
thinking is your preference. The way your filing supplies and tools feel and look is
very important to you, so invest in file folders with interesting and visually appealing patterns, colors, textures, and weight. A standard manila file folder will not
appeal to you and you will most likely not use it. Instead, consider color-coding
your file folders by the person or team involved, the project, or the type of action.

Specific Tools to Try: A traditional alphabetical or numerical filing methodology will probably not appeal to you, so consider arranging your file folders in
separate drawers or containers by project, people, action, or color. Since you
sometimes find that "out of sight is out of mind," try using open boxes, clear
storage containers, or standing divided file folder containers to keep your most
frequently used files accessible and visible. Invest in specific pens for labeling
your files so the script and colors are attractive to you.

If You're a Visualizer

Your Approach to Document Retrieval: Holistic, intuitive, integrating, and synthesizing thinking is your preference. You see the future and the big picture, so
the concept of an overly rigid retrieval system can feel restrictive. You have never
liked filing and avoid it at all costs, finding it one of the most boring and repetitive
tasks ever!

Specific Tools to Try: To avoid feeling restricted, consider corralling your papers in baskets, mail sorter trays, open boxes, or clear storage containers. Group the papers by project or idea. Within the basket, consider using colored file folders, which appeal to your senses, to further subdivide the papers for easier retrieval. Leverage your visual orientation by investing in clear file folders. You will be able to see the contents of the file and use them as a visual cue. In short, keep your system as simple and unstructured as possible.

Mountains of paper demanding attention are the bane of many people's lives. That's why you may find the advice in this chapter to be the most useful and liberating of all. And among the many secondary benefits of conquering the paperwork monster, you will find that your office and home are much cleaner, neater, and more pleasant to look at once the excess paper has been purged. Result: an environment where it's much easier to relax, focus, and concentrate on the things that matter most to you, whether that's solving the big problems that make the difference between success and failure on the job or simply enjoying the company of friends and family during an evening meal or a weekend break.

12

Harness the
Productive Power
of Your Teammates:
Delegate

"I KNOW, I REALLY SHOULD ASK FOR SOME MORE HELP AND delegate," lamented Roxanne. But—ah—the big "But" was about to get in the way again.

Roxanne is the in-house counsel and a senior vice president at one of the largest nonprofit foundations in the country. As a highly respected member of the executive team, she touches almost everything that the foundation does, her office door is a revolving door, and her workdays average twelve to fourteen hours. This pace is not sustainable and it is also unhealthy both for Roxanne and for the foundation. But Roxanne continues to resist the idea of delegating some of her work, even though she knows it is essential for her mental and physical well-being.

Roxanne is not alone. We may understand, at least intellectually, that delegating is a powerful skill that can boost productivity and build cohesive teams. Yet many of us resist it or do it poorly. There are three common reasons for this resistance—psychological, organizational, and technical.

PSYCHOLOGICAL RESISTANCE: THE URGE TO DO IT ALL

The most common obstacle to delegating is psychological—the insistence, either conscious or subconscious, on doing everything yourself. This resistance is often fear-based, so probing the nature of your fear—figuring out what you lack faith in—can help you identify the underlying cause. That is the first step to overcoming the fear and abandoning the misguided belief that you *must* do everything yourself.

It isn't only insecure young workers who suffer from psychological resistance. Even highly successful top executives can exhibit this syndrome. Katie Tyler, the CEO of hotel brand Four Seasons, admits she is a bit of a "control freak," but for the good of her and everyone around her, she tries to delegate. Her advice for others who suffer the same problem: "Sit on your hands if you have to. Get yourself to that place."[1]

Roxanne's problem, like Katie Tyler's, was psychological resistance, and what she lacked faith in was her value to the organization. Roxanne believed she had to "do it all" to prove her worth to the organization, and she resisted delegating because this sense of worth was central to her identity.

Once Roxanne recognized this psychological stumbling block, she was able to acknowledge it, explore its meaning to her, and evaluate the reality behind it. Was she actually valued by her organization? She certainly was—otherwise she would never have been promoted to a position of such importance and authority. Did her value lie in all the mundane tasks she insisted on performing personally? Not at all—it lay in her judgment, her experience, and her ability to offer wise counsel on significant legal issues.

Recognizing these truths enabled Roxanne to get past her psychological resistance to delegating and to move on to the second step to overcoming this resistance—deciding what she could and could not delegate.

Not every task you perform is suitable for delegation. Almost everyone has certain tasks they will *never* delegate, and that is entirely appropriate. The challenge is to make sound decisions as to which tasks should and should not be delegated.

Let's take Roxanne as an example. The tasks and projects she will never delegate are those that align with why the organization hired her—her legal expertise and her astute understanding of how the legal aspects of philanthropic advancement are played out in the real world.

Roxanne will also never delegate tasks and projects where she is the only person in the organization with the knowledge, skills, and expertise to complete the work and where her unique abilities are highlighted—for example, resolving complex legal concerns for clients and articulating potential legal issues regarding the structuring of donations.

Last, and most important, Roxanne will not delegate the tasks and projects that bring meaning and joy to her work. For Roxanne, this includes interacting with the donors and resolving complex legal issues so that both the donor and the organization are able to realize their goals.

These three categories of tasks that Roxanne will never delegate make sense in the context of her life and career. The first two categories include tasks to which she brings unique skills and credentials; no one else could perform them quite as well as Roxanne. And the third category includes the tasks that make her job enjoyable and meaningful. Delegating any of them would either reduce Roxanne's value to the foundation or harm her mental and spiritual well-being.

If you are striving to overcome a psychological resistance to delegating, look at your project and task list and decide which tasks you will *never* delegate. This liberating exercise will help you get very clear about your value and the unique contributions you make to your organization. And separating the tasks you must do from the ones you can consider passing on to others will also help silence that voice in your head telling you that you *must* do it all.

Roxanne and I went back to her task and project list and identified the tasks that she could and should delegate. Here are the criteria we used, which you may find helpful in making your own delegation decisions.

First, *delegate tasks that are not the highest and best use of your time*. Roxanne used to manage her calendar and schedule all her own appointments; now she delegates this task to an assistant, who can handle it easily and accurately without taking up Roxanne's time.

Second, *delegate tasks that someone else can do faster or better than you.* Roxanne has an exceptional team who are capable, eager to learn, and very tech savvy. For this reason, she now turns over a lot of research work to her team, since they can often track down in minutes the same information it would take her hours to find.

If psychological resistance is your problem, ask yourself, "What do I lack faith in? Is that fear truly justified?" If you realize that your lack of faith is unfounded—as it usually is—you can decide which tasks you should never delegate, based on your unique talents, separating them from the many other tasks that you can and should delegate. This will let you accept help from other people with the many tasks you formerly handled all alone.

ORGANIZATIONAL RESISTANCE: A SHORTAGE OF RESOURCES

The second reason many people resist delegating is that they lack the human resources needed to complete the work. In many organizations today, with resources stretched thin and budget dollars scarce, one person is often doing work that used to be handled by two or more. Under these circumstances, being told to delegate may feel like a bad joke. "Delegate? I'd love to do it! But to whom?"

If this is the reality in your organization, it may be time to get a little creative. Avery's company, a managed care and data analysis firm serving hospitals, was experiencing tremendous growth, and she and her team needed additional support simply to handle the volume of work on their desks. At the same time, Avery also needed to significantly upgrade her technology platform in response to new government regulations and her exploding practice—a costly project that took precedence over hiring an additional staff person. What to do?

Avery's solution was to hire a student intern from the local community college majoring in health care administration. Avery's colleague Laura, an alumna of the college, reached out to its career services department, wrote a job description to ensure the intern would receive credit hours, and interviewed applicants. Within a month, an exceptional young student, David, joined the team as an intern.

When Avery and I spoke a few weeks ago, David was excelling on the job, and she was considering hiring him full-time after his graduation.

Like Avery, you may need to come up with a creative way to enlist the help you need. If you work in a large company, you may not have the budget dollars for an additional full-time employee, but resources for a specific project may be available. Think outside the box. Can a temporary worker take on a task that has been bottlenecking your progress? Can you outsource some of the work to a virtual assistant—an online assistant, working remotely, who can handle specific assignments on either a per-task or hourly basis, thereby saving you the costs of a part-time or full-time employee? Can you partner with another division or department of your company—or even with an outside firm—and split the cost for a project that will benefit both organizations?

It would be great if unlimited finances let us hire all the talent we can use—but in the real world that's rarely the case. Sometimes, however, a bit of ingenuity can enable you to find an alternative solution.

TECHNICAL RESISTANCE: FIVE PRINCIPLES FOR EFFECTIVE DELEGATION

The final reason many people resist delegating is simple lack of technical know-how. Some have failed miserably when delegating in the past—the work was flawed or late, or the process of delegating proved so difficult and time-consuming that doing the work itself would have been faster and easier. Discouraged by results like these, some people give up on the whole idea of delegating. "If you want something done right," they say, "you have to do it yourself."

Unfortunately, this attitude will trap you permanently in a world of extreme busyness, unable to call on others to complement your energies, skills, and knowledge. So how do you effectively and efficiently delegate? Here are the steps I teach my clients:

- Follow the advice of achievement guru Stephen Covey: Be clear on the goal and open on the path.[2]
- Set people up for success.
- Understand your team members' Productivity Styles and delegate accordingly.
- Communicate to be heard.
- Simply follow up.

Let's consider each of these principles in turn.

BE CLEAR ON THE GOAL AND OPEN ON THE PATH

Noah was my manager at my first job out of college. One day, after I had been working for him for about three months, he approached my cubicle and said, "Carson, I need a deck updating me on the HR Service Center employee training program. Let me know when it's ready—and thanks!" And he walked away, probably thinking to himself, "Another job delegated—and one more task I can cross off my list!"

I immediately began sweating. First, I had no idea what a "deck" was, and second, I could not figure out what Noah really wanted.

I soon learned that a deck was a PowerPoint slide presentation. But I still was not clear what Noah was trying to achieve. Who was he presenting the deck to? What was its purpose? What information was important to include in the deck? I was fairly desperate to please and get it right (yes, my perfectionistic Type A tendencies were revealing themselves in all of their glory!). But what was the goal? To say I was floundering was an understatement.

Has something like this ever happened to you? Remember how you felt—anxious, unsure, and confused—and you can immediately see that this is *not* the recipe for successful delegation.

You can avoid inducing these unpleasant feelings in the person to whom you delegate a task by always being clear on the goal while being open on the path toward reaching that goal—the wise delegation advice that effectiveness expert Stephen Covey offers.

Explicitly define the purpose behind the project or task. Make sure the goals are measurable and specific; for the person assuming the project, paint a vivid picture of what success will look like. At the same time, avoid defining or dictating in minute detail how the task is to be completed. This is demoralizing and ineffective, and it stifles creativity and innovation. Provide assistance and guidance, but only if it's needed.

The goal is to delegate, not to micromanage. You want to allow your team members the space to innovate and make their own unique contributions to the work. By being open on the path, you add dignity to the delegation process and give your team members an opportunity to uniquely express themselves—both of which are great motivators.

Here's how Noah might have delegated the task to me in an effective, motivating way:

Carson, I need a PowerPoint presentation on the Human Resources (HR) Service Center employee training program. I want the presentation to outline and explain the most current changes in the employee training program developed by the HR Service Center training team. I need it to be clear, concise, and understandable by everyone in the organization—not filled with jargon that only HR experts might understand.

Jerry in the HR Service Center training department has the information you will need on the employee training program. And here are a couple of sample slide decks that show the format of our standard presentations.

If you run into any problems along the way or have any questions, feel free to ask me or Cathy, my assistant, for help. Please provide a draft of the presentation to me by Friday, February 6, at noon.

You can see the difference between this act of delegation and the vague assignment Noah originally offered. Now the goal of the project is clear, and some of the key resources I will need to complete the task have been offered and explained. At the same time, Noah has not told me precisely how to perform the tasks, what details to include, or what methods to use—he assumes I am smart enough to figure those out on my own and that I will ask him if I get stuck along the way.

That's the right way to delegate.

SET PEOPLE UP FOR SUCCESS

You might call me naïve, but my experience is that most people really want to succeed—to take on meaningful, purposeful tasks and produce high-quality work. Effective delegation occurs when you set people up for success.

The first step is to stop making flawed assumptions when you delegate a task. Ask yourself, "Where am I making assumptions about the skills and knowledge of the person to whom I am delegating the task or project? Have I assumed that they are clear on the goals of the project? Have I assumed that they understand the terms I am using, that they have the skills and knowledge needed or the time, tools, and other resources required?" Check your assumptions. When they do not match reality, take steps to fill the gaps by providing the missing knowledge, skills, tools, and resources. If you don't, you may end up with a subpar result.

Next, avoid the second delegation pitfall—the temptation to dump and run. This is a mistake that Roxanne made when she first began delegating tasks.

Eager to get started on her new life as a champion delegator, Roxanne marched into the office of her associate Denise one Thursday afternoon. "Denise," she said, "I need your help on some projects. Can you please complete the board packets for the Smith Trust board meeting on Monday and the Woods Trust board meeting on Tuesday? I also need you to revise the fourth-quarter financial statement for the Hancock Foundation by the end of business today. Thanks, Denise! I'm off to my committee meeting." And Roxanne went breathlessly flying down the hall, leaving Denise overwhelmed and confused.

Roxanne made a couple of classic errors in her dump-and-run delegation. First, she delegated everything at one time. When you do this, there is no room or time to clearly define the goal, check any assumptions, or discuss current workloads. By dumping three separate projects, each somewhat complex, on Denise's desk at once, Roxanne practically guaranteed that misunderstandings and errors would occur.

Avoid making this mistake. To reduce the risk of wasted time spent explaining, evaluating, and correcting work, select just one item on your task list that you want to delegate and invest the time needed to explain it clearly. If necessary, assist your team member in brainstorming specific strategies for completion.

Roxanne's second major gaffe was her failure to define the due date for the tasks and the limits of the authority she was delegating to Denise.

Remember my first boss, Noah? As he and I worked together, his delegation skills gradually improved. Six months into my job, he asked me to draft a PowerPoint presentation for an upcoming presentation on our communications platform capability. He clearly defined the goals and his expectations for the PowerPoint presentation: Use colorful graphics, include a minimum of six peer-reviewed studies to validate our communications platform choice, and include no more than four bullet points per slide. So far, so good.

But as Noah was leaving my desk, I asked, "When is it due?" He stopped, turned back around, and stared at me. I suddenly realized that he had not even thought about when he wanted the presentation back to review.

Avoid skipping a step the way Noah did. Never be vague or unsure about the due date. You want to ensure that your team member can properly prioritize their workload. You also want to give yourself plenty of time to review the work before the final deadline. If you have no deadline or a due date in mind, do not delegate the task or project. You are not ready to hand over the task, and you are not setting your team member up for success.

In addition, you need to define the limits of the authority you are delegating. Be clear about where your team member can make independent decisions and where they cannot. For example, Noah gave me the authority to research the studies to validate our communication platform choice. However, I did not have the authority to recommend a different communications platform based on my research. The decision had already been made, and my input was neither needed nor wanted.

Finally, as part of the process of setting up your team member for success, consider the obstacles they may face and define the problems that they can address on their own as distinguished from those that require your input. If you know you will be traveling or tied up in meetings, make sure they either know how to get in touch with you if necessary or have the authority to proceed without you so they will not sit on the task wasting time.

Everyone wants the possibility of earning a gold star for their work. When you delegate, provide all the tools needed to make it easy for your team member to earn that gold star—or two or three. When your team members succeed, so do you!

UNDERSTAND YOUR TEAM MEMBERS' PRODUCTIVITY STYLES AND DELEGATE ACCORDINGLY

Efficiency and effectiveness increase exponentially when you work with your Productivity Style rather than against it—so when you delegate, strive to understand your team member's style and work with it, not against it.

How do you determine your team members' style? You can invite them to take the Productivity Style Assessment in this book, or you can look for Productivity Style clues and cues. Each person leaves behind some cues and clues. Some are overt and others are subtle, depending on the degree of preference the individual has for a particular style.

My husband, Andrew, and I were having dinner one Saturday night with two of our closest friends, Peter and Sue, when the topic of this book came up. Our friends both asked, almost at the same time, "What is *my* Productivity Style?" Neither of them had taken the Productivity Style Assessment, so I had to rely on clues and cues to help me. I thought for a moment about the things I had learned and observed about Peter and Sue during the years of our friendship.

Peter is a highly successful serial entrepreneur. He loves extreme outdoor sports, ice climbing, technical off-course skiing, and mountain biking. He is frequently reading the latest business book and always owns the latest and greatest technology tool. In conversation, Peter likes to ask questions like "What do you think about XYZ?" and uses words and phrases like *visualize, brainstorm*, and *cutting edge*. During meetings, he takes notes by hand and draws pictures and doodles in the margins, then takes a picture of his notes and files them in Evernote on his iPad. When explaining a concept, Peter often uses pen and paper to illustrate his points as he speaks. He can manage multiple projects at one time and prefers to have a large variety of projects under way at once. He works on a given task right up to the deadline, and his calendar is not rigidly scheduled.

Sue's style is very different from Peter's. She is a stay-at-home mom who is extremely involved in volunteer activities in our community. She teaches group exercise classes and is part owner of a gym. Sue tends to fall behind on her e-mail because she prefers to connect with people by phone or in person. She adores accessories—shoes, handbags, necklaces, and earrings—and is often dressed in colorful outfits. She takes notes by hand on Post-it Notes or the backs of receipts, and her home office is filled with colorful file folders from which stacks of papers are practically exploding. She has a secret subscription to *People* magazine, which she devours each month, and she's a huge fan of *American Idol* and *Dancing with the Stars*.

Now that you've heard about the clues and cues that Peter and Sue leave behind, what do you think their Productivity Styles are?

I told Peter that I thought his Productivity Style was Visualizer, and Sue that I thought her Productivity Style was Arranger. We discussed the thinking and workflow preferences for both, and they said that my assessment sounded accurate. I based my evaluations on their work styles, how they talk about and manage time, the words and phrases they frequently use when communicating, their clothing and accessory choices, their hobbies, what they like to read, and the TV shows and movies they like to watch.

Every Productivity Style has discernible preferences in each of these areas. Use the table below as a guide to help you determine your team members' Productivity Styles. To download a copy, go to www.carson tate.com.

PRODUCTIVITY STYLE CLUES AND CUES

Clue Types	Prioritizer	Planner	Arranger	Visualizer
E-mail Style	• Succinct • Minimum number of words or phrases • Often no salutation or closing	• Bullet points or numbers to illustrate key points • Stated action steps • Due dates or time-lines	• Salutation and closing • Personal information and personal inquiry • Tendency to write longer paragraphs	• Multiple ideas conveyed at once • Often no opening or closing • Run-on or long sentences
Time Management	• Deadline = drop-dead date • Ability to focus and prioritize • Balance between work and personal life skewed at times	• Deadline = drop-dead date • Work frequently completed in advance of deadlines • Detailed, highly structured calendar	• Deadline = time frame for completion • Work and deadlines negotiated with colleagues and managers • Guide or plan for the day	• Deadline = the moment project or deliverable is turned over • Time to complete work maximized • Tendency to visualize the day
Project and Task Management	• Solves the problem first • Focuses on the outcome or goal to be achieved • Prioritizes tasks	• Organizes the project • Plans and schedules time to complete tasks • Creates timelines and project plans	• Understands who needs to be involved in the project first • Communicates and delegates • Creates visual, colorful handwritten lists	• Ideates or brain-storms about the project first • Understands the why • Creates visual, colorful, handwritten lists

Clue Types	Prioritizer	Planner	Arranger	Visualizer
Workspace	• Minimal to no visual clutter • Clean, crisp lines • Desk or work surface is frequently devoid of anything but what they are currently working on	• Organized • Every item has a place and is in its place • Project materials are labeled and out of sight when not in use	• Personal items and mementos are displayed • Music, soft lighting. • Colorful file folders, pens, and containers	• Papers, books, file folders used as visual cues • Unique or unusual personal mementos displayed • Space and tools for brainstorming
Frequently Used Words and Phrases	• "What is the goal?" • "What are the facts?" • "Get things done" • "Prioritize" • "Anticipate" • "Work smart"	• "How will this be completed?" • "Plan" • "Organize" • "Summarize" • "List"/"calendar" • "Time to complete work"	• "Who is involved on this project?" • "Communicate," "communication" • "People"/"team" • Descriptive, colorful phrases and words • Feeling phrases • Kinesthetic language—"touch," "feel," "see," "smell," "taste"	• "Why are we doing this?" • "Multitasking," "juggling" • "Work/life balance" • "See," "visualize" • "Brainstorm," "ideate" • "Vision for the end result"

Clue Types	Prioritizer	Planner	Arranger	Visualizer
Clothing and Accessories	• Conservative, tailored • Muted or dark colors • More formal and structured • Minimal to no accessories	• Conservative, tailored • Functional, practical, durable • Muted or dark colors • Practical accessories	• Trendy, stylish • Colorful • Multiple accessories • Soft, comfortable fabrics and cuts	• Trendy, stylish • Colorful • Unique, custom, or handcrafted clothing and accessories • Comfortable and functional
Hobbies	• Solo or small-group activities • Clear goal or outcome, often with a score • Golf or tennis	• Organized, structured activities	• Group activities • Crafts or activities that involve using the hands to create	• Group or solo activities • Extreme sports or adventures • Involves risk, novelty, or uncertainty like skydiving or heli-skiing
Books, TV, and Movies	• Tend to be factual or include real events or people • Discuss trends or data	• Movies tend to be historical or biographical • "How to" or instructional	• Focus on people, relationships, and stories • Full range of emotions	• Focus on the future, innovation, what's next • Exciting, risky

Our thinking preferences influence and inform not only how we structure and execute our work, but also numerous other decisions and activities in our lives. Observe and listen to your team members. You might be surprised at what you notice and how your observations can provide insights into your team members' Productivity Styles that can help you improve your delegation effectiveness.

COMMUNICATE TO BE HEARD

Each Productivity Style is associated with a unique approach to listening and communication. Now that you have a sense of your team members' Productivity Styles, you can modify the language you use to ensure that your message will be clearly heard and understood when you communicate with them. The table that follows offers some specific communication strategies.

WORK SIMPLY:
COMMUNICATING WITH TEAM MEMBERS
ACCORDING TO THEIR PRODUCTIVITY STYLE

When You're Communicating with a Prioritizer

The Prioritizer's Style: The Prioritizer's preferred style of thinking is analytical, logical, and fact-based. Accordingly, when you communicate with a Prioritizer, focus on data and facts. Be brief, succinct, clear, and precise, offering just the facts and no fluff. Think through your ideas in advance and present them in a logical format. Prioritizers prefer written materials that are direct, to the point, and technically accurate.

Delegating to a Prioritizer: When you delegate to a Prioritizer, clearly state at the beginning of the conversation the goal of the project and what you want to achieve. Then state the facts or current data on the project and provide clear references or resources to back up the data. Conclude with the due date. Expect the conversation to be brief—that is the Prioritizer's preference.

When You're Communicating with a Planner

The Planner's Style: The Planner's preferred style of thinking is organized, detailed, and planned. Accordingly, when you communicate with a Planner, stay on topic, avoid digressions, present your ideas in a sequential, organized manner, and provide detailed timelines. Provide thorough references and state any rules, procedures, or processes that may impact the task or project.

    Delegating to a Planner: When you delegate to a Planner, sequentially step through the time frame for completion at the beginning of the conversation. Then discuss any current processes or procedures that could impact the project, and conclude with follow-up procedures, since thorough, timely follow-up is important to Planners.

When You're Communicating with an Arranger

The Arranger's Style: The Arranger's preferred style of thinking is emotional, kinesthetic, and interpersonal. Accordingly, when you communicate with an Arranger, ensure that the conversation is informal, open, and warm, with no hidden agenda. The Arranger is interested in the impact of a project on others and how they will feel about it. They want to know who is involved in projects and they want team members to have equal consideration when plans are being made.

    Delegating to an Arranger: When you delegate to an Arranger, open the conversation with a personal question or comment. Then clearly articulate who is involved and how the task will impact others on the team. Conclude by asking whether there are any questions, and allow time for your Arranger team member to talk further about the project.

When You're Communicating with a Visualizer

The Visualizer's Style: The Visualizer's preferred style of thinking is holistic, integrating, and synthesizing. Accordingly, when you communicate with a Visualizer, use minimal details, provide the big picture using visuals and metaphors, and articulate how the project or task aligns with the organization's strategy.

Visualizers prefer an overview and a broad conceptual framework, so avoid getting bogged down in details.

Delegating to a Visualizer: When you are delegating to a Visualizer, open the conversation by explaining the *why* of the project or the task. Why is this project or task important to the organization? How does it fit within the broader strategy or mission of the organization? Use colorful, vivid language to convey your message. Then reinforce that you are open on the path to achieving the outcome so that the Visualizer does not feel boxed in or restricted. Conclude with a time frame for completion.

If you tailor your communication to the nuances of each Productivity Style, you can ensure that your message is clearly heard and understood. However, if you have a new team member or are working with a colleague in a different department whom you do not know well, you can make a good connection with them no matter what their preferred style may be by making sure that you address each of the following four questions in your delegation conversation—*what, how, who,* and *why.* Each of these questions appeals to a particular Productivity Style:

- Prioritizers are focused on *what* questions—What is the goal? What do you want to achieve? What are the key facts?
- Planners are focused on *how* questions—How do you want it completed? How much time do you have? How has this been done in the past?
- Arrangers are focused on *who* questions—Who is involved? Who needs to know this information? Who will be impacted by this initiative?
- Visualizers are focused on *why* questions—Why are we doing this project? Why this approach versus another approach? Why don't we consider . . . ?

By addressing each of the four questions, you will ensure that a team member from any style will understand your message.

We all communicate differently. When you delegate, speak the language of your team member's Productivity Style to ensure that your message is clearly heard and understood.

SIMPLY FOLLOW UP

You have effectively and efficiently delegated a task or project to a team member. Well done! Now you need to follow up on what you have delegated.

The first key for effective follow-up is *not* to wait until the last minute. So often, in the frantic warp speed of our typical workdays, we forget to create the time and space to follow up on what we have asked our team members to complete for us. Following up prior to the due date of the task or project provides an opportunity for you to help remove roadblocks that might prevent timely completion of the project or lead to work that is inaccurate or incomplete.

Equally critical is clear, constructive feedback *after* the project is completed. If you delegate, delegate, and delegate while never acknowledging the time and effort your team member is dedicating to the work and its positive impact on the team, your team member may begin to feel less valued and may also begin to lose trust in you. By contrast, concrete, helpful feedback, including both praise for every positive and (when necessary) suggestions for improvement on future projects, demonstrates to your team member that you are paying attention to their work and that you value their contributions.

So there is tremendous value for you and your team member in following up—a time investment that produces an incredibly high rate of return.

Establish a follow-up process at the moment you delegate the task. For example, suppose you've asked your team member to revise and update the market analysis for your presentation in three weeks. During your conversation, you might decide together to follow up in two weeks to review the first draft of the analysis. You should tell your team member specifically what you want to review: "Be ready to explain any new trends or unusual data points you plan to highlight, and also be prepared to demonstrate the format you have in mind for the presentation."

Then you should agree on how you will follow up. You might say, "Please e-mail me your draft of the presentation on Monday, and let's schedule a fifteen-minute phone call on Tuesday to discuss it."

Now you are both clear on the follow-up process, you have created space and time for reflection and discussion prior to the due date, and you have demonstrated your commitment to the project and your support of your team member.

You can also automate your follow-up using technology tools. In Outlook, Outlook for Mac, Lotus Notes, and Gmail, you can write a custom rule to automatically track your follow-up items. It works like this: Every time you send an e-mail and cc yourself on that e-mail, a copy of the e-mail is automatically sent to a designated folder (I call mine "Waiting For"). Now you have in one place all of the delegated e-mail messages requiring follow-up. You can also assign tasks in Outlook, which enables you to track and automatically be notified of the task's completion.

Delegation is one of the most crucial productivity tools in today's complex world, where only the simplest tasks can be handled by one person alone. Most projects of any scope or complexity demand the combined input of a number of people—which is why we form teams and committees, launch civic organizations and nonprofits, and build companies. Leverage the human resources around you and stop struggling to handle your workload all alone. Learn to delegate effectively, and you'll find yourself multiplying your own capabilities as well as those of your organization.

13

Work Well with Others

WORKING WITH A TEAM IS ONE OF THE GREAT JOYS OF LIFE. But it can also be one of the biggest sources of frustration.

"Why does Joanne always wait until the absolute last minute to complete her tasks? Because of her, the entire office always seems to spend the final day of any project rushing around frantically to meet the deadline!"

"Every e-mail I receive from Mark is a sentence or less—sometimes just a few letters. The last e-mail Mark sent me read 'K TX.' What the heck does that mean!?"

"I love my manager—but every time I visit her with a quick question, we have to discuss her weekend and her three children's latest incredible accomplishments. Why can't we just get to the point?"

"My colleague William drives me crazy with all of his tangents! I don't want to brainstorm new project ideas when we haven't even finished our current project!"

"Barbara is so unfriendly! She never looks me in the eye when I talk to her, and she is always all business—nothing but numbers, facts, and data. Why can't she lighten up?"

Do any of these complaints sound familiar? Is there a colleague in your office, a member of your volunteer committee, or a parent on your child's sports team who makes you want to pull your hair out in frustration?

The reason we find other people so challenging to work with is usually very simple: When your Productivity Style and the Productivity Styles of others clash, the misunderstanding and tension that result can impede you from completing your best work.

THE CLASH OF PRODUCTIVITY STYLES

On his second day as the company's new chief financial officer, Ralph walked into Claire's office unexpected and uninvited. "I've got some questions about last quarter's financials," he announced, staring at the spreadsheet in his hand. "I'm wondering why your division missed its goal by half a percent. And while you're at it, I need an explanation for these higher expenses in the human resources category."

For a long moment, Claire just stared at Ralph. It was 7:30 a.m. Claire had arrived in her office just moments before and hadn't even had a chance to pop the top on her morning cup of coffee. She felt as if she were being cross-examined by a particularly hostile attorney.

She scrambled to collect her thoughts. Of course she was willing to discuss her financials, and her division had a sound reason for missing its quarterly numbers (a recent large investment in a new leadership development program for the executive team). But Ralph's approach to getting the information he needed was off-putting at best. Claire sighed (unnoticed by Ralph), pulled up the financials on her computer, and began answering Ralph's questions, wondering how long she could put up with the new CFO's working style.

The problem is that Ralph's and Claire's styles are diametrically opposed. Ralph is a Prioritizer: analytical, linear, driven solely by data and facts. He wants Claire to provide the facts about the financial gap in a succinct and efficient manner. He is not interested in wasting precious time on chitchat or pleasantries. By contrast, Claire is an Arranger—expressive, intuitive, a highly effective communicator who works well with a team. Relationships and connections are important to her and she is adept at reading the emotional underpinnings in any situation. She wants to point out to Ralph that investing in people through high-quality training programs is essential for continued profitability and long-term success. But this is qualitative information, which is meaningless in Ralph's eyes.

In a similar way, when a Planner and a Visualizer work together, there will probably be clashes and misunderstandings, since each style's strengths oppose the other's. The Visualizer is focused on the big picture, but the Planner is focused on the details. The Visualizer sees the forest, but the Planner sees the bark on the third tree in on the right. The Visualizer is focused on the future, but the Planner is focused on the form. The Visualizer provides the context and the strategic intent of a project, leaving the frustrated Planner hungry for specific details about how to complete the project.

Your productivity and effectiveness is directly connected to your ability to work well with others. So how can you work well with others when Productivity Style differences threaten to cause misunderstandings and hostility? The key is to leverage the Productivity Style strengths of your team members—including yourself—and minimize their blind spots.

LEVERAGE YOUR COLLEAGUES' PRODUCTIVITY STYLE STRENGTHS AND MINIMIZE THEIR BLIND SPOTS

Brenda is the controller and manager of operations for my company. She has a primary Productivity Style of Prioritizer and a close secondary Productivity Style as a Visualizer, while my primary Productivity Style is that of a Planner with a close secondary Productivity Style as an Arranger. Our current roles in the company definitely play to our Productivity Style strengths. But the differences between our styles sometimes lead to mutual frustration.

Brenda and I were recently working on launching a new e-mail management course. I had outlined the plan for the launch, provided the content, and, of course, put the launch date on my calendar. However, when Brenda received the plan and the content, she started questioning the timeline because she didn't have all the data she needed from our e-commerce provider for the connection to QuickBooks. (Her Prioritizer preference was showing itself.) Then, while researching the additional data she needed, Brenda started brainstorming new ideas for the product launch, including new hosting platforms (all fueled by her secondary Visualizer preference).

When Brenda called me to suggest delaying the launch, I felt the tension building in my shoulders. "But Brenda," I protested, "we have a solid plan and we need to launch the product to meet the needs of our clients!"

"Of course," Brenda replied, "but if we can't seamlessly accept payment and if the content hosting platform isn't easy to use, the whole launch may fail! Then how will our clients feel?"

Brenda's concerns were valid and important—and so were mine. Our blind spots prevented us from understanding why we were clashing. We needed to overcome our differences by playing to each other's strengths— Brenda's strengths in analysis, ideation, innovation, fact-based decision making, and goal orientation, as well as my strengths in organization, planning, intuitive understanding of the clients' needs, and an ability to translate ideas into action.

After a few frustrated e-mails back and forth, I did what I should have done earlier: I picked up the phone and started a dialogue with Brenda about how our styles were clashing (once again!). We both began to laugh. We then revised the product launch plan, moved it out two weeks, and switched hosting platforms. As a result, the product launch was seamless and effective.

As this story illustrates, each Productivity Style has workflow strengths and blind spots. Use the tables below as a guide to help you leverage your team members' Productivity Style strengths and minimize their blind spots. Being aware of the blind spots that cause conflict and tension, potentially derailing projects, can enable you to recognize them and keep your projects on track.

WORK SIMPLY:
PRODUCTIVITY STYLE STRENGTHS

Workflow Types	Prioritizer	Planner	Arranger	Visualizer
E-mail	• Succinct • Fact-based • Clearly stated argument or theory	• Organized • Detailed • Clearly stated next action steps	• Interpersonal connection • Inclusive of all relevant stakeholders and constituencies • Well written, without run-on sentences or fragments	• Presenting context or big picture • Integrating ideas and concepts • Use of colors, fonts, symbols, and other visual cues to mark ideas
Time Management	• Prioritizes to achieve goals • Is able to focus and manage attention while minimizing distractions • Meets deadlines	• Uses a detailed, highly structured calendar • Completes work on or in advance of deadline	• Uses a general guide or plan for the day • Intuitively knows what work to complete when and for whom • Able to accommodate others' needs while still meeting deadlines	• Able to complete significant amounts of work quickly • Intersperses challenging tasks with play or fun • Works well under pressure and tight deadlines

Workflow Types	Prioritizer	Planner	Arranger	Visualizer
Task Execution	• Prioritizes tasks based on goals • Knows how long tasks will take • Lists and completes tasks in predetermined order	• Uses detailed, action-oriented task lists • Schedules time to complete tasks • Stays on task; strong need for completion	• Completes work by collaborating with others • Skilled at delegation • Prefers working with a team to solo work	• Effectively manages multiple tasks at once • Prefers a variety of tasks to repetitious tasks • Connects tasks to big-picture goals
Project Management	• Has a clear purpose, goals, metrics, and objectives • Understands budgeting and financial resources • Ensures that needed data and research are accessible • Identifies available technology tools and resources	• Has a clear plan, agendas, guidelines, and timelines • Clearly defines responsibilities and accountabilities • Identifies resources required	• Understands project team members, customers, and other stakeholders • Understands others' roles and best modes of interaction • Identifies project meeting facilitation skills available	• Has a clear vision of success • Understands how project fits into broader strategy • Willing to innovate, take risks, challenge the status quo • Identifies opportunities to create change

WORK SIMPLY:
PRODUCTIVITY STYLE POTENTIAL BLIND SPOTS

If Your Colleague Is a Prioritizer

His or her blind spots may include:

- A tendency to be controlling and rigid
- Excessive competitiveness
- Valuing speed over excellence
- Focusing on project over process

If Your Colleague Is a Planner

His or her blind spots may include:

- Rigidity
- Missed opportunities due to resistance to deviating from plans
- Lack of spontaneity
- Excessive attachment to outcome
- Valuing process over project

If Your Colleague Is an Arranger

His or her blind spots may include:

- Missing important details due to incomplete planning
- Lack of awareness of how their style impacts others
- Excessive involvement with people; taking on others' concerns and problems as their own
- Tendency to lose sight of end results
- Valuing people over project

If Your Colleague Is a Visualizer

His or her blind spots may include:

- Tendency to overlook details
- Tendency to complete work late due to lack of planning
- Excessive spontaneity and impulsiveness, which may derail project plans
- Valuing possibilities over process

WORK WELL WITH YOUR BOSS, YOUR COLLEAGUE, AND YOUR ASSISTANT

Now it's time to delve a bit deeper into the *how* of leveraging strengths and minimizing blind spots. Let's explore three of the key work relationships many business people have—with their boss, with a colleague, and with an assistant—and identify some specific techniques for mitigating Productivity Style differences in workflow and task management.

WORKING WITH YOUR BOSS

Steven, whose primary Productivity Style is Planner, was a risk manager in a financial services firm. He was organized, detailed, cautious, and never missed a deadline. When Steven reached out to me for coaching, I was unsure why, because he was very highly regarded in the company and consistently exceeded all of his goals. But during our second coaching session, I realized how hard he was working to consistently meet the expectations of his boss, Danielle. She was a maverick in the firm, known for her innovative, cutting-edge ideas, her strategic thinking, and her ability to manage multiple projects at one time. As a Visualizer, Danielle was consistently asking Steven to research one new idea after another and then integrate them into his project plans.

Steven was working nights and weekends just to keep up with Danielle's ideas. This was causing him tremendous amounts of stress. Steven was frustrated and so was Danielle thanks to their very different, conflicting Productivity Styles.

I suggested to Steven that we include Danielle in our next coaching session, and he readily agreed. I explained the concept of Productivity Style, and the two quickly realized that their differing Productivity Style strengths were causing stress, frustration, and misunderstanding. As they talked, they gradually realized how they could work together better to produce higher-quality work on time and up to the standards of their organization.

In the weeks that followed, Steven began preparing his project plans in mind-map form so Danielle could see the entire project and ideate without being distracted by the rigidity of a sequential project plan. This enabled her to contribute her ideas at the beginning of the project rather than throughout it, which derailed Steven. He would then take the mind map and convert it into a plan he could work from, incorporating Danielle's input.

Steven also built additional review time into all of his project schedules in order to give Danielle time to think about and question him on aspects of the project without making him miss his deadline. Understanding how important it was to Steven to adhere to deadlines, Danielle allotted time on her calendar to review his work.

Steven began including the context—the *why*—in all of his communications with Danielle. When writing notes, he would highlight in color any action items he needed Danielle to complete, so it was easy for her to see how she could support him.

Danielle developed the habit of brainstorming *prior to* her meetings with Steven, making it easy for her to provide enough structure to their conversations so that Steven would always be clear on the next action steps. Knowing that Steven always asks for a deadline, she began thinking about her calendar and when she actually needed the work to be completed prior to initiating a conversation with him.

Now Steven is more engaged and focused at work; he has almost completely stopped working at night and on weekends. Steven and Danielle's most recent project—an enhanced process for evaluating borrower risk—is expected to save the organization at least three million dollars this year.

If you and your boss find yourselves continually at odds over workflow processes, don't just fume or complain. Do what Steven and Danielle did: Figure out how Productivity Style differences may be short-circuiting clear communication and cooperation, and come up with specific procedural changes that will make it easier for the two of you to work together harmoniously and productively.

WORKING WITH YOUR COLLEAGUE

Sharon is vice president of the projects, retail, and risk management group at a consumer products company. After a highly successful career in sales, she was excited by the opportunity to bring her innovative big-picture thinking and customer-focused orientation to a very analytical, data-driven team. Because her team is responsible for special initiatives for the entire organization, she was frequently called upon to collaborate with her colleague, Amanda, vice president of information technology. Under Amanda's leadership over the past two years, the IT organization had become more data-driven, efficient, responsive, and linear in its approach to problem solving.

Within just a few months, three projects involving Sharon and Amanda had stalled. Both Sharon and Amanda were frustrated, because neither of them had ever missed a deadline before, and these breakdowns reflected poorly not only on them but on their teams.

When Sharon called me for help, I suggested a meeting that included Amanda. As soon as we began discussing the issues together, it became clear that Productivity Style differences were derailing their partnership. As a Visualizer, Sharon embraces risk and change; she doesn't hesitate to disrupt the status quo to find an innovative solution to a problem.

Meanwhile, as a Prioritizer, Amanda never makes a decision without significant amounts of data; she stresses efficiency and precision when managing her team. No wonder their collaboration wasn't working. Sharon would present a big-picture idea to Amanda; Amanda would then focus on validating a minute piece of data to confirm that the idea was viable. This took time and energy, which frustrated Sharon. Sharon felt as if her value to the organization was not being realized, and Amanda felt as if Sharon's unproven ideas would stress her already overworked team. Sharon was focused on the future, and Amanda was focused on the facts.

I suggested that Sharon and Amanda each create a list of their Productivity Style strengths and frustrations. Comparing the lists was quite an eye-opener for both of them. You cannot change what you are not aware of, so understanding the real nature of their conflict was the first step toward implementing a solution.

Sharon began including risk analysis data and pricing comparison models in all of her presentations to Amanda, providing enough information to convey both the crucial details and the big picture that was so important to Sharon. She also made sure that all of her communications with Amanda were succinct and logical, and abandoned the notion of conducting hourlong brainstorming strategy sessions with her.

The new flow of useful data from Sharon enabled Amanda to delegate the analysis to one of her team members, freeing herself up to think logically and analytically about the project. Leveraging this strength allowed her to identify any gaps in the project plans and proactively anticipate delays.

Sharon and Amanda's next project was not only completed on time but also attracted the attention of the CEO, who was surprised and intrigued by its innovative yet logical approach to the company's pricing control policy. Amanda and Sharon's relationship has improved as well; they now frequently seek each other's counsel on both personal and professional matters. Understanding a colleague's Productivity Style makes it much easier to accept them—and maybe even enjoy them!

WORKING WITH YOUR ASSISTANT

One of my certified coaches, Gail Angelo, was helping Joan, a senior leader in a large consulting firm, to improve her leadership effectiveness. It became clear during the coaching engagement that one of Joan's biggest opportunities lay in better utilizing her assistant.

Joan's primary Productivity Style is that of an Arranger. Expressive and energetic, with a hands-on style that she employs with both her team and her clients, Joan enjoys the "rush" of the marketplace and the wins that come from her tenacity and hard work. It is easy for her to move from one thing to another very quickly without worrying much about the details. But despite her love of lists (color-coded for better planning), Joan felt as if she was losing her ability to be in control of her time, her energy, and ultimately her effectiveness.

After studying Joan's working style, Gail identified the problem: Joan was using her assistant, Susan, only for basic tasks like organizing travel, appointments, expenses, and the calendar, not realizing that Susan was capable of much more.

Susan's primary Productivity Style is that of a Planner. Unlike Joan, she prefers to be given instructions in an organized and sequential manner, often focusing on *how* something will get done rather than *who* is involved. She carefully plans her time; is very detailed, systematic, and concise; and always prefers to complete assignments rather than leave them open-ended. She gets enormous satisfaction from the act of crossing things off her to-do list.

Unfortunately, Joan rarely paused long enough to think through how she might better utilize Susan, and while Susan knew the relationship was not as effective as it could be, she was unsure how to better meet Joan's needs.

Gail soon realized that it would be helpful to include Susan in some of the coaching sessions. In these sessions, Joan and Susan talked about the differences and similarities in their Productivity Styles and the way the differences were impacting their ability or inability to get things done. These discussions enabled them to leverage their Productivity Style strengths to maximize output.

Now, in addition to her traditional support roles, Susan acts as a liaison among Joan's colleagues who request time on her calendar. Together they have created a strategy that blocks out time for strategic and creative thinking. Susan is filtering out e-mails for Joan and continues to color-code them the way Joan prefers. She is conducting research on topics Joan is working on or are in her nice-to-do file (as opposed to her have-to-do file). As a result, Joan has reclaimed three to five additional hours a week for more strategic thinking, relevant networking, and reenergizing. Susan is engaged, fulfilled, and productive, knowing that she is making a real difference as she works on projects that utilize all her strengths.

CONTRIBUTE TO A HIGH-PERFORMANCE TEAM

Most of us have consistently participated in teams from childhood, beginning with the local youth basketball team or Girl Scout troop to the science project group or debate team in high school. The challenges and frustrations of teamwork continue in the workplace and may become even more pronounced because the stakes are so much higher: Now the value of your teamwork may impact your next promotion, bonus, or political standing in the organization. And most experts on the future of business agree that collaboration and teamwork are only going to become more important in the years and decades to come.

To ensure that you are working on and contributing to a highly functioning team, it's crucial to understand the productivity value that you and your colleagues bring to the team.

Before you join your next team—when considering a job change, a position transfer, a promotion, or a career shift—ask yourself the following questions:

- What productivity value do I bring to a team?
- What is my most significant productivity contribution?
- What do I enjoy about being part of a team?
- What do I not like about being part of a team?
- What can I do to be a more effective team member?

Some of the answers to these questions can be gleaned by considering each of the Productivity Styles and the contributions they make to a team. Examine the following chart, and think about the information presented in light of your own experiences with teamwork. Which contributions have you most consistently made to the teams you belong to? When you've been part of a particularly high-achieving team, what role did you play in its success? Most people have a persistent pattern of behavior that shapes the quality of their teamwork—it's very valuable to recognize yours.

WORK SIMPLY: CONTRIBUTING TO A TEAM BY LEVERAGING YOUR PRODUCTIVITY STYLE

If You're a Prioritizer

Your contributions to the team may include:

- Analyzing data
- Logical processing
- Diagnosing issues, problems, or challenges
- Solving challenging, complex problems
- Financial and budgetary control
- Achieving the stated goal or objective
- Clarifying issues

If You're a Planner

Your contributions to the team may include:

- Competing project work on time
- Establishing order
- Planning
- Focusing on details
- Paperwork
- Structured tasks
- Scheduling

If You're an Arranger

Your contributions to the team may include:

- Building relationships
- Facilitating team interaction
- Intuitive understanding of the political climate and/or organizational undertones
- Communication
- Persuading or selling ideas
- Listening
- Coaching

If You're a Visualizer

Your contributions to the team may include:

- Serving as a catalyst for change
- Envisioning the future
- Inventing solutions to problems
- Integrating disparate ideas
- Visualizing the big picture
- Embracing risk taking
- Ensuring variety in both thought and execution

Understanding the varying strengths that different Productivity Styles bring to a team can go a long way in helping you identify the teams to which you have the most to offer. And if you are in the position of recruiting or organizing a team, recognizing the variety of strengths that are needed to build a successful team can help you find the right assortment of team members to complement and support one another effectively.

I was once engaged by a large global pharmaceutical organization to help them revolutionize their meeting culture. But before we could begin the culture change work, I had to assist the group of physicians and scientists who had been assembled to lead the change effort in becoming a highly functioning team.

The majority of the team were Prioritizers and Planners, and their strengths had clearly helped to shape the early stages of the project. The goal of the culture change was very clear—fewer, better meetings—and the plan to achieve the outcome was detailed, structured, and logical, clearly anticipating and addressing the challenges that would arise as the change initiative was rolled out. But there were gaps in the plan, and some members of the team felt isolated and unappreciated. Friction and frustration ensued.

A bit of analysis made the problem very clear. The vocal majority, made up of Prioritizers and Planners, were not valuing the essential contributions of the Arrangers and Visualizers in the group. Without the input of these two neglected groups into communicating the vision, persuading others to change ingrained habits, and encouraging them to embrace risk, the meeting revolution they all desired would probably never happen.

So I asked the entire team to pause to evaluate the productivity value they were contributing to the change initiative. I asked the team members to get together with their primary Productivity Style counterparts to discuss the value they contributed to the team. Each Productivity Style group produced a flip chart outlining their contributions and posted it on the wall.

Then I asked the entire team to do a "productivity value walk-around" with me. We literally walked to each flip chart and reviewed the value of that style. At each chart, I asked, "What will happen if we don't recognize and include this style's productivity strengths in the project?" Little by little, the team members began to recognize the gaps in their thinking and the importance of embracing and drawing upon each Productivity Style's contributions.

The team came together and launched a highly successful meeting revolution program, which eliminated thirteen thousand hours of meetings by leveraging the strengths of *every* member of the team.

COACH YOUR TEAM MEMBERS

Change is an ever-present reality of life in the twenty-first century. (Just think about how many system updates you have made in the past six months on your smartphone!) Change is also at the core of coaching—a powerful leadership tool for responding to the changing dynamics of the world in which we all live.

I define coaching as an action-oriented, goal-focused process to improve performance, guide self-discovery, and make behavioral shifts. As a longtime practitioner of the art of coaching—and someone who has benefited from the help of a number of gifted coaches in a variety of practice arenas—I've found that it is a powerful way to improve productivity and effectiveness.

Whenever you want to help develop and improve the performance of a team or a team member, you have an opportunity to coach, whether the person on the receiving end is a colleague at work, a classmate at school, a fellow volunteer, or even your child. To maximize the positive impact of your coaching, consider the Productivity Style of the person you are coaching. In particular, use words and phrases that are most likely to inspire the person you are coaching, while avoiding words and phrases that will tend to demotivate them. You'll find some suggestions in the table below.

WORK SIMPLY:
COACHING BY PRODUCTIVITY STYLE: WORDS AND PHRASES THAT INSPIRE OR DEMOTIVATE

If You're Coaching a Prioritizer

You can inspire them by using words and phrases like:

- Accurate
- Correct
- Logical approach
- Excellent analysis
- How can I have a greater impact?

You're likely to demotivate them by using words and phrases like:

- I feel
- I believe
- Short-term focus
- Illogical approach

If You're Coaching a Planner

You can inspire them by using words and phrases like:

- Time
- Plan
- Destination
- Endgame
- What and by when

You're likely to demotivate them by using words and phrases like:

- No deadline or time frame
- Let's see what unfolds

- Open-ended
- Let's brainstorm some ideas

If You're Coaching an Arranger

You can inspire them by using words and phrases like:

- How did you just know?
- Astute insight
- You are so enthusiastic!
- Good connection
- Engage

You're likely to demotivate them by using words and phrases like:

- It would be more productive if you worked alone on this . . .
- Be more formal in your approach
- I need this in black and white
- Just the facts

If You're Coaching a Visualizer

You can inspire them by using words and phrases like:

- Innovative
- Imaginative
- Ideation
- Woo!
- Paint me a picture of your ideal future

You're likely to demotivate them by using words and phrases like:

- Can't
- Won't
- Must
- Always done this way

Another way that exceptional coaching and average coaching can often be distinguished is by the quality of the questions being asked. When coaching your teammates, colleagues, or family members, remember to ask questions that are in alignment with their Productivity Style. In the table below are questions to consider in your coaching conversations by Productivity Style.

WORK SIMPLY:
COACHING QUESTIONS BY PRODUCTIVITY STYLE

If You're Coaching a Prioritizer

Try using questions like:
- What is your goal?
- What is the focus of our conversation today?
- What accomplishments [or setbacks] have you had since our last coaching session?
- What do you want?
- How important is _____ to you?
- What will help you achieve your goal?
- What will get you moving forward?
- Where can you find data that will help you make that decision?
- What are you seeking to achieve?
- How can you do _____ better than anyone else?
- What will you do about _____?
- What will you do as a result of our conversation?

If You're Coaching a Planner

Try using questions like:
- What accomplishments [or setbacks] have you had since our last coaching session?
- How will you know whether our conversation is successful?
- How will you be able to recognize success?
- What do you want?

- What steps will you take to accomplish _____?
- What has worked for you in the past?
- How are you going to do _____?
- How can you make _____ work more effectively?
- How will you decide which step to take next?
- What will you do by when?
- What are one or two things you can do to meet this challenge?
- What are your next steps?

If You're Coaching an Arranger

Try using questions like:

- How are you today?
- How do you feel about this?
- What would you like to focus on during our time together?
- What does the feedback you received tell you about your strengths [or growth opportunities]?
- What does this feedback mean to you?
- If you were sitting in their seat, how would you view the actions you are considering?
- How is your behavior impacting others?
- How is your behavior supporting you in [or distracting you from] achieving your goals?
- What resources are available to support you in this?
- Who can support you in this?
- Who will you speak to?
- Who else needs to be involved?
- What did you gain from our time?

If You're Coaching a Visualizer

Try using questions like:

- What are you developing right now?
- What are the gaps between where you are today and where you want to be in six months?
- Paint me a picture of the ideal future state.

- What do you think about _____?
- What are you considering?
- What ideas do you have for addressing _____?
- What action can you take in this moment to help you achieve _____?
- If there was something else you could do, what would it be?
- What barriers can you foresee that will need to be addressed as you implement your next action steps?
- What was your "ah-ha" moment during our conversation?

There may be times when you find yourself wishing that everyone you work with could have the same Productivity Style as you. How clear, simple, and effortless things would be, with no need to ever explain, clarify, or translate ideas from one "language" to another!

But be careful what you wish for! As we've seen throughout this chapter, every Productivity Style has its own blind spots as well as its own unique strengths. A team whose members share the same style is likely to run up against unexpected difficulties that can derail projects— obvious problems they literally could not see because of the blind spots native to their shared style.

That's why true diversity—not just of gender, race, or ethnicity, but of Productivity Style—is such a valuable asset to an organization. The next time you feel frustrated with a colleague whose differing style leaves you confused or exasperated, take a deep breath and a second look. That person probably has a unique and valuable perspective to share that can help you and your organization achieve much more—provided you have the openness to recognize and appreciate it.

14

Lead a Meeting Revolution

HAVE YOU STARTED HOLDING MEETINGS IN THE OFFICE bathroom? You laugh, but that is exactly what happened to Roxanne.

As you recall from chapter 12, Roxanne is a senior leader at one of the largest foundations in the country. As chief legal counsel, her input is sought on virtually every transaction in the office. Her days are filled with back-to-back meetings and conference calls. She is frequently double- and even triple-booked, and a good day is one when she can actually get a break to visit the office bathroom. And that is when it happened.

Roxanne was rushing down the hall, running late for her next meeting, because the prior meeting had run long, as usual. She quickly darted into the ladies' room and made her way into one of the stalls. She was still seated there when the bathroom door opened. Roxanne heard footsteps, but of course she couldn't identify who had entered—not until the steps came closer and she heard a voice that she recognized as belonging to Susan, one of her teammates.

"Roxanne, is that you? I recognize those red shoes—they're my favorites!"

Nonplussed, Roxanne confessed, "Yes, it's me," wondering how she had gotten herself into a conversation under these awkward circumstances.

"Oh, I'm so glad I caught you!" Susan said. "I got the papers about the Hanson family trust donation. But there are some details I don't understand. Can you put me in touch with the lawyer who handles the trust? I have some questions about the tax exemption that I'm sure he can answer."

As Susan continued her interrogation, Roxanne flushed the toilet, rearranged her clothing, and emerged from the stall, red-faced. Susan was there in the bathroom with two of her colleagues. "Hi, Roxanne," Erica said; Paula just nodded as she dabbed at a small stain on her collar before the bathroom mirror.

As Roxanne washed her hands, she told Susan, "I've been in touch with the Hanson lawyer. He's very responsive and I'm sure he'll be able to help you. Sharon has his number and his e-mail."

"Oh, thanks!" Susan replied gratefully.

"I've got a question too," Erica chimed in. "It's about the orchestra grant I've been working on. Do we have a date when the funds are supposed to arrive?"

"I think so," Roxanne answered. "Randy Fowler has that information. He's out today, but he should be back tomorrow."

Paula shook her head. "No," she interjected. "I spoke to his assistant. Randy has the flu. He's going to be out all week."

"Oh, what a shame!" Erica said. "I was counting on him to help me with my presentation for the staff meeting on Friday. Roxanne, is there someone else who can take his place?"

Roxanne was considering Erica's question when the ludicrousness of the whole situation suddenly struck her.

"I have a question for the three of you," she exclaimed. "Why are we having this conversation in the ladies' bathroom?"

Susan, Erica, and Paula simply stared at Roxanne as if the answer was obvious. "Because," Susan replied, "this is the only time all day when you haven't been in a meeting!"

Roxanne is not the only manager who finds she is racing from meeting to meeting. According to one study, the average CEO spends approximately 67 percent of their time in meetings.[1] Anecdotal evidence and the complaints of my clients suggest that managers at other levels have similar schedules. The National Statistics Council reports that eleven million business meetings occur each day, and that 37 percent of employee time is spent in meetings.[2] Just look around your office. Where is everybody? If your workplace is a typical one, the answer is obvious: They are all in a meeting.

Meetings are unavoidable, and when they are conducted effectively, they can lead to innovation, higher-performing teams, and a stronger bottom line. However, too often, meetings are ineffective, irrelevant, wasteful, and costly. The fact is that the meeting culture consuming America is unsustainable and unproductive. How many meetings did you attend last week that lacked an agenda, started late, and ended late? How often did you attend a meeting without knowing why you were even there? How many meetings actually resulted in a new idea or an actionable decision? The answers tell you all you need to know about the problems with the way we manage our meetings.

Too many meetings fail to generate any meaningful return on the investment of time and energy they demand. They also undermine individual productivity. Our meeting-intensive culture forces people to complete their work in the margins of their day—early in the morning and late at night—impacting their health, motivation, and work/life balance.

Something has got to give.

IS THIS MEETING REALLY NECESSARY?

The first step to reforming our dysfunctional meeting culture is to start questioning the personal and professional value of each and every meeting you attend.

Instead of automatically accepting that next meeting request, pause and consider the meeting's return on investment for you. Will this meeting assist you in achieving your goals? How does the purpose of the meeting (if any!) align with the company's strategic priorities? What contribution can you make in the meeting? Will anyone even notice if you are not present? Will this meeting be energizing, or will it suck the life right out of you? Will this meeting be merely a rehash of the last five meetings?

Above all, is attending this meeting the highest and best use of your time right now? If not, revolt—decline the meeting request.

Remember, every time you say yes to one thing, you are saying no to something else. Because time is a commodity, the meetings you agree to attend are far from costless. That's why it's essential to begin questioning the value of every meeting.

Of course, in our meeting-centric business world, people may be surprised and disappointed to have you turn down their meeting requests. You will learn to select your meetings—to choose the meetings that are most important so that the most crucial relationships in your life are being nurtured. Sometimes the right choices are not obvious, and sometimes making them can be painful.

One of my most important clients asked me to attend a meeting in Chicago one October 31. As I always do, I evaluated the meeting using the questions listed above. "It's a high-value meeting," I said to myself, "one where I can make a meaningful contribution and one that is directly connected with my company's strategic goals." "I'll be there," I told the client.

But after I hung up the phone, I turned to my calendar to book the meeting and noticed a single word printed alongside the date: HALLOWEEN. Of course! October 31 is Halloween—a special day for my three-year-old, EC. She had already picked out her costume, Hello Kitty, and she was looking forward to attending the neighborhood party and making her trick-or-treat rounds with me in tow.

I picked up the phone and called my client back. "I'm sorry," I said, "but I just realized I had overlooked another unbreakable commitment for the thirty-first. Can we please reschedule our meeting?"

"Is your other commitment really unbreakable?" my client responded, sounding slightly irritated.

"I'm afraid so," I said. "Would it be possible to meet on the first or the second instead?" Within a few moments, we found an alternative date.

In organizing our complex calendars, it's inevitable that we may disappoint people from time to time—but by scheduling a meeting in Chicago for October 31, I was disappointing the wrong person. That is why I could not let it stand.

Of course, everyone needs to make these kinds of decisions according to a unique set of personal values and goals. Halloween trick-or-treating is not an unbreakable commitment in everyone's calendar. For you, what matters most may be an upcoming seminar where you will learn a crucial skill you want to use as a springboard into your next position, or a day dedicated to exercise and meditation that you have planned for weeks as a way of recharging after a stressful year at work. The key is to focus on your most important goals—whatever they are—and to have the courage to say no to meetings that do not help you pursue those goals.

It is also equally important to remember your Productivity Style and the Productivity Styles of your colleagues and team members, because meetings have different value for each style. My professional colleague Nicole shared this story with me:

A few years ago, I had a colleague who was obsessed with "keeping people in the loop" and having every team member attend every meeting. This inefficiency drove me insane and led to several clashes. I see now that the reason my colleague acted in this way, which I considered irrational and counterproductive, wasn't because he was thoughtless or didn't value people's time. It was because of his intense need to feel connected to and validated by others. He was proud of our company and wanted nothing more than to be perceived as a valuable and contributing member.

Nicole's colleague most likely had a primary preference as an Arranger, which helps to explain his strong need to make personal connections with others. Meetings filled this need for him. In contrast, a Prioritizer views meetings merely as opportunities to collect and present data and facts in a very efficient manner; a Planner values meetings if they help him understand processes and procedures; and a Visualizer uses meetings to ideate, explore, and integrate concepts. Each Productivity Style brings different goals and needs to the meeting process. Recognize these differences in yourself and others as you ask whether a particular meeting is really necessary.

It is time for a meeting revolution. Start your revolution today. Question the value of every meeting, consider your Productivity Style meeting needs and those of your colleagues, and, when you must, choose to disappoint the *right* people.

UNDERSTAND YOUR MEETING ALTERNATIVES

There are really only six types of meetings—informational meetings, decision-making meetings, problem-solving meetings, brainstorming meetings, team-building meetings, and instruction or skill-development meetings. Understanding the differences is an important first step in improving the way you plan and participate in meetings.

- *Informational meetings* are meetings where information is shared, and no action is required from the meeting attendees other than to digest and process the information.
- *Decision-making meetings* are designed to make a decision. Key leaders and stakeholders who have the necessary information and authority are present, and the meeting concludes with a decision.

- *Problem-solving meetings* are meetings to address a specific business issue. Data and background information on the problem are presented, potential solutions to the problem are discussed, and the
  meeting ideally concludes with agreed-upon action steps to either
  resolve the problem or gather additional information on it.
- *Brainstorming meetings* are ideation sessions designed to innovate,
  create, and explore novel ideas related to current business challenges
  or opportunities. These meetings tend to be long, involve multiple
  constituencies and stakeholders, and frequently produce a list of
  ideas to be implemented by another team or group.
- *Team-building meetings* are designed to strengthen the relationships
  on a team. These meetings may be off-site events that involve non-
  business activities like volunteering to build a house together, completing a ropes course, or celebrating a significant personal event like
  a birthday or the birth of a child.
- *Instruction or skill-development meetings* are held to teach and develop new skills. These skills may be soft skills like communication
  and presentation delivery, or technical skills like how to complete a
  loan request or use a new customer database program.

To lead your meeting revolution, the first step is to get very clear on
the types of meetings you are leading or attending and then look for
meeting alternatives. These can save you and your team members enormous amounts of time.

Perhaps the most unnecessary type of meeting is the informational
meeting. Conveying information can be accomplished in many different
ways. For example, instead of holding a Monday morning staff meeting
where information is shared and people talk about their weekends, consider a weekly update sent via e-mail instead. When I worked for Bristol-
Myers Squibb, my team received a weekly voicemail from David, our
manager, with all of the information we needed for that week. David's
voicemails were succinct, timely, and very useful. Ask colleagues in other
companies how they communicate information and updates. Information

can be posted on your company's internal message boards and/or intranet site. You can even consider going "old school" by posting a paper flyer on the doors of the bathroom stalls, on the refrigerator in the office break room, or on a bulletin board in the hall. Get creative—you have nothing to lose but a weekly gathering that needlessly consumes an hour or more of your team's valuable time.

If you feel that an informational meeting is imperative, consider the divide-and-conquer approach used by one of my clients. The company's sales division holds useful but time-consuming monthly update meetings where recent sales metrics are presented, new product features are discussed, and company news is shared. To improve the efficiency of the meetings, the manager decided that his team members would take turns attending the meetings. Now two members attend the meeting, take notes, compare and consolidate their notes to ensure that no essential details are missed, and then e-mail an update to the team. The team members who attend the meeting know that they are responsible for delivering accurate information to their teammates. As a result, they are fully engaged and present—no checking e-mail or instant messages during the meeting. Result: No one on the team has missed a product update or a company announcement, and the team is exceeding their sales targets each month.

Decision-making and problem-solving meetings generally do not have viable meeting alternatives. Dialogue and discussion, essential components of each of these meetings, cannot be replicated outside of a meeting format. But targeted premeeting preparation can streamline and shorten meetings of these kinds. For example, sending the data, background, and any collateral materials on the decision or problem prior to the meeting enables participants to prepare effectively for it. Precious meeting time can be spent on discussion rather than orienting and grounding everyone in the context and history.

Brainstorming and team-building meetings also require a live, collaborative format. However, the effectiveness of the meeting can be enhanced if premeeting materials are sent in advance of the meeting and participants are encouraged to ideate beforehand.

Skill development does not have to be confined to a traditional in-person classroom format. There are robust self-paced online programs and platforms available to teach a wide variety of skills. Define clearly the goals and objectives of the training and use these to guide your thinking as you explore alternative delivery methods.

Finally, when evaluating meeting alternatives, consider the primary Productivity Style of the participants and try to leverage that style's strengths.

For example, Prioritizers are information junkies who cannot get enough facts and data. Informational meetings fuel their addiction, as long as they are short and succinct. Ask your Prioritizer colleagues to suggest alternative information delivery channels to replace an informational meeting. They will happily share their ideas on how to disseminate and collect information in the most efficient and effective manner.

Planners love instructional or skill-development meetings, which give them a chance to learn new information and processes. Ask your Planner colleagues to suggest an alternative to the traditional instructional or skill-development meeting, because their focus on process and form make them ideally suited to determine how to teach new skills. You may be surprised by what they come up with.

For a Visualizer, a brainstorming meeting is invigorating, exciting, and stimulating. However, it is not the meeting itself that is so stimulating, it is the act of brainstorming. Ask a Visualizer to suggest an alternative form of brainstorming that could be done virtually, remotely, or in a completely different way. Leverage the innovative talents of your Visualizer colleagues and you may discover a very novel way to brainstorm.

Consider meeting alternatives. They can jump-start your revolution by eliminating a significant fraction of the meetings you now hold. Imagine all you can accomplish during the extra hours in your day!

MEETING SUCCESS DEPENDS ON YOUR PLANNING

It was eleven o'clock, and Alex was already attending his fourth meeting of the day. But his mood was surprisingly upbeat. "At least this meeting won't be a waste of time," he thought as he settled into his chair. "Everyone in the room received the product safety data from the last round of prototype testing a week ago. All we have to do is discuss the results and make a decision on the next phase of product development. We'll have a clear forward path for the next three months, and the whole meeting shouldn't take longer than fifteen minutes." He smiled at his six colleagues as they joined him around the conference table.

Twenty minutes later, however, Alex's mood had soured. The discussion he expected hadn't materialized. Instead, the room was silent as Alex's six colleagues flipped through the pages of data from the product safety tests. It was clear that none of the meeting participants had analyzed the data prior to the meeting; they were reading it now for the first time. And there was no telling whether they'd be prepared to make a decision about future steps without additional review and analysis. Alex groaned in frustration as he glanced at his watch. "Another wasted hour!" he thought.

Alex's experience—one that most of us have shared—reflects a vital truth about meetings: The success of any meeting depends on premeeting reflection and planning. This means that the role of the meeting leader is particularly crucial.

When you are the leader of a meeting, to drastically improve your chances of conducting an effective, efficient meeting, start by reflecting on the following questions in advance:

- Why do we need to meet? What is the purpose of the meeting? Which of the six meeting types does it fit?
- What is the outcome I want to achieve as a result of this meeting?

- Is there an alternative format I can use to achieve the outcome?
- If a meeting is essential, what is the ideal format to achieve the meeting outcomes—an in-person meeting, a virtual meeting, or a combination of the two? Due to the physical location of the meeting participants, an in-person meeting may not be possible. However, if it is possible to meet in person, I strongly encourage you to do so or to use videoconferencing technology so that you can see the participants. A significant portion of our communication is nonverbal, and if you cannot see the people in the meeting, you may miss the subtle cues indicating understanding, agreement, misunderstanding, and/or disagreement.
- Who needs to attend the meeting?
- What information do I need from the attendees?
- What do the attendees need to know or complete in advance of the meeting to achieve the meeting outcome?
- What expectations do I have for the meeting attendees regarding preparation and participation? How will I communicate these expectations?

Answering all these questions and methodically acting on the answers will go a long way toward ensuring that the meeting focuses on—and achieves—its real purpose.

When you are a meeting participant, you still have an important responsibility beforehand. As always, you should evaluate the meeting's value and its return on investment for you before accepting the invitation. If you decide to attend, reflect on the following questions:

- What is the unique contribution I can make in this meeting?
- What preparation is required?
- What do I need to do prior to the meeting to ensure I can be engaged, focused, and fully present?

Whether you are a meeting leader or an ordinary attendee, premeeting reflection and planning is a strategic and high-value investment of your time. Remember to leverage your Productivity Style strengths in your planning and premeeting reflection to make this process work for you. Commit to making every meeting you lead or attend effective, productive, and impactful—and use advance planning and reflection to make sure it happens.

UNLEASH THE POWER OF A PERFECT AGENDA

A meeting without an agenda is like a ship without a rudder. Without an agenda, there is no way to guide the conversation to achieve the meeting's goal. Revolt against agendaless meetings—always ask for an agenda in advance. If the leader cannot provide one, you should either decline the meeting or (if you feel you must attend anyway) accept the fact that there is a high probability that your time investment will yield a poor return.

When you lead a meeting, create what I call a POWER agenda:

- Purpose
- Outcomes
- Who
- Execution
- Responsibility

A POWER agenda will ensure that you are clear on the purpose and outcomes for the meeting and guarantee that you have a thoughtful, organized plan to achieve them. Here's how it works:

- *Purpose.* Clearly state at the top of the agenda the meeting purpose. For example, "Purpose: To analyze quarterly social media metrics."

- *Outcomes.* Below the purpose, list the meeting outcomes—the actual results you are aiming for, which will determine the success or failure of the meeting. For example, "Outcomes: To determine a new Twitter strategy to increase our number of followers; to determine frequency of Facebook postings; and to identify content themes that generate the most conversation on LinkedIn." Then, using the outcomes as your guide, list the topic areas and discussion points or questions to guide the discussion. For example, "Topic: Twitter—What was last month's most frequently retweeted tweet? How many followers do we have? How are they finding us? Using this data, what do we need to do differently to attract additional followers?"

- *Who.* Next to each topic, identify who will lead this topic discussion and how long the topic will be discussed during the meeting.

- *Execution.* At the bottom of the agenda, leave room to list the execution or next action steps that will be taken as a result of the meeting.

- *Responsibility.* Identify who is responsible for each action item and when they will be expected to communicate to the meeting participants what they have accomplished.

In drafting your POWER agenda, leverage your own Productivity Style. For example, if you are a Prioritizer or a Planner, create a traditional agenda—linear and detailed, with bullet points in a document format. By contrast, if you are Visualizer, try brainstorming and mind-mapping the agenda using Post-it Notes, colored markers, or an online mind-mapping program like the ones mentioned in chapter 7. You could even use the first three minutes of the meeting to sketch your mind map on a whiteboard for the entire group, explaining it as you go. (See figures 14.1 and 14.2 for two sample POWER agendas, one using the traditional bulleted format, the other created using the mind-mapping technique.) If you are an Arranger, use a dictation service like Copytalk to dictate your agenda, then let Copytalk transcribe it and e-mail it to you.

```
AGENDA: Planning Meeting for Annual Sales Conference

PURPOSE: To start the planning process for next year's
sales conference, to be held January 17-18.

OUTCOMES: To create a master list of planning activities,
who is responsible for each, and a timeline for their
completion.

TOPICS:

    ▪ SITE SELECTION: Same location as last year (ballroom
      at Empire Hotel)? Or consider alternative sites?
      TOPIC LEADER: Jill  TIME: 15 minutes
    ▪ PROGRAM DEVELOPMENT: Detailed schedule for both days
      will be needed, including complete list of
      presentations, product demonstrations, and speakers.
      TOPIC LEADER: Randy  TIME: 20 minutes
    ▪ KEYNOTE SPEAKER: Ideas for a dynamic kickoff
      speaker? Budget available? TOPIC LEADER: Dana  TIME:
      10 minutes
    ▪ TRAVEL AND HOTEL ARRANGEMENTS: Who will work with
      our travel department to coordinate these plans? Any
      support or help needed? TOPIC LEADER: Sangeet  TIME:
      5 minutes
    ▪ COMMUNICATIONS: Team needed to take charge of
      informing all participants about our plans and
      responding to questions/suggestions. TOPIC LEADER:
      Nora  TIME: 10 minutes

EXECUTION AND RESPONSIBILITY:
```

Figure 14.1. A POWER agenda using the traditional bulleted format.

A POWER agenda can help ensure that a meeting stays on track, achieves its stated goals, and concludes with agreed-upon next action steps. It also enables participants to fully prepare for the meeting and make meaningful contributions.

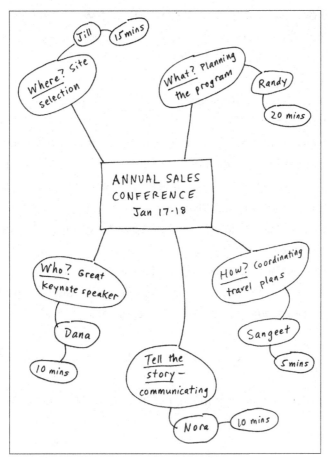

Figure 14.2. A POWER agenda using the mind-mapping technique.

INVITE THE RIGHT PEOPLE (AND *ONLY* THE RIGHT PEOPLE)

Gina walked into the conference room. She found that all of the chairs at the table were already occupied, and the chairs along the sides were beginning to fill up as well—twenty seats in all. She thought to herself, *"All* of these people were invited to this meeting?" Scanning the room, she noticed that the people with the authority to make the decisions required during the meeting were not in the room, but their team members were present. Gina squeezed into one of the few remaining seats and thought to herself, "This is going to be a long meeting—and I bet we're going to leave the room without making a decision."

Gina is obviously an experienced meeting attendee. She understands how the attendance at a meeting can crucially impact its effectiveness and impact.

If you are in charge of organizing a meeting, it is imperative to invite the right people and *only* the right people to the meeting. Now, if you are an Arranger this can be challenging, because you want to be inclusive and ensure that connection and collaboration are occurring on the team. However, remember that inviting too many people—or the wrong people—can and will derail your meeting.

To begin thinking about who should be on the list, start by recognizing that there are four types of meeting attendees: *the decision maker, the influencer, the resource person,* and *the executer.*

- *The decision maker* is the person with the authority to make decisions.
- *The influencer* has the pull and network within the organization to advocate and popularize meeting decisions and initiatives.
- *The resource person* has specific knowledge, skills, and expertise needed to inform the decisions and create plans for executing those decisions.
- *The executer* has the knowledge, skills, resources, and authority to successfully complete the work resulting from the meeting.

An ideal meeting has each of these types of meeting attendees in attendance. Of course, one person can represent multiple roles, while more than one representative of a specific role may be required. For example, you may need three executers to complete a complex project discussed during the meeting.

If you are leading a meeting, ask yourself the following questions to determine who really needs to attend:

- What is the meeting outcome?
- Who in the organization must be present to achieve the meeting outcome?
- Who is the decision maker?
- Who is the influencer?
- Who is the resource person?
- Who is the executer?
- If there are people who will not be invited to the meeting but who have been invited to similar meetings in the past, how will you communicate your rationale for excluding them in this instance?

With the answers to these questions in mind, carefully consider the optimal number of attendees to achieve the meeting objective. The number should align with the desired outcome. For example, if the meeting is an information-sharing meeting, it's likely that communication will be one way, with minimal interaction. That means the group size can be unlimited—for example, when important news affecting everyone in a large organization must be communicated, an information-sharing meeting may be held in a large auditorium holding hundreds of people, perhaps with remote video links to other company sites where thousands of other employees can listen in.

On the other hand, if the meeting is a brainstorming one, no more than twenty to thirty-five attendees is optimal. A larger group can help with idea proliferation, but if the group is closer to thirty-five attendees, consider planning smaller breakout sessions to ensure that all participants have the opportunity to contribute ideas.

Problem-solving meetings ideally include twelve to fifteen attendees, limited to the key stakeholders. For decision-making meetings, consider scheduling sessions with six to fourteen attendees, perhaps broken down into smaller teams, to evaluate and select options first. Then hold a final meeting, limited to three to six decision makers, to make the final decision.

Determining whom to invite to a meeting can be challenging,

politically charged, and time-intensive. However, without the right people in the meeting, nothing will be accomplished, and everyone who attends will waste the most precious commodity—their time. Invite the right people and *only* the right people to your meetings.

DETERMINE THE IDEAL LENGTH FOR YOUR MEETING

How often have you left a meeting and thought to yourself, "We could have concluded this meeting fifteen minutes ago—or even an hour ago"? At some point, we all stopped carefully considering the ideal length for a meeting and succumbed to the default setting in our calendars, allocating one hour for every meeting, regardless of its purpose. It is time to break from the pack. Start questioning the length of all of the meetings you lead and attend.

If you are leading a meeting, carefully consider the purpose, outcomes, and format to determine its ideal length. If the purpose of your meeting is to brainstorm a product to compete directly with your number one competitor, then you will probably need a large amount of time. If the purpose is to communicate the new expense policy and show how to use the new reporting program, then a few minutes is probably sufficient.

If you are leading a virtual meeting by telephone or computer network, be cognizant that you will probably only have the partial attention of your far-flung, invisible attendees due to multitasking. That means that if the meeting exceeds forty-five to sixty minutes, you are guaranteed a significant deterioration in attention and focus. So for meetings of this kind, shorter is definitely better.

In practically every case, your goal should be to keep meetings as focused, limited, and brief as possible. According to John Medina, author of *Brain Rules,* the average adult's attention span is ten minutes. Once a discussion lasts longer than that, it's necessary to do something emotionally relevant to regain people's attention.[3] No wonder people joke about experiencing "Death by PowerPoint"! A ninety-minute PowerPoint presentation meeting violates the way our brains actually work, destroying the purpose of a meeting and wasting everybody's time.

So consider simply shortening all of your regularly scheduled meetings by fifteen minutes. This change automatically leads to a reduction in chatter, off-topic rambling, and rehashing of previous points—all common occurrences that undermine the effectiveness of the meeting.

One of my clients, an aerospace company, has revolutionized its meeting culture by establishing a default meeting format of fifteen-minute meetings *without chairs*. If there is a very specific reason for a longer meeting, the time may be extended; if there are team members who are unable to stand, the team members sit in a circle facing each other with no tables. Otherwise the default format applies. Since revolutionizing its culture, the company now holds fewer meetings that are more productive, impactful, and engaging.

Recently, a colleague and I led a four-hour visioning session for a company planning its own meeting revolution. The leadership team was skeptical that we could create a vision and begin mapping an action plan to achieve it in only four hours. But by the end of our session, not only had the team mapped out its vision for the future, but it had also formed innovation teams and started outlining action plans for achieving the vision. What's more, the session ended fifteen minutes early!

How did it happen? Planning and preparation. The participants completed a presession survey and received multiple communications about the meeting and their expected participation. We developed and used a POWER agenda, the right participants were invited, and we shortened each exercise and activity slightly to create just enough tension to keep people engaged and moving forward.

You too may be skeptical that shorter meetings can be as effective and productive as longer ones. Give it a try. You may be delightfully surprised by the results—and I promise you that none of your colleagues will be heard complaining, "Gee, I'm disappointed that today's meeting was so short!"

ENGAGE *ALL* MEETING PARTICIPANTS

I glanced around the room as the meeting droned on. A few people were halfheartedly taking notes; others looked as if they were daydreaming or wondering when lunch would be served. Then my attention was caught by a faint snorting sound from my left. I turned toward the sound and saw a gray-suited man three seats away with his head bobbing gently up and down and his eyes closed. Could it be? Yes—he was asleep! Another faint snore emerged, the first of several emitted in a gentle, rhythmic pattern as a light snooze turned into a full-blown nap. His colleagues on either side were oblivious—one was rapidly typing into her smartphone, the other doodling on a yellow pad.

"Where am I?" I wondered. "Have I been transported back in time to my most boring class in junior high school?"

No. Sad to say, this was a state-of-the-business update meeting at a Fortune 500 company, and at the lectern the president had been reading his PowerPoint slides for over sixty minutes in a very dry, monotonous voice. No wonder his entire audience was disengaged.

Engaging all the participants in your meeting is essential, and actually very simple. As we have discussed, every Productivity Style has its own communication preferences. The simplest way to ensure that you are engaging and communicating effectively with everyone is to ensure that you answer the *what, how, who,* and *why* questions for each discussion item on your agenda. In this way, you'll appeal to the communication preferences of all your attendees, regardless of their Productivity Style. The table that follows provides the specific guidance you will need.

WORK SIMPLY:
STRATEGIES TO ENGAGE ALL MEETING PARTICIPANTS BY PRODUCTIVITY STYLE

To Engage a Prioritizer

Prioritizers are focused on data, facts, and figures; they want to know the answers to *what* questions: What is the goal? What is the objective? What are the key facts? What data or reference material is available?

To Engage a Planner

Planners are focused on process, order, and structure; they want to know *how* the ideas will actually be implemented: How will we accomplish the goal? When is the due date? How many people are involved? How will we approach this problem or issue?

To Engage an Arranger

Arrangers are focused on people, the team, and communication among participants in any project; they want answers to *who* questions: Who is involved? Who needs to know this information? Who is the audience, and how do they prefer to receive information?

To Engage a Visualizer

Visualizers are focused on the big picture, novel ideals, the conceptual framework, and the ways this meeting is connected to the strategic purpose of the organization; they want answers to *why* questions: Why is this important? Why is this idea or approach being explored? Why are the participants involved? Why do they need to know?

One of my clients, a global construction company, was pitching their services to a large health care system in Washington, D.C.—a new industry for them and therefore a significant opportunity. Lacie, their head of business development, was preparing the presentation and prepping the team for the upcoming meeting on Thursday. I was in their office on Tuesday, working with the leadership team on communicating effectively using individual Productivity Styles, when Lacie suddenly blurted out, "Wait a second! Our health care presentation only answers the *what* and *how* questions—we haven't addressed the *who* or the *why!*"

Lacie was right. The company's presentations were always focused on the facts, figures, and data of the projects; they routinely included pages of cost estimates and safety data, as well as multiple slides outlining the project plan and critical decision points. This was all important and useful information. But what Lacie had realized was that she and the team had not spent any time discussing *who* would be using the new buildings and their reactions to the spaces, or *why* these new buildings would appeal to critically ill patients and their families as well as serve the health of the entire community.

Result: As written, the presentation would likely resonate with the Prioritizers and Planners in the room, while leaving the Arrangers and Visualizers bored and unmoved.

Lacie and her team revised the presentation to include *who* and *why* information. They added additional color, pictures, and quotations from satisfied customers to round out what was originally a very analytical, linear presentation.

When I checked back in with Lacie a few weeks later, she was ecstatic. Her company had received the bid and would be constructing the health care system's new cardiac care building. "We never had such a successful proposal presentation!" Lacie declared. "Every single person in the room said that we were the obvious choice for the project. They loved us!"

As you plan and prepare for your meetings make sure that you have answered the *what, how, who,* and *why* questions for each item on your agenda, thereby maximizing your chances to engage and effectively communicate with all meeting participants.

WHO HAS THE A? FOLLOW UP TO MAXIMIZE YOUR MEETING ROI

A meeting can be carefully planned and expertly led, but if the leader and meeting participants do not execute on the action steps that result, the entire meeting will still be a waste of time.

To maximize the return on investment (ROI) from your meeting, use these two simple strategies: Determine who has the "A," then streamline meeting follow-up. Let's consider each strategy in turn.

Paul Joyce, a colleague and exceptional consultant, taught me the nuances around true accountability. Paul and his team have designed a robust process, called the Accountability Map, for determining roles, responsibilities, and accountability on leadership teams.

To populate the Accountability Map, the leadership team is interviewed and asked a series of questions about their roles, performance criteria, and current projects. Paul and his team then build a spreadsheet highlighting where there are redundancies and accountability gaps. When they review the map with the senior team, they discuss these redundancies and gaps. For each specific initiative or deliverable, they ask, "Who has the A?"

The A, of course, stands for accountability. As Paul explains, only one person can be truly accountable for a particular initiative. The A does not mean that they must personally perform all the work; it means that they own and are responsible for making sure that the work is successfully completed, no matter who handles any specific task involved.

Simple? Yes. But at times I have seen clients ask two or three people to be accountable for a project. This kind of diffusion of responsibility never works; it inevitably results in nothing being done, with each of the two or three "accountable" individuals assuming that "someone else" would take charge. Only one person can have the A. So for each action step that arises during your meeting, pause and determine who is accountable for leading, guiding, and ensuring the successful completion of this action step. Do not move forward to the next item until you have determined who has the A.

Once you have determined who has the A, discuss follow-up procedures. When is the action item due? In what form? Do all of the participants need an update? If so, how will this update be delivered? In a group e-mail? Orally at the next meeting? Posted on the company's SharePoint site or in another project management program? Will one person on the team receive all updates, incorporate them into the project plan or the next meeting agenda, and disseminate this document to the team? Or will you leverage your project management, collaboration tool, or existing e-mail system and have one person on your team responsible for inputting the tasks into the tool, assigning the tasks, and tracking follow-up?

All of these options may be viable, depending on the ways you and your team members are accustomed to communicating. How you choose to track your next action steps and follow up on your meeting action items is entirely up to you. However, in order to ensure your success, I recommend the following:

- Have one person in the meeting responsible for taking the meeting minutes and capturing the next action steps. This is a strength of Planners, so leverage that strength if you have a Planner in the meeting.
- Be clear. Vague, ambiguous action steps only create frustration and waste time. This is a strength of Prioritizers, so use that strength if you have a Prioritizer in the meeting. For example, you might ask Bill, "Please summarize our agreed-upon next action steps."
- Be consistent. Follow the same process for tracking and following up on next action steps after every meeting. Ask your Planner colleagues to either recommend a process or implement the process. This is another one of their strengths.
- Leverage the technology available to you, or create and use a next action steps template if you are not currently using a particular project

management or collaboration tool. Refer back to the task execution tools in chapter 7 as well as the project management tools listed in chapter 8.

Execute! Ensure that the time you invest in meetings generates a high ROI by determining who is accountable for each action step, and then decide on a clear, consistent follow-up process.

Yes, meetings can be time-consuming, boring, unfocused, and frustrating. We have all been there. But it does not have to be that way. Lead a meeting revolution where you work! You may become a hero to the team members and colleagues whom you help to liberate from the shackles of meeting dysfunction!

15

Put It All Together

IN THE PAGES OF THIS BOOK, I HAVE PRESENTED AN ARRAY OF tools and strategies related to every aspect of your life. But they are all in service of a single key message: *Work simply to live fully.*

Busyness is the noise that gets in your way. Turn down the noise by understanding and using your productive brain. Stop fighting against your natural wiring and what you know to be true for you. Instead, change the ways you work and live so that you can be the best you—creative, productive, energized, and happy.

Yes, it can be very difficult in the middle of a crazy Wednesday to dial down the noise to achieve want you really want. At times you just do what you must do—sleep, eat, work, feed the children—putting one foot in front of the other on what feels like a never-ending forced march. However, you and I both know that there is much more to life. There is joy, dancing, serving others, making a meaningful contribution to your community, stimulating work, chocolate, wine, long walks on the beach, and laughing so hard that your sides ache.

My wish for you is to claim it—to claim your purpose and live a rich, full life. Put everything together in this book in the way that works for you and watch your dreams come true. Here are a few suggestions that can help you do it.

GET CLEAR

"It is hard to see if your windshield is dirty." This is a lesson I learned from one of my favorite teachers, Sonia Choquette. Her advice: Examine what is holding you back and clouding your vision. Acknowledge it and then remove the dirt.

Is there any dirt and grime on your windshield? What is getting in the way of you seeing clearly? Where have you fallen prey to the busyness epidemic? What is driving your busyness? Is it shaped by your need to feel important, worthy, and valuable, and the abiding fear that the "real me" falls short? Is it fueled by the imperative that you stay at the office to be seen even if your most meaningful work is already finished? Is it technically driven busyness, where your tools, systems, strategies, and techniques for understanding, organizing, and managing work have simply failed to keep up with changing demands? Or is your busyness a combination of these?

Olivia, an attorney and book agent, was frantically busy juggling the demands of her career, her two children, her husband, her mother, her sister, her friends, the parent-teacher organization, her blog, and her volunteer commitments. At times, all these demands felt as if they were all in competition with one another. Olivia's windshield had become almost completely caked over with dust, dirt, and grime. She had tried the usual strategies to stop being busy—an e-mail management course, a new planner, and ideas and tips from friends and colleagues. None of it worked for more than a few days, because Olivia had not addressed what was driving her busyness.

Olivia's busyness was driven by the belief that if she was not always available to and for her clients, then she was not providing value and was unworthy of her compensation. It was also driven by tools and systems that were not aligned to her Productivity Style and the way she actually worked. Only after examining both the psychological and technical drivers of her busyness did Olivia begin to make lasting changes that would help her create the life she wanted.

Take a look at the dirt and grime that impedes your vision. Acknowledge it, and then take the necessary steps to scrub your windshield clean. Until it is clean, it is going to be difficult for you to find greater personal freedom, creativity, and joy. And isn't that the real goal?

EMBRACE YOUR PRODUCTIVITY STYLE

T-shirts labeled "One size fits all" never fit properly. The arm holes are too small, the neck opening is too large, or the sleeves are too long.

The same applies to one-size-fits-all approaches to personal productivity. Maybe you have tried to use a calendar tool you received in a time management workshop or those colored Post-it notes that a friend recommended. If the results were disappointing, the fault is not yours—it's the fault of tools and techniques that do not match your Productivity Style.

So instead of fighting against your natural thinking, learning, and communicating preferences, work with them. Identify your Productivity Style and then embrace it. Use your understanding to guide the choices you make to manage your attention, invest your time, get work done, tame your inbox, and design your workspace in ways that are customized for *you*—not for someone else.

KNOW WHERE YOU REALLY WANT TO GO

At the beginning of each new coaching engagement, I give my client a magic wand—an imaginary one, of course. "Ta-da!" I declare. "Today, everything in your life is exactly the way you want it!" This never fails to elicit a smile and a laugh. Who *wouldn't* want a magic wand accompanied by a promise like that?

But then the work begins, starting with some serious questions. Now that your life is exactly the way you want it, what has changed? What does your life—professional and personal—look like and feel like? What are you doing? Who are you doing it with?

It is amazing to listen to the shift in my clients' voices as they describe their magic-wand life. There is a new tone reflecting feelings of excitement, joy, fun, meaning, and purpose.

So now it's your turn. You have just been handed a magic wand. What do you really want? What are your dreams? Do not get bogged down in *shoulds*—you *should* want this because you are the partner in a consulting firm, you *should* want that because you are a loving husband or wife, son or daughter, you *should* want fill-in-the-blank because that is what everyone wants. Don't *should* all over yourself. Instead, imagine what you *really* want—and get ready to go for it.

SET YOUR GOALS AND ALIGN YOUR TIME SPEND

Once you get to the point where you can see, feel, taste, and touch your magic-wand life, set your goals and align your time spend to make that life a reality.

Write your READY goals—Realistic, Exciting, Action-oriented, Directive, and Yours. Then Aim your time spend, matching it to your goals with your calendar as the primary tool. Think carefully about each task or project you are considering putting on your calendar. Ask yourself, "How does this task or project move me one step closer toward achieving my goals?"

Be vigilant—do not allow tasks or projects onto your calendar that do not move you closer to your goals.

INVEST YOUR TIME WISELY TO ACHIEVE YOUR GOALS

How are you investing your time to achieve your goals? Look at your calendar—your time investment statement. What does it show you about your time spend? Are you giving away your time? If so, stop! Maximize the hours in each day by choosing time investment tactics that work for your Productivity Style. Time is a nonrenewable resource. Invest it wisely to achieve your goals.

FOCUS ON THE REAL WORK THAT IS ALIGNED TO YOUR GOALS

There is work—the routine, time-filling work most of us spend our days performing—and then there is your *real* work, the work that takes you one step closer to achieving your goals. Reshape your task list to focus on the real work you should be doing.

First, examine your assumptions. Where are you letting assumptions guide your decision-making process about the work that needs to be completed? Are assumptions that may be false, misleading, or unsupported getting in the way of you completing the work that is aligned with your personal goals?

Next, look at your current to-do list. What do you need to *stop* doing? Take a hard, critical look at your projects and tasks and ask yourself whether each project is still relevant, directly tied to your goals, and offers a significant return on your time investment. Eliminate the projects and tasks that deserve to be cut—no one is going to miss them, least of all you.

Then ask, "What do I need to *start* doing? What projects and tasks need to be added to my to-do list that will enable me to achieve my goals?" Put them on the list.

Leave the busy work to someone else, someone who does not want your magic-wand life. Focus on the real work that you are meant to do.

STOP REACTING AND START RESPONDING

You are in the driver's seat of your life. Stop reacting and start responding—thoughtfully, purposefully, and consciously.

Start by taking control of your work routines. Decide what work to complete by considering three variables—your time, the resources or tools available, and your energy level. Turn off the rings, pings, and buzzes on all of your devices. Make technology a tool that serves you, not a dictator to which you bow.

Then take control of your inbox. Use the E-mail Agility Circle to clear out your inbox, convert e-mails into tasks, forward them to the appropriate colleagues, or simply delete them. And use all of the e-mail technology tools to make your inbox work *for you*. Leverage every bell, whistle, and tool provided to you to simplify and streamline your e-mail communication.

Next, stop pushing papers. Build a retrieval system that lets you access any piece of information you want in seconds.

Finally, revolutionize your approach to meetings. If attending a particular meeting is not the highest and best use of your time, say no. Remember, every time you say yes to one thing, you are saying no to something else.

Reacting all day long is exhausting—and it does not help create your magic-wand life. Start responding instead.

ASK FOR HELP

People want to help. It took me a very long time to really believe this and turn down the voice inside me that says, "I have to do it all." But it's true—people want to be of service, to contribute, and to share their talents with others.

So ask for help. Learn to delegate effectively. Determine what you can and should delegate, avoid dumping and running, and set up your colleagues for success. In the end, both you and your organization will accomplish much more if you overcome your resistance to delegating and instead take full advantage of all the skills, talent, and knowledge your fellow team members have to offer.

DO NOT NEGLECT YOUR MAINTENANCE

Would you spend a day planting new plants in your backyard, investing both your time and money—and then fail to water them? Of course not.

Like those plants, your success is a living thing, which is why careful, regular maintenance is essential to your success. Planning is your maintenance, and the simplest and best way to think about it is in layers—from monthly planning down to weekly and daily planning.

Monthly planning maintains the big-picture view of your goals, commitments, and priorities, ensuring that your calendar is aligned with what really matters to you.

Weekly planning helps you focus on the projects and tasks you need to tackle now. It prevents your brain from having to remember and remind you of what you need to do—an unnatural task for which the brain is poorly suited. Weekly planning lets you review your projects, gather and process the stuff that has accumulated during the week, and ensure that it is properly organized.

Finally, daily planning ensures a laserlike focus on what you want to accomplish during the day. It helps you minimize distractions and control the competing projects that often come up.

Maintenance is essential to living your magic-wand life. Do not neglect it—or yourself.

Epilogue

Unlimited Achievement

THE BUSYNESS EPIDEMIC IS PERVASIVE AND SADLY DEMOCRATIC.
It affects us all, with symptoms that vary based on who we are and the type of work we do. Time, freedom, and meaning are the costs.

Thankfully, there is an alternative. When you work from your strengths, acknowledging your unique Productivity Style, and align your work and your tools to support you, it is easier to manage your days and weeks. When you recognize time as a nonrenewable resource and get clear on your priorities, it is easier to say yes to the things that really matter and no to the countless distractions vying for your attention. When you can work with uninterrupted focus, it is easier to tap into your latent, dormant creativity. And slowly, ever so slowly, you notice a shift in the conditions of your life. You are working simply and living fully.

Let's check back in with Andi, Brigham, Colin, Samantha, and Emily—the clients we first met back in chapters 1 and 2—and see how their lives have changed.

Andi realized that she could not outwork her work. She was going to have to radically change how she thought about her work, how she structured her workdays, and how she cared for herself and her family. She redesigned her professional and personal life from the ground up, establishing new boundaries around her work time and personal time. Realizing that self-care was vital, she made a commitment to running four times a week and eating healthy. She mastered crock-pot cooking and hired a housekeeper. Andi, Bill, and Christopher now spend their weekends boating on the lake near their home, playing outside, and enjoying one another. Andi was recently promoted to managing partner of the local office.

When we met for lunch recently, which we enjoyed without Andi checking her iPhone once, she told me that she had a wardrobe consultant coming over that evening to freshen up her look for spring to complement her chic new haircut. She looked lighter, freer, more confident, and excited. She was performing at the top of her game.

You may recall that Brigham had been working long hours that felt unproductive and unsatisfying. Something had to change—and change fast. Brigham and I worked together, reframing his understanding of his role and his unique contribution to his event-planning company. He completely redesigned his calendar, creating days dedicated to specific types of work as well as an entire day each week reserved for brainstorming, thinking, reading magazines, and writing. This weekly Brigham day has renewed his passion for his work and helped him reignite his natural creativity. As a result, his cutting-edge ideas about event management were recently featured in a popular trade magazine and the *New York Times*. What's more, his company is on track this year to have its most profitable year ever. Brigham is looking forward to what comes next for his company and himself.

Colin's legal practice was growing so rapidly that he was unable to keep up and had started turning prospective clients away. He and I prepared a strategy to build virtual platforms and infrastructure to support his expanding business. He took on a partner—a smart, analytical, hungry young attorney who was able to take over a significant portion of his caseload. He also hired an executive assistant and a personal assistant, and he redesigned his paralegal's job, tying a portion of her compensation to the firm's profitability, which prompted her to streamline her workflow and increase her billable hours by 30 percent.

Energized by these changes, Colin found a new office in an office building filled with other entrepreneurs that provided administrative support, a fully stocked kitchen, and well-appointed conference rooms. The printer that used to ride in the backseat of his car now sits on a credenza. Colin and his wife, Susan, have started attending concerts again and bought season tickets to their alma mater's football games. Colin has stopped eating sleeves of Girl Scout cookies for lunch, he looks ten years younger than when we started working together, and this month will be his most profitable to date.

Samantha had been disappointed when she did not receive the promotion she'd been hoping for, despite her long hours and personal sacrifices. As we looked deeper into her cognitive thinking style, how she worked and communicated, it became apparent that she was not speaking the language of her company's leaders. When Samantha would talk to her manager and the senior leaders, she would present big ideas and gloss over or overlook the tactics involved in implementing her ideas. She went to work to modify the way she communicated. She started communicating more effectively, writing clearer, more succinct, streamlined e-mails and presenting her ideas and new concepts using matrices and project plans via pictures rather than vague, high-level strategy.

George, Samantha's manager, says that something has shifted in her: "She's more responsive, she completes her work on or before deadlines, and she just successfully launched a groundbreaking IT training program. It's quite a change for the better!" Best of all, Samantha has gotten back to watching New England Patriots games without her computer open in front of her, as well as attending her son's baseball games and enjoying time with him on the weekends.

Emily was completely burned out from long hours, poor results, and lack of time to recharge. She had to change—and she did. She developed new workflow processes and communication strategies. She shifted how she invested her time, how she handled the incessant flow of e-mails, and the tactical execution of her work. She reduced her work hours to sixty a week and started receiving positive feedback on her work performance. She also started spending more time with her two little girls and her husband. She and Tom now have a regular weekly date night, and the family recently traveled to the beach for their first-ever vacation together. Emily has found her own simplicity and is finally living fully.

As for me, I no longer see busyness as a way to prove myself to the world. I have limited my travel and spend no more than three nights a week away from my family. I can now play in the backyard with EC for hours, focused, present, and fully available, not worried or distracted by my work or what needs to be done. I am also more deeply engaged with my clients and I am providing them with more impactful support. Andrew and I play more, I am running more, and I am spending more time with my friends. I am clear on why I am here and how I am to serve.

I am still a work in progress, still traveling on my journey to work simply and live fully. There are days and weeks where I spin out of control, overwhelmed and hooked by my psychological need to prove myself by doing it all. When this happens, I take a deep breath and remember that tomorrow is a new day, a day for a fresh start. And I start again.

Andi, Brigham, Colin, Samantha, Emily, and I all have very different lives, with varying interests, goals, priorities, and dreams. But we all have one thing in common: Busyness no longer defines us, ensnares us, derails us, undermines us. We are finally free to engage fully and meaningfully in life.

Now is the time for you to let your light fully shine in the world—to be a beacon of hope, inspiration, and encouragement for others, even as you pursue the goals that make your life richer, more meaningful, and more rewarding.

Today is your day. Work simply. Live fully.

Additional Tools to Work Simply

If you want additional resources and tools to work simply, visit the book's Web site:

www.carsontate.com

On the site, you can find resources like these:

- **Online Productivity Style Assessment.** Share the link with your colleagues, friends, and family. Let them identify their Productivity Style and use the strategies in the book to help you work and communicate more simply and effectively.

- **Application Materials**
  - Time value log template
  - Time investment tactics by Productivity Style
  - Task and project tactics by Productivity Style
  - How to convert e-mails to tasks
  - Clues and cues by Productivity Style

- **Productivity Style Differences Conversation Guide.** Get access to a conversation guide designed to help you discuss the different Productivity Styles on your team and how to more effectively work together (PDF format).

Acknowledgments

I'd like to thank my husband, Andrew, for his love, unfailing support, and encouragement, and my daughter, EC, for her love, laughter, and ability to keep me in the beautiful present moment. To Georgi Dienst and Allison Hickmon for being my soul sisters. To Sabrina Tully for being my "believing eyes." To Gail Angelo, John Bennett, Donna DeChant, Ryan Dienst, and Beth Purdy for their wise and thoughtful feedback and suggestions.

To Katherine Beaumont for believing in me and this book. To Brettne Bloom for guiding me and sharing her incredible wisdom and resources. To Niki Papadopoulos, my talented editor, for her insightful feedback and suggestions and the entire staff at Penguin for your dedication and tireless support. To Karl Weber for helping me shape this book into a presentable manuscript, and to all my clients for lending me your stories and allowing me to serve you.

Notes

Chapter 1: Work Smarter, Not Harder

1. John de Graaf, ed., *Take Back Your Time: Fighting Overwork and Time Poverty in America* (San Francisco: Berrett-Koehler, 2003).
2. W. Van Eerde, "Procrastination at Work and Time Management Training," *Journal of Psychology* 137 (2003): 421–34; B. J. C. Claessens, "Perceived Control of Time: Time Management and Personal Effectiveness at Work" (unpublished doctoral dissertation, Technische University Eindhoven, Netherlands); T. H. Macan, "Time Management: Test of a Process Model," *Journal of Applied Psychology* 79 (1994): 381–91; G. Slaven and P. Totterdall, "Time Management Training: Does It Transfer to the Workplace?" *Journal of Managerial Psychology* 8 (1993): 20–28; C. Orpen, "The Effect of Time Management Training on Employee Attitudes and Behavior: A Field Experiment," *Journal of Psychology* 128 (1994): 393–96.
3. A. M. Tripoli, "Planning and Allocating: Strategies for Managing Priorities in Complex Jobs," *European Journal of Work and Organizational Psychology* 7 (1998): 455–76.
4. E. Cools and H. Van den Broeck, "Development and Validation of the Cognitive Style Indicator," *Journal of Psychology* 141, no. 4 (2007): 359–87.

Chapter 3: What's Your Productivity Style?

1. Readers interested in learning more about this fascinating field of research can begin with the following seminal articles: E. Cools and H. Van den Broeck, "Development and Validation of the Cognitive Style Indicator," *Journal of Psychology* 141, no. 4 (2007): 359–87; J. Hayes and C. W. Allison, "Cognitive Style and Its Relevance for Management Practice," *British Journal of Management* 5 (1994): 53–71; R. G. Hunt et al., "Cognitive Style and Decision Making," *Organizational Behavior and Human Decision Processes* 44 (1989): 436–52; M. Kozhevnikov, "Cognitive Styles in the Context of Modern Psychology: Toward an Integrated Framework of Cognitive Style," *Psychological Bulletin* 133, no. 3 (2007): 464–81.

2. F. E. Bloom, A. Lazerson, and L. Hofstader, *Brain, Mind and Behavior* (New York: W. H. Freeman, 1985).

3. Ned Herrmann, *The Creative Brain* (Kingsport, TN: Ned Herrmann Group, 1989).

4. Carson F. Tate, "Whole Brain Thinking and Knowledge-Worker Productivity" (master's thesis, McColl School of Business, Queens University, Charlotte, NC, 2011).

Chapter 4: Manage Your Attention

1. Jonathan B. Spira and Joshua B. Feintuch, "The Cost of Not Paying Attention: How Interruptions Impact Worker Productivity," Basex, Inc., September 2005.

2. Katherine Bindley, "Distractions at Work: Employees Increasingly Losing Focus; Some Companies Combating the Problem," *Huffington Post,* December 13, 2012, http://www.huffingtonpost.com/2012/12/13/work-distractions-employees-lose-focus-companies-problem_n_2294054.html.

3. "Do Collaboration and Social Tools Increase or Drain User Productivity?" harmon.ie, http://harmon.ie/Downloads/DistractionSurveyResults.

4. Susan Weinschenk, "Why We're All Addicted to Texts, Twitter and Google," *Brain Wise,* September 11, 2012, http://www.psychologytoday.com/blog/brain-wise/201209/why-were-all-addicted-texts-twitter-and-google.

5. Winifred Gallagher, *Rapt: Attention and the Focused Life* (New York: Penguin, 2009).

6. Eilene Zimmerman, "Distracted? It's Time to Hit the Reset Button," *New York Times,* November 19, 2011, http://www.nytimes.com/2011/11/20/jobs/to-avoid-distractions-at-work-hit-the-reset-button.html?_r=0.

7. Ibid.

8. Tony Schwartz, *The Way We're Working Isn't Working: The Four Forgotten Needs That Energize Great Performance* (New York: Free Press, 2010), 191.

9. "Time Management Tips from Martha," *Helping You Organize* (blog), October 18, 2010, http://lelahwithanh.blogspot.com/2010/10/time-management-tips-from-martha.html.

10. Zimmerman, "Distracted?"

11. "Tory Burch: Balance Is Hard," Yahoo Entertainment, March 10, 2014, http://sg.entertainment.yahoo.com/news/tory-burch-balance-hard-010000640.html.

12. Robert Solow, "We'd Better Watch Out," *New York Times Book Review*, July 12, 1987, 36; Erik Brynjolfsson, "The Productivity Paradox of Information Technology," *Communications of the ACM* 36, no. 12 (1993): 66–77; Yaacov Cohen quoted in Jolie O'Dell, "Social Media Distractions Are Costing Businesses Major Money," *Mashable*, May 27, 2011, http://mashable.com/2011/05/27/digital-distraction-survey/.

13. Pamela Karr-Wisniewski and Ying Lu, "When More Is Too Much: Operationalizing Technology Overload and Exploring Its Impact on Knowledge Worker Productivity," *Computers in Human Behavior* 26 (March 2010): 1061–72.

14. O'Dell, "Social Media Distractions Are Costing Businesses Major Money."

15. "New Ask.com Study Reveals Workplace Productivity Killers," PR Newswire, May 7, 2013, http://www.prnewswire.com/news-releases/new-ask-com-study-reveals-workplace-productivity-killers-206398681.html.

16. Ibid.

Chapter 5: Set Your Priorities

1. "A View from the Top: Advice from the Super Successful," Forbes.com, http://www.forbes.com/pictures/lmj45mlmg/a-view-from-the-top-advice-from-the-super-successful-5/.

Chapter 6: Invest Your Time Wisely

1. Randy Pausch, *The Last Lecture* (New York: Hyperion, 2008).

2. "Randy Pausch Lecture: Time Management," YouTube, http://youtube.com/oTugjssqOT0.

3. "LinkedIn CEO Jeff Weiner on Time Management," WSJ Live, January 15, 2012, http://on.wsj.com/L4PVMU.

4. "How Entrepreneurs Can Manage Own Time," Livemint.com, April 11, 2011, http://www.livemint.com/Opinion/n2y2ujRKMY39nV24J7pn2M/How-entrepreneurs-can-manage-own-time.html.

5. Eilene Zimmerman, "Distracted? It's Time to Hit the Reset Button," *New York Times*, November 19, 2011, http://www.nytimes.com/2011/11/20/jobs/to-avoid-distractions-at-work-hit-the-reset-button.html?_r=0.

6. David Allen, *Getting Things Done* (New York: Penguin, 2003).

Chapter 7: Free Your Brain with a Master TASK List

1. Erin Schulte, "What's on the Paper List That Keeps Aaron Levie So Productive?" *Fast Company,* December 2013–January 2014, 119; available at http://www.fastcompany.com/3021586/most-productive-people-box-aaron-levie.

Chapter 8: Get More Done: Complete Tasks and Projects with Ease

1. "GE's Jeff Immelt on Leadership, Global Risk and Growth," Wharton .com., April 30, 2013, http://knowledge.wharton.upenn.edu/article/ges-jeff-immelt-on-leadership-global-risk-and-growth/.

Chapter 9: Tame Your Inbox

1. Aaron Mandelbaum, "Email Overload: 2012 Email Stats," Yahoo Small Business Advisor, February 24, 2013, http://smallbusiness.yahoo.com/advisor/email-overload-2012-email-stats-231631861.html; "Email Statistics Report, 2012–2016," Radicati.com, http://www.radicati.com/wp/wp-content/uploads/2012/04/Email-Statistics-Report-2012-2016-Executive-Summary.pdf.
2. "Richard Branson on Time Management," *Entrepreneur,* September 28, 2011, http://entrepreneur.com/article/220418.

Chapter 10: Shape Your Space for Mental and Physical Freedom

1. Carleen Hawn, "Pixar's Brad Bird on Fostering Innovation at Pixar," Gigaom .com, April 17, 2008, http://gigaom.com/2008/04/17/pixars-brad-bird-on-fostering-innovation/.
2. Peter Hartlaub, "Creativity Thrives in Pixar's Animated Workplace," SF-Gate.com, June 13, 2010, http://articles.sfgate.com/2010-06-13/news/2190 8813_1_storieschronicle-exclusive.
3. Josh Weber, Stanley Holmes, and Christopher Palmeri, "'Mosh Pits' of Creativity," Businessweek.com, http://www.businessweek.com/magazine/content/05_45/b3958078.htm.
4. "Microsoft—Pioneer Studios Office," Office Snapshots, http://www.office snapshots.com/2010/12/07/microsoft-pioneer-studios-office/.
5. Susan Cain, *Quiet: The Power of Introverts* (New York: Random House, 2012), 84.
6. Aoife Brennan, Jasdeep S. Chugh, and Theresa Kline, "Traditional Versus Open Office Design," *Environment and Behavior* 34, no. 3 (May 2002): 279–99.
7. Jay L. Brand and Thomas J. Smith, "Effects of Reducing Enclosure on Perceptions of Occupancy Quality, Job Satisfaction, and Job Performance in Open-Plan Offices," *Proceedings of the Human Factors and Ergonomics Society 49th Annual Meeting* (2005): 818–21.

8. Sara Varlander, "Individual Flexibility in the Workplace: A Spatial Perspective," *Journal of Applied Behavioral Science* 48, no. 1 (May 2011): 33–61.

9. T. Thanem, S. Varlander, and S. Cummings, "Open Space = Open Minds?: The Ambiguities of Pro-Creative Office Design," *International Journal of Work Organisation and Emotion* 4, no. 1 (2011): 78–98.

10. Eric Sundstrom, R. Kring Herbert, and David W. Brown, "Privacy and Communication in an Open-Plan Office: A Case Study," *Environment and Behavior* 14, no. 3 (May 1982): 379–92.

Chapter 11: Stop Pushing Papers

1. "Facts About Paper: The Impact of Consumption," The Paperless Project, http://www.thepaperlessproject.com/facts-about-paper-the-impact-of-consumption/.

2. "Time Management Statistics," Key Organization Systems, http://www.keyorganization.com/time-management-statistics.php?id=53.

3. "Document Imaging Facts and Figures," Arrowheadsoftware.com, http://www.arrowheadsoftware.com/docinfo.htm.

4. Hazel Thornton, "The 80/20 Rule Is Your Friend," *Organized for Life* (blog), February 18, 2013, http://www.org4life.com/the-8020-rule-is-your-friend/.

Chapter 12: Harness the Productive Power of Your Teammates: Delegate

1. "A View from the Top: Advice from the Super Successful," Forbes.com, http://www.forbes.com/pictures/lmj45,lmg/a-view-from-the-top-advice-from-the-super-successful-5/.

2. Stephen R. Covey, *The 7 Habits of Highly Effective People: Powerful Lessons in Personal Change, Anniversary Edition* (New York: Simon & Schuster, 2013).

Chapter 14: Lead a Meeting Revolution

1. Rachel Emma Silverman, "Where's the Boss? Trapped in a Meeting," *Wall Street Journal*, February 14, 2012, http://online.wsj.com/news/articles/SB10001424052970204642604577215013504567548.

2. Rosemary DiDio Brehm, "You're Probably Wondering Why I've Called You All Here . . . ," BABM.com, http://www.babm.com/management/Are_Your_Business_Meetings_Efficient_And_Effective.htm.

3. John Medina, *Brain Rules: 12 Principles for Surviving and Thriving at Work, Home, and School* (Seattle: Pear Press, 2008).

Index

Printed in the United States
by Baker & Taylor Publisher Services